"Reading has always been my home, my sustenance, my great invincible companion."

Anna Quindlen, *How Reading Changed My Life*

Dear Colleagues,

This book is a celebration. Last year, every K-3 classroom in New York City received approximately 300 books to read, to discuss, and to treasure. The more than four million books distributed citywide further our efforts to enhance literacy instruction and underscore the importance of classroom libraries in a comprehensive approach to literacy. This teachers guide is designed to help educators make the best use of those libraries.

Extensive research shows that students who read often tend to read well. Classroom libraries ensure that students have books that match their interests and current reading levels. Our schools must expose them to the sweep of literature that readers need to grow, which is why upper grades classrooms will receive libraries this fall.

The write-ups contained in this book reflect the best thinking of teachers from every corner of New York City. Their suggestions and observations have been guided by exemplary knowledge of the teaching of literacy, authentic experience using these books with their own students, and a keen awareness of the importance of literacy-rich classroom environments. Wise and skillful as they are, they know the value of daily opportunities to read real books with support and guidance from thoughtful teachers in ensuring our children meet high standards. They also recognize that books can serve many instructional purposes throughout the school day — for reading aloud to and with children, in guided reading and word study lessons, in author and genre studies - for which this book can serve as a roadmap.

As we move forward with our Children First initiative, I hope that you will find this guide useful. Today, kids and teachers in K-3 classrooms across our city hold an invaluable instructional resource in their hands. Through this initiative, we can support all of New York City's young children in acquiring strong reading habits and help them realize the extraordinary pleasure of sitting down with a great book.

Best wishes as you read — and learn — with your students,

Diana Lam
Deputy Chancellor for Teaching and Learning

A Special New York City Edition

This special New York City edition of *A Field Guide to the Classroom Library* was made possible by the generosity of several supporters of the New York City public schools. These include the Teachers College Reading and Writing Project, Heinemann, and Books *for* Children project funders Alan and Gail Levenstein. It was produced under the auspices of Diana Lam, Deputy Chancellor for Teaching and Learning and Peter P. Heaney, Jr., Executive Director, Division of Instructional Support.

The Mayor's Classroom Library collections provided to New York City teachers in Kindergarten – Grade 3 were funded by the mayor's office. The Books *for* Children project included the development of classroom library lists and this companion series of field guides. Our appreciation is extended to Lucy McCormick Calkins and the members of the Teachers College Reading and Writing Project for including us in this collaborative effort. Our thanks also go to Heinemann publishing and Kate Montgomery, editor.

These materials were developed primarily by the dozens of teachers and staff developers who make up the Teachers College Reading and Writing Project community. Revisions, additions and editorial work, and the supplementary materials found in the last section of this guide were developed by the New York City Department of Education in collaboration with Teachers College.

The project coordinator at the Department of Education was Adele Schroeter, Office of Research, Development and Dissemination, Division of Instructional Support. In addition to the Teachers College Reading and Writing Project community, contributors included: Gabriel Feldberg, Renée Dinnerstein, Patricia Tanzosh, Sharon Nurse, Daniel Feigelson and Denise Levine, Division of Instructional Support; Eve Litwack, teacher, CSD 15; Theresa Burns, editor; Cheryl Tyler, K-2 staff developer, CSD 10; Barbara Rosenberg, teacher, CSD 2; and Lisa Ripperger, literacy consultant.

Special thanks to Gabriel Feldberg, Office of Research, Development and Dissemination, for writing, reviewing, revising and formatting materials.

Assistance in preparing this manuscript for publication was provided by the Office of Instructional Publications, Nicholas A. Aiello, Ph.D., Director; and Christopher Sgarro, Editor in Chief. Sherrhonda Daniels, Office of Research, Development and Dissemination, provided assistance with the typing and editing of this guide.

A Field Guide to the Classroom Library Ⓒ

A Field Guide to the Classroom Library C

Lucy Calkins

and

*The Teachers College
Reading and Writing
Project Community*

HEINEMANN
Portsmouth, NH

Heinemann
A division of Reed Elsevier Inc.
361 Hanover Street
Portsmouth, NH 03801–3912
www.heinemann.com

Offices and agents throughout the world

Library of Congress Cataloging-in-Publication Data
Calkins, Lucy McCormick.
   A field guide to the classroom library / Lucy Calkins and the Teachers
College Reading and Writing Project community.
       v. cm.
   Includes bibliographical references and index.
   Contents: [v. 3] Library C : grades 1–2
   ISBN 0-325-00497-8
   1. Reading (Elementary)—Handbooks, manuals, etc.   2. Children—Books and reading—Handbooks, manuals, etc.   3. Children's literature—Study and teaching (Elementary)—Handbooks, manuals, etc.   4. Classroom libraries—Handbooks, manuals, etc.   I. Teachers College Reading and Writing Project (Columbia University).   II. Title.

LB1573 .C183 2002
372.4—dc21   2002038767

Editor: Kate Montgomery
Production: Abigail M. Heim
Interior design: Catherine Hawkes, Cat & Mouse
Cover design: Jenny Jensen Greenleaf Graphic Design & Illustration
Manufacturing: Louise Richardson

Printed in the United States of America on acid-free paper

06   05   04   03   02   1   2   3   4   5

This field guide is dedicated to

Gaby Layden

The Field Guides to the Classroom Library *project is a philanthropic effort. According to the wishes of the scores of contributors, all royalties from the sale of these field guides will be given back entirely to the project in the continued effort to put powerful, beautiful, and thoughtfully chosen literature into the hands of children.*

Contents

Acknowledgments

The entire Teachers College Reading and Writing Project community has joined together in the spirit of a barn-raising to contribute to this gigantic effort to put the best of children's literature into the hands of children.

There are hundreds of people to thank. In these pages, I will only be able to give special thanks to a few of the many who made this work possible.

First, we thank Alan and Gail Levenstein who sponsored this effort with a generous personal gift and who helped us remember and hold tight to our mission. We are grateful to Annemarie Powers who worked tirelessly, launching the entire effort in all its many dimensions. Annemarie's passionate love of good literature shines throughout this project.

Kate Montgomery, now an editor at Heinemann and a long-time friend and coauthor, joined me in writing and revising literally hundreds of the field guides. Kate's deep social consciousness, knowledge of reading, and her commitment to children are evident throughout the work. How lucky we were that she became a full-time editor at Heinemann just when this project reached there, and was, therefore, able to guide the project's final stages.

Tasha Kalista coordinated the effort, bringing grace, humor, and an attention to detail to the project. She's been our home base, helping us all stay on track. Tasha has made sure loose ends were tied up, leads pursued, inquiries conducted, and she's woven a graceful tapestry out of all the thousands of books, guides, and people.

Each library is dedicated to a brilliant, passionate educator who took that particular library and the entire effort under her wing. We are thankful to Lynn Holcomb whose deep understanding of early reading informed our work; to Mary Ann Colbert who gave generously of her wisdom of reading recovery and primary texts; to Kathleen Tolan who championed the little chapter books and made us see them with new eyes; to Gaby Layden for her expertise in the area of nonfiction reading; to Isoke Nia for passionate contributions to our upper grade libraries; and to Kathy Doyle who knows books better than anyone we know.

We thank Pam Allyn for her dedication to this effort, Laurie Pessah for working behind the scenes with me, and Beth Neville for keeping the Project on course when this undertaking threatened to swamp us.

Finally, we are grateful to Mayor Guiliani for putting these libraries into every New York City school. To Judith Rizzo, Deputy Chancellor of Instruction, Adele Schroeter, Director of Office of Research, Development and Dissemination, Peter Heaney, Executive Director of the Division of Instructional Support, and William P. Casey, Chief Executive for Instructional Innovation, we also offer our heartfelt thanks for contributing their wisdom, integrity, and precious time to making this miracle happen.

Contributors

Christina Adams
Lisa Ali Chetram
Pam Allyn
Francine Almash
Janet Angelillo
Liz Arfin
Anna Arrigo
Laura Ascenzi-Moreno
Maureen Bilewich
Melissa Biondi
Pat Bleichman
Christine Bluestein
Ellen Braunstein
Dina Bruno
Theresa Burns
Lucy Calkins
Adele Cammarata
Joanne Capozzoli
Laura Cappadona
Justin Charlebois
Linda Chen
Mary Chiarella
Danielle Cione
Erica Cohen
Mary Ann Colbert
Kerri Conlon
Denise Corichi
Danielle Corrao
Sue Dalba
Linda Darro
Mildred De Stefano
Marisa DeChiara
Erica Denman
Claudia Diamond
Renee Dinnerstein
Kathy Doyle
Lizz Errico
Rosemarie Fabbricante
Gabriel Feldberg
Holly Fisher

Sofia Forgione
Judy Friedman
Elizabeth Fuchs
Jerilyn Ganz
Allison Gentile
Linda Gerstman
Jessica Goff
Iris Goldstein-
    Jackman
Ivy Green
Cathy Grimes
David Hackenburg
Amanda Hartman
Grace Heske
Caren Hinckley
Lynn Holcomb
Michelle Hornof
Anne Illardi
Maria Interlandi
Erin Jackman
Debbie Jaffe
Helen Jurios
Kim Kaiser
Tasha Kalista
Beth Kanner
Michele Kaye
Laurie Kemme
Hue Kha
Tara Krebs
Joan Kuntz Verdino
Kathleen Kurtz
Lamson Lam
Gaby Layden
Karen Liebowitz
Adele Long
Cynthia Lopez
Natalie Louis
Eileen Lynch
Theresa Maldarelli
Lucille Malka

Corinne Maracina
Jennifer Marmo
Paula Marron
Marjorie Martinelli
Esther Martinez
Debbie Matz
Teresa Maura
Leah Mermelstein
Melissa Miller
Kate Montgomery
Jessica Moss
Janice Motloenya
Marie Naples
Marcia Nass
Beth Neville
Silvana Ng
Isoke Nia
Jennie Nolan
    Buonocore
Lynn Norton Manna
Beth Nuremberg
Sharon Nurse
Liz O'Connell
Jacqueline O'Connor
Joanne Onolfi
Suzann Pallai
Shefali Parekh
Karen Perepeluk
Laurie Pessah
Jayne Piccola
Laura Polos
Annemarie Powers
Bethany Pray
Carol Puglisi
Alice Ressner
Marcy Rhatigan
Khrishmati Ridgeway
Lisa Ripperger
Barbara Rosenblum
Jennifer Ruggiero

Liz Rusch
Jennifer Ryan
Karen Salzberg
Elizabeth Sandoval
Carmen Santiago
Karen Scher
Adele Schroeter
Shanna Schwartz
India Scott
Marci Seidman
Rosie Silberman
Jessica Silver
Miles Skorpen
Joann Smith
Chandra Smith
Helene Sokol
Gail Wesson Spivey
Barbara Stavetski
Barbara Stavridis
Jean Stehle
Kathleen Stevens
Emma Suarez Baez
Michelle Sufrin
Jane Sullivan
Evelyn Summer
Eileen Tabasko
Patricia Tanzosh
Lyon Terry
Kathleen Tolan
Christine Topf
Joseph Turzo
Cheryl Tyler
Emily Veronese
Anne Marie Vira
Marilyn Walker
Gillan White
Alison Wolensky
Michelle Wolf
Eileen Wolfring

Introduction: What Is This Field Guide?

Lucy Calkins

When I was pregnant with my first-born son, the Teachers College Reading and Writing Project community organized a giant baby shower for me. Each person came with a carefully chosen book, inscribed with a message for baby Miles. Since then, we have commemorated birthdays, engagements, graduations, and good-byes by searching the world for exactly the right poem or picture book, novel or essay, and writing a letter to accompany it. Inside the letter, it says "This is why I chose this piece of literature precisely for you." In this same way, the book lists and the written guides that accompany them in this field guide have become our gift to you, the teachers of our nation's children. We have chosen, from all the books we have ever read, exactly the ones we think could start best in your classroom, and with these books, we have written notes that explain exactly why and how we think these texts will be so powerful in your children's hands.

The book lists and guides in this field guide are the Teachers College Reading and Writing Project's literacy gift to New York City and to the nation. When, two years ago, patrons Alan and Gail Levenstein came to us asking if there was one thing, above all others, which could further our work with teachers and children, we knew our answer in a heartbeat. We couldn't imagine anything more important than giving children the opportunity to trade, collect, talk over, and live by books. We want children to carry poems in their backpacks, to cry with Jess when he finds out that his friend Leslie has drowned, to explore tropical seas from the deck of a ship, to wonder at the life teeming in a drop of water. We want our children's heroes to include the wise and loving spider Charlotte, spinning her web to save the life of Wilbur, and the brave Atticus Finch.

We told the Levensteins that for teachers, as well as for children, there could be no finer gift than the gift of books for their students. We want teachers to be able to read magnificent stories aloud as the prelude to each school day, and to know the joy of putting exactly the right book in the hands of a child and adding, with a wink, "When you finish this book, there are more like it." We want teachers to create libraries with categories of books that peak their students' interests and match their children's passions, with one shelf for Light Sports Books and another shelf for Cousins of the Harry Potter books, one for Books That Make You Cry and another for You'll-Never-Believe-This Books. With this kind of a library, how much easier it becomes to teach children to read, to teach them what they need to become powerful, knowledgeable, literate people!

Even as we embarked on the effort to design magnificent classroom libraries, we knew that the best classroom library would always be the one assembled by a knowledgeable classroom teacher with his or her own students in mind. But, in so many cities, twenty new teachers may arrive in a school in a single year, having had no opportunity to learn about children's books at all. Even though some teachers have studied children's books, they may not be the ones given the opportunity to purchase books. Or, too often, there is no time to make book selections carefully—funds are discovered ten minutes before they must be spent or be taken from the budget. For these situations, we knew it would be enormously helpful to have lists and arrangements of recommended books for classroom libraries. Even without these worries, we all know the value of receiving book recommendations from friends. And so, our commitment to the project grew.

Our plan became this: We'd rally the entire Project community around a gigantic, two-year-long effort to design state-of-the-art classroom libraries and guides, exactly tailored to the classrooms we know so well. Simultaneously, we'd begin working with political, educational, and philanthropic leaders in hopes that individuals or corporations might adopt a school (or a corridor of classrooms) and create in these schools and classrooms the libraries of our dreams. Sharing our enthusiasm, colleagues at the New York City Board of Education proposed that idea to the mayor. Two years later, that dream has come true—In his January 2001 state of the city address, Mayor Giuliani promised $31.5 million of support to put a lending library in every New York City classroom, kindergarten through eighth grade.

Hearing this pronouncement, educational leaders from around the city joined with us in our philanthropic effort. People from the New York City Board of Education reviewed the lists and added suggestions and revisions. The Robin Hood Foundation, which had already been involved in a parallel effort to develop *school* libraries, contributed their knowledge. Readers from the Teachers Union and from the Office of Multicultural Education and of Early Childhood Education and of Literacy Education all joined in, coordinated by Peter Heaney, Executive Director of the Division of Instructional Support, and Adele Schroeter, Director of the Office of Research, Development and Dissemination. The book selections for the classroom libraries became even more carefully honed, and the written guides became richer still.

Over the past few months, boxes upon boxes of books have arrived across New York City, and in every classroom, children are pulling close to watch, big-eyed, as one exquisite, carefully chosen book after another is brought from the box and set on the shelf. Each teacher will receive between three and four hundred books. With most of these books, there will be a carefully crafted guide which says, "We chose this book because . . ." and "On page . . ." and "You'll notice that . . ." and "If you like this book, these are some others like it. . . . " I cannot promise that in every town and city across the nation the effort to put literature in the hands of students and guidance in the hands of their teachers will proceed so smoothly. But I'm hoping these book lists and these ready-made libraries bearing a stamp of approval will catch the eye of funders, of generous patrons, and of foresighted school leaders. And, every penny that comes to the authors from the sale of these field guides will go directly back into this project, directly back into our efforts to get more books into children's hands.

In the meantime, we needn't be idle. We'll comb through the book sales at libraries, and we'll write requests to publishers and companies. In a letter home to our children's parents, we might say, "Instead of sending in cupcakes to honor your child's birthday, I'm hoping you'll send a book. Enclosed is a list of suggestions." We can and will get books into our children's hands, by hook or by crook. And we can and will get the professional support we need for our reading instruction—our vitality and effectiveness as educators depend on it.

About the Books

When hundreds of teachers pool their knowledge of children's books as we have here, the resulting libraries are far richer than anything any one of us could have imagined on our own. We're proud as peacocks of these selections and of the accompanying literary insights and teaching ideas, and can't wait to share them both with teachers and children across the country. Here is a window into some of the crafting that has gone into the book selections:

- We suggest author studies in which the texts that students will study approximately match those they'll write and will inform their own work as authors.

- In upper-grade libraries, we include books that are relatively easy to read, but we have tried to ensure that they contain issues of concern to older children as well.

- We include books that might inform other books in the same library. For example, one library contains three books about dust storms, another contains a variety of books on spiders.

- We know that comprehension and interpretive thinking must be a part of reading from the very beginning, so we include easy to read books that can support thoughtful responses.

- We try to match character ages with student ages, approximately. For example, we have put the book in which Ramona is five in the library we anticipate will be for kindergartners, and put fourth-grade Ramona in the library we anticipate will be for fourth graders.

- We include complementary stories together when possible. For example, Ringgold's *Tar Beach* and Dorros' *Abuela* appear in the same library, anticipating that readers will recognize these as parallel stories in which the narrator has an imagined trip.

- We have never assumed that books in a series are all of the same level. For example, we have determined that some of the *Frog and Toad* books are more challenging, and this is indicated in our libraries.

- We understand that books in a series cannot always be easily read out of sequence. Because we know the *Magic Treehouse* series is best read in a particular sequence, for example, we have been careful with regard to the books we select out of that series.

- We selected our libraries to reflect multicultural values and bring forth characters of many different backgrounds and lives.

■ We try to steer clear of books that will not meet with general public approval. We do not believe in censorship, but we do believe that books purchased en masse should not bring storms of criticism upon the unsuspecting teacher.

At the same time that we are proud of the work we've done, we also know that there are countless magnificent books we have omitted and countless helpful and obvious teaching moves we have missed. We are certain that there are authors' names we have inadvertently misspelled, opinions expressed with which we don't all agree, levels assigned that perhaps should be different, and so on. We consider this work to be a letter to a friend and a work in progress, and we are rushing it to you, eager for a response. We are hoping that when you come across areas that need more attention, when you get a bright idea about a guide or booklist, that you will write back to us. We have tried to make this as easy as possible for you to do—just go to our website and contact us!

Choosing the Library for Your Class

We have created seven libraries for kindergarten through sixth grade classrooms. The libraries are each assigned a letter name (A–G) rather than a grade-level in recognition of the fact that the teacher of one class of fourth graders might find that Library D is suited to her students, and another fourth grade teacher might opt for Library E or Library F.

In order to determine which classroom library is most appropriate for a particular class in a particular school, teachers need to determine the approximate reading levels of their students in November, after the teachers have had some time to assess their students as readers. Teachers can compare the book the middle-of-the-class reader tends to be reading with the books we note for each level, and choose the library that corresponds to that average text level. More detail follows this general description. In shorthand, however, the following equivalencies apply:

Library Ⓐ is usually Kindergarten
Library Ⓑ is usually K or 1st grade
Library Ⓒ is usually 1st or 2nd grade
Library Ⓓ is usually 2nd or 3rd grade
Library Ⓔ is usually 3rd or 4th grade
Library Ⓕ is usually 4th or 5th grade
Library Ⓖ is usually 5th or 6th grade

The system of saying, "If in November, your children are reading books like these," usually doesn't work for kindergarten children. Instead, we say Library A is suitable if, in November, the average student cannot yet do a rich, story-like, emergent (or pretend) reading of a familiar storybook, nor can this child write using enough initial and final consonants that an adult can "read" the child's writing.

It is important to note that all of the books in any given library are not at the same level of difficulty. Instead, we have created a mix of levels that tend to represent the mixed levels of ability of readers in the classes we have studied. The composition of the libraries, by level, is described on pages liii–lxii.

Once you have chosen the library that best corresponds to the average level of your students as readers, you will need to decide which components of the library best suit your curriculum. Each library is divided into components—a core and some modules. The core is the group of books in the library we regard as essential. Each library also contains six modules, each representing a category of books. For example, in each library there is a module of nonfiction books, and in the upper-grade libraries there are modules containing five copies each of ten books we recommend for book clubs. Each module contains approximately fifty titles. The exact quantity from module to module varies slightly because we have tried to keep the cost of each module approximately equal. This means, for example, that the nonfiction module that contains more hardcover books has fewer books overall.

There are a variety of ways to assemble a library. Some teachers will want to purchase the entire library—the core plus the six modules. Sometimes, teachers on the same grade level in a school each purchase the same core but different modules, so a greater variety of books will be available across the hall for their students. In New York City, teachers automatically received the core of their library of choice, 150 books, and then could choose three of the six possible modules.

The Contents of Each Library

Researchers generally agree that a classroom should contain at least twenty books per child. Obviously, the number of books needs to be far greater than this in kindergarten and first grade classrooms, because books for beginning readers often contain fewer than 100 words and can generally only sustain a child's reading for a short while. We would have liked to recommend libraries of 750 titles but decided to select a smaller number of books, trusting that each teacher will have other books of his or her choice to supplement our recommendations.

Because we predict that every teacher will receive or buy the core of a library and only some teachers will receive any particular module, we tried to fill the core of the libraries with great books we couldn't imagine teaching, or living, without. Because we know children will borrow and swap books between classrooms, it is rare for books to be in the core of more than one library, even though some great books could easily belong there.

Usually, these classroom libraries include enough books from a particularly wonderful series to turn that series into a class rage, but the libraries frequently do not contain all the books in a series. Often, more books in the series are included in Modules One and Two, which always contain more books for independent reading, divided into the same levels as those in the core. Our expectation is that once readers have become engrossed in a series, teachers or parents can help them track down sequels in the school or public library.

Within the core of a library, we include about a dozen books of various genres that could be perfect for the teacher to read aloud to the class. These are all tried-and-true read aloud books; each title on the read-aloud list is one that countless teachers have found will create rapt listeners and generate rich conversation.

In every library we have included nonfiction books. They were not chosen to support particular social studies or science units; that would be a different and admirable goal. Instead, our team members have searched for nonfiction texts that captivate readers, and we imagine them being read within the reading workshop. The nonfiction books were chosen either because their topics are generally high-interest ones for children (animals, yo-yo tricks, faraway lands, disgusting animals), or because they represent the best of their genre.

Each library contains about fifteen books that could be splendid mentor texts for young writers. That is, they contain writing that students could emulate and learn from easily since it is somewhat like the writing they are generally able to create themselves.

In each core library, an assortment of other categories is included. These differ somewhat from one library to another. Libraries D and E, for example, contain many early chapter books, but since it is also crucial for children at this level to read the richest picture books imaginable, the core contains a score of carefully chosen picture books. Some cores also contain a set of books perfect for an author study. The categories are indicated on the book lists themselves, and under "Teaching Uses" in the guides.

The vast majority of books in each library are single copies, chosen in hopes that they will be passed eagerly from one reader to another. The challenge was not to find the number of books representing a particular level, but instead to select irresistible books. The chosen books have been field tested in dozens of New York City classrooms, and they've emerged as favorites for teachers and children alike.

The few books that have been selected in duplicate are ones we regard as particularly worthwhile to talk over with a partner. We would have loved to suggest duplicate copies be available for half the books in each library—if libraries had more duplicates, this would allow two readers to move simultaneously through a book, meeting in partnerships to talk and think about the chapters they've read. The duplicate copies would allow readers to have deeper and more text-specific book talks, while growing and researching theories as they read with each other. Duplicates also help books gain social clout in a classroom—allowing the enthusiasm of several readers to urge even more readers to pick the book up. If teachers are looking for ways to supplement these libraries, buying some duplicate copies would be a perfect way to start.

Many of the libraries contain a very small number of multiple (four or five) copies of books intended for use in guided reading and strategy lessons. Once children are reading chapter books, we find teachers are wise to help children into a new series by pulling together a group of four readers, introducing the text, and guiding their early reading. Teachers may also want to offer extra support to children as they read the second book in a series, and so we suggest having a duplicate of this next book as well, so that each child can read it with a partner, meeting to retell and discuss it.

The Levels Within the Libraries

We've leveled many, but purposely not all, of the books in every classroom library. The fact that we have leveled these books doesn't mean that teachers should necessarily convey all of these levels to children. We expect teachers will often make these levels visible on less than half of their books (through the use of colored tabs), giving readers the responsibility of choosing appropriate books for themselves by judging unmarked books against the template of leveled books. "This book looks a lot like the green dot books that have been just-right for me, so I'll give it a try and see if I have a smooth read," a reader might say. It is important that kids learn to navigate different levels of difficulty within a classroom library on their own or with only minimal support from a teacher.

We do not imagine a classroom lending library that is divided into levels as discrete as the levels established by Reading Recovery© or by Gay Su Pinnell and Irene Fountas' book, *Guided Reading: Good First Teaching for All Children* (Heinemann, 1996). These levels were designed for either one-to-one tutorials or intensive, small group guided reading sessions, and in both of these situations a vigilant teacher is present to constantly shepherd children along toward more challenging books. If a classroom lending library is divided into micro-levels and each child's entire independent reading life is slotted into a micro-level, some children might languish at a particular level, and many youngsters might not receive the opportunities to read across a healthy range of somewhat-easier and somewhat-harder books. Most worrisome of all, because we imagine children working often with reading partners who "like to read the same kinds of books as you do," classroom libraries that contain ten micro-levels (instead of say, five more general levels) could inadvertently convey the message that many *children* as well as many *books* were off-limits as partners to particular readers.

There are benefits to micro-levels, however, and therefore within a difficulty level (or a color-dot), some teachers might ascribe a plus sign to certain books, signifying that this book is one of the harder ones at this level. Teachers can then tell a child who is new to a level to steer clear of the books with plus signs, or to be sure that he or she receives a book introduction before tackling a book with this marker.

When assigning books to levels, we have tried to research the difficulty levels that others have given to each text and we have included these levels in our guides. Fairly frequently, however, our close study of a particular text has led us to differ somewhat from the assessments others have made. Of course leveling books is and always will be a subjective and flawed process; and therefore teachers everywhere *should* deviate from assigned levels, ours and others, when confident of their rationale, or when particularly knowledgeable about a reader. You can turn to the tables at the back of this section, on pages xxix–lxvi, to learn more about our leveling system.

Building the Libraries

When we started this project two years ago, we initiated some intensive study groups, each designed to investigate a different terrain in children's literature. Soon, a group led by Lynn Holcomb, one of the first Reading Recovery teachers in Connecticut, was working to select books for a K–1 library. Members of this group also learned from Barbara Peterson, author of *Literary Pathways: Selecting Books to Support New Readers* (Heinemann, 2001), who conducted groundbreaking research at Ohio State University, examining how readers actually experience levels of text complexity. The group also learned from Gay Su Pinnell, well-known scholar of literacy education and coauthor with Irene Fountas of many books including *Guided Reading*. Of course, the group learned especially from intensive work with children in classrooms. The group searched for books that:

- Represent a diverse range of shapes, sizes, authors, and language patterns as possible. The committee went to lengths to be sure that when taken as a whole, primary-level libraries looked more like libraries full of real books than like kits full of "teaching materials."

- Use unstilted language. A book that reads, "Come, Spot. Come, Spot, come," generally would not be selected.

- Contain many high frequency words. If one book contained just one word on a page ("Scissors/paste/paper/etc.") and another book contained the reoccurring refrain of "I see the scissors./ I see the paste." we selected the second option.

- Carry meaning and were written to communicate content with a reader. If the book would probably generate a conversation or spark an insight, it was more apt to be included than one that generally left a reader feeling flat and finished with the book.

- Represent the diversity of people in our world and convey valuable messages about the human spirit.

A second group, under the leadership of Kathleen Tolan, an experienced teacher and staff developer, spent thousands of hours studying early chapter books and the children who read them. This group pored over series, asking questions: Is each book in the series equally difficult? Which series act as good precursors for other series? Do the books in the series make up one continuous story, or can each book stand alone? What are the special demands placed on readers of this series?

Yet another group, led by Gaby Layden, staff developer at the Project, studied nonfiction books to determine which might be included in a balanced, independent reading library. The group studied levels of difficulty in nonfiction books, and found authors and texts that deserved special attention. Carefully, they chose books for teachers to demonstrate and for children to practice working through the special challenges of nonfiction reading.

Meanwhile, renowned teacher-educator Isoke Nia, teacher extraordinaire Kathy Doyle, and their team of educators dove into the search for the very best chapter books available for upper-grade readers. Isoke especially helped us select touchstone texts for writing workshops—books to help us teach children to craft their writing with style, care, and power.

Teacher, staff developer, and researcher Annemarie Powers worked full-time to ensure that our effort was informed by the related work of other groups across the city and nation. We pored over bibliographies and met with librarians and literature professors. We searched for particular kinds of books: books featuring Latino children, anthologies of short stories, Level A and B books which looked and sounded like literature. We researched the classrooms in our region that are especially famous for their classroom libraries, and took note of the most treasured books we found there. All of this information fed our work.

Reading Instruction and the Classroom Library: An Introduction to Workshop Structures

These classroom libraries have been developed with the expectation that they will be the centerpiece of reading instruction. When I ask teachers what they are really after in the teaching of reading, many answer, as I do, "I want children to be lifelong readers. I cannot imagine anything more important than helping children grow up able to read and loving to read. I want students to initiate reading in their own lives, for their own purposes."

There is, of course, no one best way to teach reading so that children become lifelong readers. One of the most straightforward ways to do this is to embrace the age-old, widely shared belief that children benefit from daily opportunities to read books they choose for their own purposes and pleasures (Krashen 1993, Atwell 1987, Cambourne 1993, Smith 1985, Meek 1988).

More and more, however, we've come to realize that students benefit not only from opportunities to read, read, read, but also from instruction that responds to what students do when they are given opportunities to read. I have described the reading workshop in my latest publication, *The Art of Teaching Reading* (Calkins 2001). The reading workshop is an instructional format in which children are given long chunks of time in which to read appropriate texts, and also given explicit and direct instruction. Teachers who come from a writing workshop background may find it helpful to structure the reading workshop in ways that parallel the writing workshop so that children learn simultaneously to work productively inside each of the two congruent structures. Whatever a teacher decides, it is important that the structures of a reading workshop are clear and predictable so that children know how to carry on with some independence, and so that teachers are able to assess and coach individuals as well as partnerships and small groups.

Many teachers begin a reading workshop by pulling students together for a minilesson lasting about eight minutes (unless the read aloud is, for that day, incorporated into the minilesson, which then adds at least twenty minutes). Children then bring their reading bins, holding the books they are currently reading, to their assigned "reading nooks." As children read independently, a teacher moves among them, conferring individually with a child or bringing a small group of readers together for a ten- to fifteen-minute guided reading or strategy lesson. After children have read independently for about half an hour, teachers ask them to meet with their partners to talk about their books and their reading. After the partners meet, teachers often call all the readers in a class together for a brief "share session" (Calkins 2001). The following table shows some general guidelines for the length of both independent reading and the partnership talks based on the approximate level of the texts students are reading in the class.

How Long Might a Class Have Independent Reading and Partnership Talk?		
Class Reading Level	*Independent Reading Duration*	*Partnership Talk Duration*
Library A	10 minutes	20 minutes
Library B	15 minutes	20 minutes
Library C	20 minutes	20 minutes
Library D	30 minutes	10 minutes
Library E	40 minutes	10 minutes
Library F	40 minutes	10 minutes
Library G	40 minutes	10 minutes

Periodically, the structure of the minilesson, independent reading, partnership, and then share time is replaced by a structure built around book clubs or "junior" book clubs, our own, reading-intensive version of reading centers.

Minilessons

During a minilesson, the class gathers on the carpet to learn a strategy all readers can use not only during the independent reading workshop but also throughout their reading lives. The content of a minilesson comes, in part, from a teacher deciding that for a period of time, usually a month, he needs to focus his teaching on a particular aspect of reading. For example, many teachers begin the year by devoting a month to reading with stamina and understanding (Calkins 2001). During this unit, teachers might give several minilessons designed to help children choose books they can understand, and they might give others designed to help readers sustain their reading over time. Another minilesson might be designed to help readers make more time for reading in their lives or to help them keep a stack of books-in-waiting to minimize the interval between finishing one book and starting another.

The minilesson, then, often directs the work readers do during independent reading. If the minilessons show students how to make sure their ideas are grounded in the details of the text, teachers may establish an interval between independent reading time and partnership conversations when children can prepare for a talk about their text by marking relevant sections that support their ideas.

Sometimes minilessons are self-standing, separate from the interactive read aloud. Other minilessons include and provide a frame for the day's read aloud. For example, the teacher may read aloud a book and direct that day's talk in a way that demonstrates the importance of thinking about a character's motivations. Then children may be asked to think in similar ways about their independent reading books. Perhaps, when they meet with a partner at the end of reading, the teacher will say, "Please talk about the motivations that drive your central characters and show evidence in the text to support your theories."

Conferences

While children read, a teacher confers. Usually this means that the teacher starts by sitting close to a child as he or she continues reading, watching for external behaviors that can help assess the child. After a moment or two, the teacher usually says, "Can I interrupt?" and conducts a few-minute-long conversation while continuing the assessment. A teacher will often ask, "Can you read to me a bit?" and this, too, informs any hunches about a child and his or her strengths and needs as a reader. Finally, teachers intervene to lift the level of what the child is doing. The following table offers some examples of this.

General Examples of the Conferring That Can Help Readers Grow	
If, in reading, the child is . . .	*Teachers might teach by . . .*
able to demonstrate a basic understanding of the text	nudging the child to grow deeper insights, perhaps by asking: ■ Do any pages (parts) go together in a surprising way? ■ Why do you think the author wrote this book? What is he (she) trying to say? ■ If you were to divide the book into different sections, what would they be? ■ How are you changing as a reader? How are you reading this book differently than you've read others? ■ What's the work you are doing as you read this?
talking mostly about the smallest, most recent details read	generalizing what kind of book it is, giving the child a larger sense of the genre. If it is a story, we can ask questions that will work for any story: ■ How is the main character changing? ■ How much time has gone by? ■ What is the setting for the story? If the text is a non-narrative, we could ask: ■ What are the main chunks (or sections) in the text? ■ How would you divide this up? ■ How do the parts of this text go together? ■ What do you think the author is trying to teach you?
clearly enthralled by the story	asking questions to help the reader tap into the best of this experience to use again later. ■ What do you think it is about this story that draws you in? ■ You seem really engaged, so I'm wondering what can you learn about this reading experience that might inform you as you read other books. ■ When I love a book, as you love this one, I sometimes find myself reading faster and faster, as if I'm trying to gulp it down. But a reading teacher once told me this quote. "Some people think a good book is one you can't put down, but me, I think a good book is one you must put down—to muse over, to question, to think about." Could you set some bookmarks throughout this book and use them to pause in those places to really think and even to write about this book? Make one of those places right now, would you?

Partnerships

When many of us imagine reading, we envision a solitary person curled up with a book. The truth is that reading is always social, always embedded in talk with others. If I think about the texts I am reading now in my life and ask myself, "Is there something *social* about my reading of those texts?" I quickly realize that I read texts because people have recommended them. I read anticipating conversations I will soon have with others, and I read noticing things in this one text that I have discussed with others. My reading, as is true for many readers, is multilayered and sharper because of the talk that surrounds it.

There are a lot of reasons to organize reading time so that children have opportunities to talk with a reading partner. Partner conversations can highlight the social elements of reading, making children enjoy reading more. Talking about books also helps children have more internal conversations (thoughts) as they read. Putting thoughts about texts out into the world by speaking them allows other readers to engage in conversation, in interpretations and ideas, and can push children to ground their ideas in the text, to revise their ideas, to lengthen and deepen their ideas.

For young children, talking with a partner usually doubles the actual unit of time a child spends working with books. In many primary classrooms, the whole class reads and then the teacher asks every child to meet with a partner who can read a similar level of book. Each child brings his bin of books, thus doubling the number of appropriate books available to any one child. The child who has already read a book talks about it with the other child, giving one partner a valuable and authentic reason to retell a book and another child an introduction to the book. Then the two readers discuss how they will read together. After the children read aloud together, the one book held between them as they sit hip to hip, there is always time for the partners to discuss the text. Sometimes, teachers offer students guidance in this conversation.

More proficient readers need a different sort of partnership because once a child can read short chapter books, there are few advantages to the child reading aloud often. Then too, by this time children can sustain reading longer. Typically in third grade, for example, individuals read independently for thirty minutes and then meet with partners for ten minutes to talk over the book. Again, the teacher often guides that conversation, sometimes by modeling—by entertaining with the whole-class read-aloud text—the sort of conversations she expects readers will have in their partnerships.

Book Clubs

Teaching children to read well has a great deal to do with teaching children to talk well about books, because the conversations children have in the air between one another become the conversations they have in their own minds as they read. Children who have talked in small groups about the role of the suitcase in Christopher Paul Curtis's book, *Bud, Not Buddy* will be far more apt to pause as they read another book, asking, "Might *this* object play a significant role in this book, like the suitcase did in *Bud, Not Buddy*?"

When we move children from partnership conversations toward small-group book clubs, we need to provide some scaffolding for them to lean on at first. This is because partnerships are generally easier for children to manage than small group conversations. It is also generally easier for students to read for thirty-minute reading sessions with ten-minute book talks than it is to read for a few days in a row and then sustain extended book talks, as they are expected to do in book clubs.

Children need some support as they begin clubs. One way to do this is to begin with small book club conversations about the read aloud book—the one book we know everyone will be prepared to talk about. Another way to get started with book clubs is for the teacher to suggest that children work in small groups to read multiple copies of, say, a mystery book. The teacher will plan to read a mystery book aloud to the class during the weeks they work in their clubs. Meanwhile, each group of approximately four readers will be reading one mystery that is at an appropriate level for them. The whole class works on and talks about the read-aloud mystery, and this work then guides the small group work. On one day, for example, after reading aloud the whole-class mystery, the teacher could immerse the class in talk about what it's like to read "suspiciously," suspecting everything and everyone. For a few days, the class can try that sort of reading as they listen to the read aloud. Meanwhile, when children disperse to their small groups to read their own mysteries, they can read these books "suspiciously."

Eventually the book clubs can become more independent. One small group of children might be reading several books by an author and talking about what they can learn from the vantage point of having read so many. Another group might read books that deal with a particular theme or subject. Either way, in the classrooms I know best, each book club lasts at least a few weeks. Teachers observe, and coach and teach into these talks, equipping kids with ways to write, talk, and think about texts. However, teachers neither dominate the clubs nor steer readers toward a particular preordained interpretation of a text. Instead, teachers steer readers toward ways of learning and thinking that can help them again and again, in reading after reading, throughout their lives.

Library Ⓒ Contents Description

Library C consists of

I.	Independent Reading & Partner Reading (Levels 2–8)	Level 2	23 Titles	23 Texts
		Level 3	42 Titles	43 Texts
		Level 4	73 Titles	73 Texts
		Level 5	75 Titles	80 Texts
		Level 6	71 Titles	92 Texts
		Level 7	22 Titles	27 Texts
		Level 8	22 Titles	33 Texts
	Nonfiction		33 Titles	33 Texts
	Poetry		15 Titles	15 Texts
II.	Guided Reading		8 Titles	32 Texts
III.	Reading Centers/Literature Circles		33 Titles	37 Texts
IV.	Author Study		10 Titles	10 Texts
V.	Read Alouds		30 Titles	30 Texts
VI.	Texts to Support the Writing Process		9 Titles	9 Texts
	Total Number of Texts in Library C		**466 Titles**	**537 Texts**

(Because of substitutions made in the ordering process, this number may not be precise.)

Library ❸ Book List

Group Description	Level	#	Author	Title	ISBN	Publisher	Quantity	Heinemann Write-Up
CORE								
Independent Reading		1	Chin, Theresa	I Am A Cat		Rigby	1	
	2	2	Selway, Martina	Don't Forget to Write	824986369	Hambleton-Hill Publishing	1	Y
		1	Bancroft, Gloria	Bubbles Everywhere	780288785	Wright Group	1	
		2	Canizares, Susan	Dancing	43904569X	Scholastic Inc.	1	
		3	Chanko, Pamela	Markets	439045541	Scholastic Inc.	1	
		4	Cutting, Brian	My Cat	780237870	Wright Group	1	
		5	Cutting, Jillian	Family, The	780264029	Wright Group	1	
		6	Frost, Helen	Baby Birds	736802223	Pebble Books	1	
		7	Giles, Jenny	Ball Games		Rigby	1	
		8	Randell, Beverly	Bumper Cars, The	763515086	Rigby	1	Y
		9	Randell, Beverly	Photo Book, The	435067265	Rigby	1	Y
		10	Williams, Rebel	Who Lives in this Hole?	780290690	Wright Group	1	
	3	1	Barrie, Nicola	Pizza, The	780265521	Wright Group	1	
		2	Cowley, Joy	Mrs. Wishy Washy	399233911	Wright Group	1	Y
		3	Cutting, Jullian	Grandpa	780264053	Wright Group	1	
		4	Depree, Helen	My Friend		Wright Group	1	
		5	McCoy, David	I Can Swim	81362035X	Modern Curriculum	1	
		6	Peters, Catherine	Willy the Helper	669445177	Houghton Mifflin	1	
		7	Raschka, Chris	Yo! Yes?	531071081	Orchard Books	1	
		8	Rau, Dana	Box Can Be Many Things, A	516261533	Children's Press	1	
		9	Ruckfield, Liyola	Bird Feeder	1572576952	Wright Group	1	
		10	Wall, Julia	All By Myself	780265661	Wright Group	1	
	4	1	Aliki	I Wish I Was Sick Too	68809354X	William Morrow & Co	1	

Group Description	Level	#	Author	Title	ISBN	Publisher	Quantity	Heinemann Write-Up
		2	Anholt, Catherine & Laurence	All About You	590469886	Scholastic Inc.	1	Y
		3	Barton, Byron	I Want to be an Astronaut	64432807	Harper Collins	1	
		4	Bonsall, Crosby	And I Mean It, Stanley	644046X	Harper Collins	1	Y
		5	Carelli, Dawn	Dr. Green	669445339	Houghton Mifflin	1	
		6	Gelman, Rita Golden	More Spaghetti I Say	590457837	Scholastic Inc.	1	Y
		7	Gisler, David & Tom Dunnington	Addition Annie	516020072	Children's Press	1	
		8	Hoban, Julian & Lillian Hoban	Amy Loves the Wind	60224029	Harper Collins	1	
		9	Hutchins, Pat	Titch	689716885	Simon & Schuster	1	Y
		10	Jackson, Marjorie	Mai-Li's Surprise	1572740205	Richard C. Owen Publishers	1	
		11	Marzollo, Jean	I'm a Caterpillar	590847791	Scholastic Inc.	1	Y
		12	McKissack, Patricia	Messy Bessey	516270036	Children's Press/Rookie Readers	1	Y
		13	Minarik, Else Holmelund	Cat and Dog	60242213	Harper Collins	1	
		14	Moffat, Judith	Who Stole the Cookies?	590065971	Scholastic Inc.	1	
		15	Moss, Sally	Peter's Painting	1572550139	Mondo Publishing	1	
		16	Porter, Gracie	Questions, Questions, Questions	780289889	Wright Group	1	
		17	Pyers, Greg	Animal Feet	763560952	Rigby	1	
		18	Randell, Beverly	Lion and the Mouse, The	435067435	Rigby	1	Y
		19	Semple, Cheryl	Pancakes for Supper	732702011	Wright Group	1	Y
		20	Silverstein, Shel	Giving Tree, The	60256656	Harper Collins	1	
		21	West, Colin	"Pardon?" Said the Giraffe	397321732	Harper Collins	1	Y
		22	Ziefert, Harriet	Nicky Upstairs and Downstairs	140368523	Penguin Publishing	1	Y
	5	1	Ahlberg, Janet & Allan	Each Peach, Pear, Plum	14050639X	Penguin Putnam	1	Y

Group Description	Level	#	Author	Title	ISBN	Publisher	Quantity	Heinemann Write-Up
		2	Brown, Marc	DW All Wet	316112682	Little Brown & Co	1	
		3	Cowley, Joy	Horrible Thing with Hairy Feet, The	868677035	Rigby	1	Y
		4	Cowley, Joy	Little Yellow Chicken, The	780149941	Wright Group	1	Y
		5	Fowler, Allan	All Along the River	516460196	Children's Press	1	Y
		6	Fox, Mem	Hattie and the Fox	689716117	Simon & Schuster	1	Y
		7	Fox, Mem	Zoo Looking	1572550104	Mondo Publishing	1	
		8	Hoff, Syd	Sammy the Seal	64442705	Harper Trophy	1	Y
		9	Hutchins, Pat	You'll Soon Grow Into Them, Titch	688115071	Mulberry Books	1	Y
		10	Iversen, Sandra	Baby Elephant's Sneeze	780265726	Wright Group	1	Y
		11	Jonas, Ann	Quilt, The	140553088	Penguin Publishing	1	
		12	Jonas, Ann	Reflections	688061400	William Morrow & Co	1	
		13	Kraus, Robert	Come Out and Play Little Mouse	688140262	William Morrow & Co	1	
		14	Kraus, Robert	Whose Mouse Are You?	689711425	Simon & Schuster	1	
		15	Lawrence, Lucy	Buffy's Tricks	732700698	Rigby	1	Y
		16	McDuff, Dona	Chicken Pox!	669445355	Clarion Books	1	
		17	Minarik, Else Holmelund	Father Bear Comes Home	64440141	Harper Collins	1	
		18	Nodset, Joan	Who Took the Farmer's Hat	64431746	Harper Collins	1	Y
		19	Noonan, Diana	My Friend Jess	780212266	Wright Group	1	
		20	Robinson, Fay	Vegetables, Vegetables!	516460307	Children's Press	1	Y
		21	Stevens, Janet	Town Mouse and the Country Mouse, The	823407330	Holiday House	1	Y
		22	Vaughan, Marcia	Where Does the Wind Go?	1572550074	Mondo Publishing	1	
		23	Wells, Rosemary	Max's Chocolate Chicken	140566724	Penguin Putnam	1	
		24	Wild, Margaret	Rosie and Tortoise	789426307	DK Publishing	1	Y
		25	Ziefert, Harriet	Harry Series/Harry Goes to Day Camp	140370005	Penguin Putnam	1	

Group Description	Level	#	Author	Title	ISBN	Publisher	Quantity	Heinemann Write-Up
	6	1	Adler, David	Young Cam Jansen Series/and the Dinosaur Game	140377794	Viking Penguin	1	Y
		2	Adler, David	Young Cam Jansen Series/the Ice Skate Mystery	141300124	Penguin Putnam	1	Y
		3	Aliki	We Are Best Friends	68807037X	William Morrow & Co	1	
		4	Asch, Frank	Bear Shadow/Moonbear Series	590440543	Scholastic Inc.	1	
		5	Barrett, Judith	Animals Should Definitely Not Wear Clothing	689708076	Simon & Schuster	1	Y
		6	Bourgeois, Brenda	Franklin Goes to School	590254677	Scholastic Inc.	1	
		7	Bridwell, Norman	Count on Clifford	590442848	Scholastic Inc.	1	
		8	Byars, Betsy	My Brother, Ant	14038345X	Penguin Puffin	1	
		9	Carle, Eric	Tiny Seed, The	590425668	Scholastic Inc.	1	Y
		10	Cole, Joanna	Bony Legs	590405160	Scholastic Inc.	1	
		11	de Paola, Tomie	Charlie Needs a Cloak	671664670	Simon & Schuster	1	
		12	Fowler, Allan	Hard to See Animals	516262599	Children's Press	1	
		13	Isadora, Rachel	South African Night, A	688113907 (hc)	William Morrow & Co	1	
		14	James, Simon	Dear Mr. Blueberry	689807686	Simon & Schuster	1	Y
		15	Kessler, Leonard	Here Comes the Strikeout	64440117	Harper Trophy	1	
		16	Lobel, Arnold	Frog and Toad Series/Days with Frog and Toad	64440583	Harper Collins	1	Y
		17	Marshall, Val	Postman Pete	1572551097	Mondo Publishing	1	
		18	Minarik, Else Holmelund	Little Bear Series/A Kiss for Little Bear	64440508	Harper Collins	1	Y
		19	Rylant, Cynthia	Henry and Mudge Series/In the Sparkle Days	689810199	Simon & Schuster	1	
		20	Rylant, Cynthia	Mr. Putter & Tabby/Pick the Pears	590330527	Harcourt Brace	1	Y
		21	Tolkien, J.R.R.	Hole in Harry's Pocket, The	395177111	Houghton Mifflin	1	

Group Description	Level	#	Author	Title	ISBN	Publisher	Quantity	Heinemann Write-Up
	7	1	Alphin, Elaine	Bear for Miguel, A	64442349	Harper Collins	1	
		2	Bemelmans, Ludwig	Madeline's Rescue	140502076	Penguin Putnam	1	Y
		3	Bridwell, Norman	Clifford the Big Red Dog	59044297X	Scholastic Inc.	1	
		4	Burns, Marilyn	Greedy Triangle, The	590489917 (hc)	Scholastic Inc.	1	
		5	Byars, Betsy	Golly Sisters Ride Again	64442071	Harper Collins	1	
		6	Denton, Terry	Gasp!	1572552239	Mondo Publishing	1	
		7	Fowler, Allan	It Could Still Be Water	51646003X	Children's Press	1	
		8	Havill, Juanita	Jamaica's Find	590425048	Scholastic Inc.	1	Y
		9	Henkes, Kevin	Lilly's Purple Plastic Purse	688128971 (hc)	Greenwillow Books	1	Y
		10	Hoban, Lillian	Arthur's Birthday Party	64442802	Harper Collins	1	Y
		11	Hoban, Lillian	Arthur's Halloween Costume	64441016	Harper Trophy	1	Y
		12	Lionni, Leo	Swimmy	590430491	Scholastic Inc.	1	Y
		13	McMullan, Kate	Fluffy Series/Fluffy's 100th Day of School	590523090	Scholastic Inc.	1	
		14	Paterson, Katherine	Smallest Cow in the World, The	64441644	Harper Collins	1	
		15	Ross, Pat	M&M Series/Meet M&M	140387315	Penguin Puffin	1	Y
		16	Ross, Pat	M&M Series/The Big Bag	394943406	Pantheon Books	1	
		17	Rylant, Cynthia	Mr. Putter & Tabby Paint the Porch	152017879	Harcourt Brace	1	
		18	Sharmat, Marjorie Weinman	Nate the Great and the Phony Clue	440463009	Bantam Doubleday Dell	1	Y
		19	Sharmat, Marjorie Weinman	Nate the Great and the Snowy Trail	440462762	Bantam Doubleday Dell	1	Y
	8	1	Cazet, Denys	Minnie & Moo Go to the Moon	789425378	DK Publishing	1	
		2	Cosby, Bill	Little Bill Series/Best Way to Play	590956175	Scholastic Inc.	1	
		3	Fowler, Allan	Good Mushrooms and Bad Toadstools	516263633	Children's Press	1	

Group Description	Level	#	Author	Title	ISBN	Publisher	Quantity	Heinemann Write-Up
		4	McCloskey, Robert	Blueberries for Sal	14050169X	Penguin Puffin	1	Y
		5	Stewart, Sarah	Gardener, The	374325170	Farrar Strauss & Giroux	1	Y
		6	Yolen, Jane	Commander Toad Series/the Big Black Hole	698114035	Putnam Publishing	1	Y
	9	1	de Paola, Tomie	Here We All Are	399234969	Penguin Publishing	1	
		2	de Paola, Tomie	On My Way	399235833	Penguin Putnam	1	
	10	1	Martin, Jacqueline Briggs	Snowflake Bentley	395861624	Houghton Mifflin	1	Y
Teaching Writing		1	Baylor, Byrd	I'm in Charge of Celebrations	689806205	Simon & Schuster	1	Y
		2	Cisneros, Sandra	Hairs: Pelitos	679890076	Alfred A. Knopf	1	Y
		3	Farber, Norma	These Small Stones	6024013X	Harper Collins	1	
		4	Rockwell, Anne	I Fly	517885697	Crown Publishers	1	
		5	Spinelli, Eileen	Night Shift Daddy	786824247	Hyperion Books	1	
Poetry		1	Adoff, Alfred	In for Winter, Out for Spring	152014926	Harcourt Brace	1	
		2	Hopkins, Lee Bennett	Sports! Sports! Sports! A Poetry Collection	64437132	Harper Collins	1	
		3	multiple authors	Sing a Song of Popcorn	59043974X	Scholastic Inc.	1	
		4	Yolen, Jane	Sky Scrape/City Scape	1563971798	Boyds Mills Press	1	
Read-Aloud Texts		1	Atwater, Richard	Mr. Popper's Penguins	590477331	Little Brown & Co	1	Y
		2	Blume, Judy	SuperFudge	440484332	Bantam Doubleday Dell	1	Y
		3	Browne, Anthony	Piggybook	67980837X	Alfred A Knopf	1	
		4	Bunting, Eve	Picnic in October, A	152016562	Harcourt Brace	1	
		5	Carlson, Nancy	Arnie and the Skateboard Gang	67085722X	Viking Penguin	1	
		6	Cleary, Beverly	Ramona and Her Mother	38070952X	Avon Books	1	Y
		7	Cooney, Barbara	Miss Rumphius	140505393	Penguin Putnam	1	Y
		8	de Paola, Tomie	Art Lesson, The	39921688X	Putnam & Grosset	1	Y
		9	Golenbock, Peter	Teammates	152842861	Harcourt Brace	1	Y

Group Description	Level	#	Author	Title	ISBN	Publisher	Quantity	Heinemann Write-Up
		10	Hughes, Shirley	Able's Moon	789446014	Scholastic Inc.	1	Y
		11	Hughes, Ted	Iron Giant, The	375801537	Alfred A. Knopf	1	Y
		12	Kimmel, Eric A.	Herschel & the Hanukkah Goblins	823411311	Holiday House	1	Y
		13	Lindgren, Astrid	Pippi Longstocking	140309578	Penguin Putnam	1	Y
		14	Lionni, Leo	Fish is Fish	590400061	Scholastic Inc.	1	Y
		15	McLerran, Alice	Roxaboxen	140544755	Penguin Publishing	1	Y
		16	Milne, A.A.	Winnie the Pooh	140361219	Penguin Putnam	1	
		17	Polacco, Patricia	Thundercake	698115813	Putnam Publishing	1	Y
		18	Rylant, Cynthia	All I See	531070484	Orchard Books	1	
		19	Rylant, Cynthia	Angel for Solomon Singer, An	531070824	Orchard Books	1	Y
		20	Steig, William	Amazing Bone, The	374403589	Farrar Strauss & Giroux	1	Y
		21	Yashima, Taro	Crow Boy	14050172X	Penguin Putnam	1	

MODULE 1: More Independent and Partnership Reading: Filling in the Lower Portion of the Library

Group Description	Level	#	Author	Title	ISBN	Publisher	Quantity	Heinemann Write-Up
	2	1	Ballinger, Margaret	What Has Stripes?	439116678	Scholastic Inc.	1	
		2	Hoenecke, Karen	Spaceship	1879835428	Kaeden Corporation	1	
		3	Layne, Henry	Where Do You Play?	322001544	Wright Group	1	
		4	Pasternac, Susana	In the City	590273728	Scholastic Inc.	1	
		5	Peters, Catherine	My Dog Willy	669445185	Clarion Books	1	
	3	1	Bancroft, Gloria	On the Computer	780288920	Wright Group	1	
		2	Benjamin, Cynthia	Footprints in the Sand	59044087X	Scholastic Inc.	1	Y
		3	Buxton, Jane	Going to Lucy's House	780263286	Wright Group	1	
		4	Christiansan, Nancy	Who Am I?	590461923	Scholastic Inc.	1	
		5	Cutting, Brian	Seeds, Seeds, Seeds	780202473	Wright Group	1	
		6	Franco, Betsy	Bo & Peter	590273752	Scholastic Inc.	1	
		7	Giles, Jenny	My Dad	763526762	Rigby	1	

Group Description	Level	#	Author	Title	ISBN	Publisher	Quantity	Heinemann Write-Up
		8	Hoff, Syd	Captain Cat	64441768	Harper Collins	1	Y
		9	Kneidel, Sally	Who Lays Eggs?	322001706	Wright Group	1	Y
		10	Lawrence, Lucy	Mr. Wind	73270068X	Rigby	1	
		11	Nayer, Judy	Tree Can Be, A	590962817	Scholastic Inc.	1	
		12	Podoshen, Lois	Artist, The	1572741376	Richard C. Owen Publishers	1	Y
		13	Randell, Beverly	Blackberries	435049186	Rigby	1	Y
		14	Robinson, Fay	When Do You Feel?	322001692	Wright Group	1	
		15	Scarffe, Bronwen	Oh No!	1879531585	Mondo Publishing	1	
		16	Simpson, T.	Well-fed Bear, The	868677647	Rigby	1	Y
		17	Stephens, V.	I Love Mud and Mud Loves Me	590273817	Scholastic Inc.	1	
	4	1	Boss, Kittie	Cat Tails	1572741392	Richard C. Owen Publishers	1	Y
		2	Bovetz, Marcie	Slice of Pizza, A	322001854	Wright Group	1	
		3	Capucilli, Alyssa	Biscuit	64442128	Harper Collins	1	
		4	Coughlan, Cheryl	Flies	736802401	Pebble Books	1	Y
		5	Durkee, Andrew	Hand-Me-Downs, The	669445320	Houghton Mifflin	1	
		6	Galdone, Paul	Three Billy Goats Gruff, The	899190359	Houghton Mifflin	1	Y
		7	Hall, Kirsten	Bad Bad Day, A	590254960	Scholastic Inc.	1	
		8	Henkes, Kevin	Shhhh	688079865	Greenwillow Books	1	
		9	Kroniger, Stephen	If I Crossed the Road	68981190X	Simon & Schuster	1	
		10	Maccarone, Grace	Itchy Itchy Chicken Pox	590449486	Scholastic Inc.	1	
		11	McKissack, Patricia	Messy Bessey's Closet	516020919	Children's Press	1	
		12	Podoshen, L.	Paco's Garden	1572742356	Richard C. Owen Publishers	1	
		13	Porter, Gracie	Running	780291883	Wright Group	1	Y
		14	Pyers, Greg	Changing Shape	763560979	Rigby	1	
		15	Ramsey, Joe	Wolves	32201714	Wright Group	1	
		16	Randell, Beverly	Baby Hippo	763515124	Rigby	1	Y

Group Description	Level	#	Author	Title	ISBN	Publisher	Quantity	Heinemann Write-Up
		17	Randell, Beverly	Duck with a Broken Wing	763515213	Rigby	1	
		18	Randell, Beverly	Mushrooms for Dinner	435067338	Rigby	1	
		19	Slack, Paula	Face Painting	780228642	Wright Group	1	
		20	Sloan, P.	Women at Work	780233956	Wright Group	1	
		21	Warren, Celia	Grandpa's Clues	763566314	Rigby	1	
		22	Zolotow, Charlotte	William's Doll	64430677	Harper Trophy	1	
	5	1	Aker, Suzanne	What Comes in 2s, 3s, and 4s?	671792474	Simon & Schuster	1	
		2	Bennet, Jill	Teeny Tiny	698116135	Putnam	1	
		3	Birchall, Brian	Pig William's Midnight Walk	155624620X	Wright Group	1	
		4	Bissett, Isabel	First, Take the Flour…	763560995	Rigby	1	
		5	Bloksberg, Robin	Night the Lights Went Out, The	669445428	Houghton Mifflin	1	
		6	Butler, Dorothy	My Brown Bear Barney	688177239	William Morrow & Co	1	
		7	Capucilli, Alyssa	Happy Thanksgiving, Biscuit!	694012211	Harper Collins	1	
		8	Cowley, Joy	Letters for Mr. James	780249720	Wright Group	1	
		9	Cowley, Joy	Little Brown House, The	79010685X	Rigby	1	
		10	Freeman, Marcia	Maple Trees	736800921	Pebble Books	1	
		11	Gray, Nigel	Country Far Away, A	531070247	Orchard Books	1	
		12	Hubbard, Woodleigh	My Crayons Talk	805061509	Henry Holt & Co	1	
		13	Medearis, Angela Shelf	100th Day of School, The	59025944X	Scholastic Inc.	1	
		14	Paradise, Susan	My Daddy	1886910502	Front Street	1	
		15	Parsons, John	Polar Bears	78024592X	Wright Group	1	
		16	Preller, James	Hiccups for Elephant	590485881	Scholastic Inc.	1	
		17	Reid, Mary	How Have I Grown?	590292986	Scholastic Inc.	1	
		18	Riley, Kana	New Citizens	322018501	Wright Group	1	
		19	Scarffe, Bronwen	Manners of a Pig, The	1572551038	Mondo Publishing	1	

Group Description	Level	#	Author	Title	ISBN	Publisher	Quantity	Heinemann Write-Up
		20	Vandine, JoAnn	Little Mouse's Trail Tale	1879531593	Mondo Publishing	1	
		21	Warren, Adrian	Walking by the Rio	1572741538	Richard C. Owen Publishers	1	
		22	Ziefert, Harriet	Henny Penny	140381880	Penguin Puffin	1	

MODULE 2: More Independent and Partnership Reading: Filling in the Middle of the Library

Group Description	Level	#	Author	Title	ISBN	Publisher	Quantity	Heinemann Write-Up
	6	1	Asch, Frank	Bears Bargain/Moonbear Series	671678388	Simon & Schuster	1	
		2	Barrett, Judi	Cloudy with a Chance of Meatballs	689707495	Simon & Schuster	1	
		3	Bauer, Marion	Alison's Puppy	786811404	Hyperion Books	1	
		4	Bokoske, Sharon	Dolphins (Step into Reading Books Series: A Step 2 Book)	679844376	Random House	1	
		5	Boon, Kevin	Frogs	780245725	Wright Group	1	
		6	Boon, Kevin	Lizards	780245822	Wright Group	1	
		7	Curtis, Matt	Six Empty Pockets	51626253X	Children's Press	1	
		8	Fowler, Allan	Biggest Animal Ever, The	5164600013	Children's Press	1	
		9	Fowler, Allan	Icebergs, Ice Caps, and Glaciers	516262572	Childrens Press/Rookie Read-About Science	1	
		10	Fowler, Allan	It's a Fruit, It's a Vegetable, It's a Pumpkin	516460390	Childrens Press/Rookie Read-About Science	1	
		11	Fowler, Allan	Really Big Cats	516263676	Childrens Press/Rookie Read-About Science	1	
		12	Fowler, Allan	Where Land Meets Sea	51626155X	Childrens Press/Rookie Read-About Science	1	
		13	Fowler, Allan	Woolly Sheep and Hungry Goats	516060147	Children's Press	1	
		14	Hoff, Syd	Horse in Harry's Room, The	64440737	Harper Collins	1	
		15	Hoff, Syd	Oliver	6028708X	Harper Collins	1	Y
		16	Holub, Joan	Pajama Party	448417391	Grosset & Dunlap	1	
		17	Lobel, Arnold	Martha the Movie Mouse	64433188	Harper Trophy	1	Y
		18	Lobel, Arnold	Mouse Soup	64440419	Harper Trophy	1	Y

Group Description	Level	#	Author	Title	ISBN	Publisher	Quantity	Heinemann Write-Up
		19	Maestro, Betsy	Taxi: A Book of City Words	39554811X	Houghton Mifflin	1	
		20	Meharry, Dot	Uncle Carlos' Barbeque	780265971	Wright Group	1	
		21	Michaels, Jade	Perla's Family	1586530267	Mondo	1	
		22	Minarik, Else Holmelund	Little Bear Series/Little Bear's Visit	64440230	Harper Trophy	1	Y
		23	Robinson, Fay	Solid, Liquid, Or Gas?	516460412	Childrens Press/Rookie Read-About Science	1	
		24	Rylant, Cynthia	Henry and Mudge Series/and Annie's Good Move	590040537	Simon & Schuster	1	
		25	Rylant, Cynthia	Henry and Mudge Series/and the Best Day of All	689813856	Simon & Schuster	1	Y
		26	Zion, Gene	Harry and the Lady Next Door	64440087	Harper Trophy	1	
	7	1	Bemelmans, Ludwig	Madeline Series/Madeline in America	590043064	Scholastic Inc.	1	Y
		2	de Paola, Tomie	Popcorn Book, The	823405338	Holiday House	1	
		3	Henkes, Kevin	Chester's Way	688154727	Mulberry Books	1	
		4	Henkes, Kevin	Julius, the Baby of the World	688143881	Mulberry Books	1	Y
		5	Hoban, Lillian	Arthur's Honey Bear	64440338	Harper Collins	1	Y
		6	Hoban, Lillian	Arthur's Pen Pal	6444032X	Harper Collins	1	
		7	Hoban, Lillian	Case of the Two Masked Robbers, The	64441210	Harper Trophy	1	
		8	Hoban, Russell	Frances Books Series/Bedtime for Frances	64434516	Harper Collins	1	
		9	Johnson, Donald B.	Henry Hikes to Fitchburg	395968674	Houghton Mifflin	1	
		10	Keats, Ezra Jack	Maggie and the Pirate	590448528	Scholastic Inc.	1	Y
		11	Kent, Jack	Bremen Town Musicians, The	590423649	Scholastic Inc.	1	
		12	Littledale, Freya	Peter and the North Wind	590407562	Scholastic Inc.	1	

Group Description	Level	#	Author	Title	ISBN	Publisher	Quantity	Heinemann Write-Up
		13	Minarik, Else Holmelund	No Fighting No Biting	6444015X	Harper Collins	1	
		14	Noble, Trinka	Day Jimmy's Boa Ate the Wash, The	140546235	Dial Books	1	
		15	Parish, Peggy	Dinosaur Time	64440370	Harper Collins	1	
		16	Paulsen, Gary	Tortilla Factory, The	152016988	Harcourt Brace	1	Y
		17	Pellegrini, Nina	Families are Different	823408876	Holiday House	1	
		18	Ross, Pat	M&M Series/Super Child Afternoon	140321454	Penguin Putnam	1	
		19	Rylant, Cynthia	High Rise Private Eyes/Case of the Climbing Cat	688163106	Greenwillow Books	1	Y
		20	Scieszka, Jon	True Story of the 3 Little Pigs, The	140544518	Penguin Putnam	1	
		21	Sharmat, Marjorie Weinman	Big Fat Enormous Lie, A	590967991	Scholastic Inc.	1	
		22	Sharmat, Marjorie Weinman	Nate the Great and the Tardy Tortoise	440412692	Bantam Doubleday Dell	1	
		23	Van Leeuwen, Jean	Amanda Pig, School Girl	141303573	Penguin Putnam	1	
		24	Van Leeuwen, Jean	Tales of Oliver Pig	140365494	Penguin Puffin	1	
		25	Wood, Audrey	Little Penguin's Tale	152474765	Harcourt Brace	1	Y

MODULE 3: More Independent and Partnership Reading: Filling in the Upper Portion of the Library

Group Description	Level	#	Author	Title	ISBN	Publisher	Quantity	Heinemann Write-Up
	8	1	Aliki	Fossils Tell of Long Ago	64450937	Harper Trophy	1	Y
		2	Anno, Mitsumas	Anno's Magic Seeds	698116186	Penguin Putnam	1	
		3	Brown, Marc	Arthur Chapter Books Series/Muffy's Secret Admirer	316122300	Little Brown & Co	1	
		4	Cole, Joanna	Hungry Hungry Sharks	394874714	Random House	1	
		5	Cosby, Bill	Little Bill Series/One Dark and Scary Night	590514768	Scholastic Inc.	1	
		6	Cosby, Bill	Little Bill Series/Meanest Thing to Say	590956167	Scholastic Inc.	1	

Group Description	Level	#	Author	Title	ISBN	Publisher	Quantity	Heinemann Write-Up
		7	Dadey, Debbie	Bailey School Kids Series/Hercules Doesn't Pull Teeth	590258095	Scholastic Inc.	1	
		8	Dadey, Debbie	Triplet Trouble and the Field Day Disaster	590581074	Scholastic Inc.	1	
		9	Fowler, Allan	Best Way to See a Shark, The	516460323	Children's Press	1	
		10	Howe, James	Pinky & Rex Series/the New Neighbors	689812965	Simon & Schuster	1	
		11	Hurwitz, Johanna	Russel Rides Again	688166652	Beech Tree	1	
		12	Kline, Suzy	Horrible Harry Series/Horrible Harry's Secret	590466372	Scholastic Inc.	1	
		13	Kuskin, Karla	Philharmonic Gets Dressed, The	6443124X	Harper Collins	1	
		14	Merrill, Claire	Seed is a Promise, A	590434543	Scholastic Inc.	1	
		15	Osborne, Mary Pope	Magic Tree House Series/Afternoon on the Amazon	679863729	Random House	1	
		16	Parish, Herman	Amelia Bedelia Series/Good Driving, Amelia Bedelia	38072510X	Avon Books	1	
		17	Parish, Peggy	Amelia Bedelia Series/Good Work, Amelia Bedelia	380728311	Avon Books	1	Y
		18	Patterson, Francine	Koko's Kitten	590444255	Scholastic Inc.	1	
		19	Ryder, Joanne	My Father's Hand	68809189X	William & Morrow	1	Y
		20	Rylant, Cynthia	Bird House, The	59047345X	Scholastic Inc.	1	
		21	Steig, William	Doctor de Soto	374418101	Farrar Strauss & Giroux	1	
		22	Ziefert, Harriet	New Coat for Anna, A	590416685	Scholastic Inc.	1	
	9	1	Aardema, Verna	Bringing the Rain to Kapiti Plain	140546162	Penguin Publishing	1	
		2	Betancourt, Jeanne	Ten True Animal Rescues	590681176	Scholastic Inc.	1	
		3	Brisson, Pat	Summer My Father Was 10, The	1563978296	Boyds Mills Press	1	
		4	Brown, Marcia	Stone Soup: An Old Tale	689711034	Simon & Schuster	1	
		5	Cameron, Ann	Stories Huey Tells, The	679885595	Alfred A. Knopf	1	

Group Description	Level	#	Author	Title	ISBN	Publisher	Quantity	Heinemann Write-Up
		6	Cleary, Beverly	Socks	380709260	William Morrow & Co	1	
		7	Donnelly, Judy	Titanic: Lost . . . and Found	394886690	Random House	1	
		8	Erickson, Russell	Toad for Tuesday	688163254	William Morrow & Co	1	
		9	Fletcher, Ralph	Grandpa Never Lies	395797705	Houghton Mifflin	1	
		10	Giff, Patricia Reilly	Ballet Slippers Series/Glass Slipper for Rosie	141301597	Puffin	1	
		11	Greene, Carol	Pocahontas: Daughter of a Chief	516042033	Children's Press	1	
		12	Hurwitz, Johanna	Class President	67988999X	Random House	1	
		13	Hurwitz, Johanna	Summer with Elisa	688170951	Harper Collins	1	
		14	Kline, Suzy	Song Lee/and the "I Hate You" Notes	141303034	Penguin Putnam	1	
		15	Landon, Lucinda	Meg MacKintosh Series/Case of the Curious Whale Watch	1888695013	Secret Passage Press	1	
		16	MacBride, Roger Lea	Little House Chapter Books/ Adventures of Rose and Swiney-Rose #4	64421082	Harper Trophy	1	
		17	Parks, Rosa & Jim Haskins	I Am Rosa Parks	141307102	Dial Books	1	
		18	Peet, Bill	Ant and the Elephant, The	590617257	Houghton Mifflin	1	
		19	Roy, Ron	A to Z Mysteries/Empty Envelope (#5)	679890548	Random House	1	
		20	Smith, Janice Lee	Adam Joshua Capers Series/Show and Tell War	6442006X	Harper Collins	1	
		21	Warner, Gertrude	Boxcar Children Series/Guide Dog Mystery	590569015	Scholastic Inc.	1	
		22	Weeks, Sarah	Follow the Moon	60244429	Harper Collins	1	

MODULE 4: Genre and Author Studies

Group Description	Level	#	Author	Title	ISBN	Publisher	Quantity	Heinemann Write-Up
Author Studies		1	Cohen, Miriam	Best Friends	689713347	Simon & Schuster	1	
		2	Cohen, Miriam	It's George	440411645	Bantam Doubleday Dell	1	

Group Description	Level	#	Author	Title	ISBN	Publisher	Quantity	Heinemann Write-Up
		3	Cohen, Miriam	Jim Meets the Thing: Welcome to First Grade!	44041167X	Bantam Doubleday Dell	1	
		4	Cohen, Miriam	Second Grade Friends	590474634	Scholastic Inc.	1	
		5	Cohen, Miriam	When Will I Read?	688840736	Greenwillow	1	
		6	de Paola, Tomie	26 Fairmount Avenue	698118642	Putnam Publishing	1	Y
		7	de Paola, Tomie	Baby Sister, The	698117735	Penguin Putnam	1	
		8	de Paola, Tomie	Legend of the Poinsettia, The	590486799	Scholastic Inc.	1	Y
		9	de Paola, Tomie	Oliver Button is a Sissy	156681404	Harcourt Brace	1	
		10	de Paola, Tomie	Strega Nona	671666061	Aladdin	1	
		11	Hutchins, Pat	Changes, Changes	689711379	Simon & Schuster	1	Y
		12	Hutchins, Pat	Doorbell Rang, The	590411098	Scholastic Inc.	1	
		13	Hutchins, Pat	Good Night Owl	689713711	Aladdin	1	
		14	Hutchins, Pat	My Best Friend	688114857	Harper Collins	1	
		15	Hutchins, Pat	Rosie's Walk	20437501	Simon & Schuster	1	Y
		16	Johnson, Angela	Daddy Calls Me Man	531071758	Orchard Books	1	
		17	Johnson, Angela	Do Like Kyla	531070409	Orchard Books	1	Y
		18	Johnson, Angela	Julius	531071022	Orchard Books	1	Y
		19	Johnson, Angela	Leaving Morning, The	531070727	Orchard Books	1	Y
		20	Johnson, Angela	Tell Me a Story Mama	531070328	Orchard Books	1	
Biographies		1	Brenner, Martha	Abe Lincoln's Hat	679849777	Random House	1	
		2	Davidson, Margaret	Story of Jackie Robinson	440400198	Bantam Doubleday Dell	1	
		3	Lundell, Margo	Girl Named Helen Keller, A	590479636	Scholastic Inc.	1	
		4	Parks, Rosa & Jim Haskins	I Am Rosa Parks	141307102	Dial Books	1	
		5	Parlin, J.	Amelia Earhart	440401178	Dell Publishing	1	
		6	Ringgold, Faith	My Dream of Martin Luther King	517885778	Crown	1	

Group Description	Level	#	Author	Title	ISBN	Publisher	Quantity	Heinemann Write-Up
Memoir		1	Clifford, Eth	Remembering Box, The	688117775	Houghton Mifflin	1	Y
		2	Crews, Donald	Big Mama's	590221213	Scholastic Inc.	1	
		3	Pomerantz, Charlotte	Chalk Doll, The	64433331	Harper Collins	1	
		4	Sisnett, Ana	Two Mrs. Gibsons	892391359	Children's Press	1	
		5	Zolotow, Charlotte	This Quiet Lady	688175279	William Morrow & Co	1	Y
List Books		1	Moss, Thylias	I Want To Be	140562869	Penguin Puffin	1	
		2	Rylant, Cynthia	When I Was Young in the Mountains	140548750	Penguin Publishing	1	
		3	Zolotow, Charlotte	I Like to Be Little	64432483	Harper Collins	1	
		4	Zolotow, Charlotte	My Friend John	385326513	Bantam Doubleday Dell	1	Y
Nonfiction Texts		1	Fowler, Allan	Life in a Pond	516202189	Children's Press	1	
		2	Jenkins, Martin	Chameleons Are Cool	763601446	Candlewick Press	1	
		3	Lindbergh, Reeve	What Is the Sun?	1564026094	Candlewick Press	1	
		4	Neye, Emily	Butterflies	448419661	Penguin Putnam	1	
		5	Ryder, Joanne	Snails Spell	140508910	Penguin Putnam	1	Y
Poetry		1	Chandra, Deborah	Balloons and Other Poems	374404925	Farrar Strauss & Giroux	1	
		2	Graham, Joan Bransfield	Flicker Flash	39590501X	Houghton Mifflin	1	
		3	Greenfield, Eloise	Honey, I Love	64430979	Harper Collins	1	Y
		4	Greenfield, Eloise	Night On Neighborhood Street	140556834	Penguin	1	Y
		5	Grimes, Nikki	Shoe Magic	531302865	Scholastic Inc.	1	
		6	Hopkins, Lee Bennett	Pterodactyls and Pizza	440844681	Scholastic Inc.	1	
		7	Stevenson, James	Cornflakes	688167187	Greenwillow Books	1	

MODULE 5: Talking Across Books

Group Description	Level	#	Author	Title	ISBN	Publisher	Quantity	Heinemann Write-Up
New York City		1	Dorros, Arthur	Abuela	140562257	Penguin Puffin	1	
		2	Kent, Deborah	New York City	516260723	Grolier	1	

Group Description	Level	#	Author	Title	ISBN	Publisher	Quantity	Heinemann Write-Up
		3	Konigsburg, E.L.	*Amy Elizabeth Explores Bloomingdales*	68983201X	Simon & Schuster	1	
		4	Maestro, Betsy	*Story of the Statue of Liberty*	688087469	William Morrow & Co	1	
		5	Rotner, Shelley	*Citybook*	531071065	Orchard	1	
Ocean Animals		1	Burton, French & Jones	*Ocean Animals*	1583440747	Benchmark Books	1	
		2	Ryder, Joanne	*Winter Whale*	688131107	William Morrow & Co	1	
		3	Smith, Sue	*Exploring Saltwater Habitats*	1879531321	Mondo Publishing	1	
		4	Swartz, Stanley	*Octopuses, Squid & Cuttlefish*	768503515	Dominie Press	1	
		5	Swartz, Stanley	*Sea Turtles*	768503531	Dominie Press	1	
		6	Wallace, Karen	*Gentle Giant Octopus*	76360318X	Candlewick Press	1	
		7	Wu, Norbert	*Fish Faces*	805053476	Henry Holt & Co	1	
Rural Communities		1		*If You're Not from the Prarie*			1	
		2		*Living in the Mountains*			1	
		3		*Work Song*			1	
		4	MacLachlan, Patricia	*What You Know First*	64434923	Harper Trophy	1	Y
Sports		1	Blackstone, Margaret	*This Is Baseball*	805051694	Henry Holt & Co	1	
		2	Brenner, Richard	*Sammy Sosa*	688170846	William Morrow & Co	1	
		3	Gibbons, Gail	*My Soccer Book*	688171389	William Morrow & Co	1	
		4	Kelley, James	*Baseball*	789452413	DK Publishing	1	
		5	Smith, Michael	*Sports Are Fun*	817282696	Steck-Vaughn	1	
Water		1	Berger, Melvin	*Amazing Water*	1567841295	Newbridge Educational Publishing	1	
		2	Biddulph, Fred & Jeanne	*Clouds, Rain and Fog*		Wright Group	1	
		3	Cutting, Brian & Jillian	*Clouds*	780250052	Wright Group	1	

Group Description	Level	#	Author	Title	ISBN	Publisher	Quantity	Heinemann Write-Up
		4	Fowler, Allan	It Could Still Be Water	51646003X	Children's Press	1	
		5	Parks, Brenda	Water Changes	1567849288	Newbridge Educational Publishing	1	
Weather/ Natural Disaster		1	Biddulph, Fred & Jeanne	Wind and Storms		Wright Group	1	Y
		2	Branley, Franklyn M.	Flash, Crash, Rumble, and Roll	64451798	Harper Collins	1	
		3	Branley, Franklyn M.	Tornado Alert	64450945	Harper Collins	1	
		4	Burton, French & Jones	Power of Nature, The			1	
		5	Hopping, Lorraine	Hurricanes!	590463780	Scholastic, Inc.	1	Y
		6	Iversen, Sandra	Storm, The	780234499	Wright Group	1	Y
MODULE 6: Character Studies								
Alexander		1	Viorst, Judith	Alexander & the Terrible, Horrible, No Good, Very Bad Day	689711735	Simon & Schuster	1	Y
		2	Viorst, Judith	Alexander, Who Used to be...	689711999	Simon & Schuster	1	
		3	Viorst, Judith	Alexander, Who's Not (Do You Hear Me? I Mean It!) Going to Move	689820895	Simon & Schuster	1	
Amelia Bedelia		1	Parish, Peggy	Amelia Bedelia and the Baby	380727951	Avon Books	1	
		2	Parish, Peggy	Amelia Bedelia Series/Helps Out	380534053	Harper Trophy	1	Y
		3	Parish, Peggy	Amelia Bedelia Series/the Surprise Shower	64440192	Harper Trophy	1	Y
		4	Parish, Peggy	Amelia Bedelia Series/Amelia Bedelia	64441555	Harper Trophy	1	Y
Arthur		1	Hoban, Lillian	Arthur's Back to School Day	64442454	Harper Trophy	1	
		2	Hoban, Lillian	Arthur's Funny Money	64440486	Harper Collins	1	
		3	Hoban, Lillian	Arthur's Prize Reader	64440494	Harper & Row	1	
Dragon		1	Pilkey, Dav	Dragon's Series/Dragon's Fat Cat	531070557	Orchard Books	1	

Group Description	Level	#	Author	Title	ISBN	Publisher	Quantity	Heinemann Write-Up
		2	Pilkey, Dav	Dragon's Series/Dragon's Halloween	531059901	Orchard Books	1	
		3	Pilkey, Dav	Dragon's Series/Dragon Gets By	531070816	Orchard Books	1	
Fox		1	Marshall, Edward	Fox Series/Fox at School	140365443	Penguin Puffin	1	Y
		2	Marshall, Edward	Fox Series/Fox Be Nimble	140368426	Penguin Puffin	1	Y
		3	Marshall, Edward	Fox Series/Fox on Stage	140380329	Penguin Puffin	1	
		4	Marshall, Edward	Fox Series/Fox Outfoxed	140381139	Viking Penguin	1	
Franklin		1	Bourgeois, Brenda	Franklin Goes to School	590254677	Scholastic Inc.	1	
		2	Bourgeois, Brenda	Franklin Is Bossy	590477579	Scholastic Inc.	1	
		3	Bourgeois, Brenda	Franklin Is Messy	590486861	Scholastic Inc.	1	
		4	Bourgeois, Brenda	Franklin Plays the Game	590226312	Scholastic Inc.	1	
Frog and Toad		1	Lobel, Arnold	Frog and Toad Series/Frog and Toad All Year	64440591	Harper Collins	1	Y
		2	Lobel, Arnold	Frog and Toad Series/Frog and Toad Are Friends	64440206	Harper Trophy	1	Y
		3	Lobel, Arnold	Frog and Toad Series/Frog and Toad Together	64440214	Harper Trophy	1	Y
George and Martha		1	Marshall, James	George and Martha	395199727	Houghton Mifflin	1	
		2	Marshall, James	George and Martha Back In Town	395479460	Regnery Publishing	1	
		3	Marshall, James	George and Martha Encore	395253799	Houghton Mifflin	1	
		4	Marshall, James	George and Martha Round and Round	395584108	Houghton Mifflin	1	
Lyle		1	Waber, Bernard	Funny Funny Lyle	395602874	Houghton Mifflin	1	
		2	Waber, Bernard	Lovable Lyle	395198585	Houghton Mifflin	1	
		3	Waber, Bernard	Lyle and the Birthday Party	395174511	Houghton Mifflin	1	
		4	Waber, Bernard	Lyle, Lyle Crocodile	440844053	Scholastic Inc.	1	
Madeline		1	Bemelmans, Ludwig	Madeline and the Bad Hat	140566481	Penguin Putnam	1	
		2	Bemelmans, Ludwig	Madeline and the Gypsies	140566473	Penguin Putnam	1	

Group Description	Level	#	Author	Title	ISBN	Publisher	Quantity	Heinemann Write-Up
Miss Nelson		3	Bemelmans, Ludwig	Madeline Series/Madeline	140501983	Penguin Putnam	1	Y
		1	Allard, Harry	Miss Nelson Has a Field Day	395486548	Houghton Mifflin	1	
		2	Allard, Harry	Miss Nelson is Back	39541668X	Houghton Mifflin	1	
		3	Allard, Harry	Miss Nelson is Missing	590118773	Scholastic Inc.	1	Y
Poppleton		1	Rylant, Cynthia	Poppleton	59084783X	Scholastic Inc.	1	Y
		2	Rylant, Cynthia	Poppleton Everyday	590848534	Scholastic Inc.	1	
		3	Rylant, Cynthia	Poppleton in Spring	590848224	Scholastic Inc.	1	Y

MODULE 7: Shared Reading and Read Aloud

Group Description	Level	#	Author	Title	ISBN	Publisher	Quantity	Heinemann Write-Up
Big Books—1 Big Book + 4 Small Copies		1	Galdone, Paul	Henny Penny	899192254	Clarion Books	1	
		2	Guarino, Deborah	Is Your Mama a Llama?	590447254	Scholastic Inc.	1	
		3	Krauss, Ruth	Carrot Seed, The	64432106	Harper Trophy	1	
		4	Sendak, Maurice	Chicken Soup with Rice	6443253X	Harper Trophy	1	
		5	Sharp, Paul	Paul the Pitcher	51642064X	Children's Press	1	
Books About Reading		1	Bunting, Eve	Wednesday Surprise, The	395547768	Clarion Books	1	
		2	Mora, Pat	Tomas and the Library Lady	375803491	Alfred A. Knopf	1	
		3	Stewart, Sarah	Library, The	374443947	Farrar Strauss & Giroux	1	Y
		4	Winch, John	Old Woman Who Loved to Read	823413489	Holiday House	1	
Books About Writing		1	Christelow, Eileen	What Do Authors Do?	395866219	Houghton Mifflin	1	
		2	Parker, Steve	It's A Frog's Life	1575842505	Reader's Digest	1	
		3	Schotter, Roni	Nothing Ever Happens on 90th St.	531071367	Orchard Books	1	
		4	Stewart, Sarah	Gardener, The	374325170	Farrar Strauss & Giroux	1	Y
Chapter Books		1	Dahl, Roald	James & the Giant Peach	140374248	Penguin Publishing	1	

Group Description	Level	#	Author	Title	ISBN	Publisher	Quantity	Heinemann Write-Up
		2	DeGross, Monalisa	Donovan's Word Jar	64420892	Harper Trophy	1	
		3	Estes, Eleanor	Hundred Dresses, The	156423502	Harcourt Brace	1	
		4	Lewis, C.S.	Chronicles of Narnia/Lion, the Witch and the Wardrobe	64409422	Harper Trophy	1	Y
Journeys		1	George, Lindsay	Around the World	688152694	Greenwillow	1	
		2	Moss, Marissa	Amelia Hits the Road	1562477900	Pleasant Company	1	
		3	Rylant, Cynthia	Tulip Sees America	590847449	Scholastic Inc.	1	Y
		4	Williams, Vera	Stringbean's Trip to the Shining Sea	688167012	William Morrow & Co	1	
Qualities of Good Writing		1	Child, Lauren	I Will Never Not Ever Eat a Tomato	763611883	Candlewick Press	1	
		2	Johnson, Angela	Down the Winding Road	789425963	DK Publishing	1	
		3	Lirch, Tanya	My Duck	439206707	Scholastic Inc.	1	Y
		4	Pilkey, Dav	Paperboy, The	531071391	Orchard Books	1	
		5	Zolotow, Charlotte	Do You Know What I'll Do?	6027879X	Harper Collins	1	Y

Benchmark Books for Each Text Level

TC Level	Benchmarks: Books that Represent Each Level
1	*A Birthday Cake* (Cowley) *I Can Write* (Williams) *The Cat on the Mat* (Wildsmith)
2	*Rain* (Kaplan) *Fox on the Box* (Gregorich)
3	*It Looked Like Spilt Milk* (Shaw) *I Like Books* (Browne) *Mrs. Wishy-Washy* (Cowley)
4	*Rosie's Walk* (Hutchins) *The Carrot Seed* (Krauss) *Cookie's Week* (Ward)
5	*George Shrinks* (Joyce) *Goodnight Moon* (Brown) *Hattie and the Fox* (Fox)
6	*Danny and the Dinosaur* (Hoff) *Henry and Mudge* (Rylant)
7	*Nate the Great* (Sharmat) *Meet M&M* (Ross)
8	*Horrible Harry* (Kline) *Pinky and Rex* (Howe) *Arthur Series* (Marc Brown)
9	*Amber Brown* (Danziger) *Ramona Quimby, Age 8* (Cleary)
10	*James and the Giant Peach* (Dahl) *Fudge-A-Mania* (Blume)
11	*Shiloh* (Naylor) *The Great Gilly Hopkins* (Paterson)
12	*Bridge to Terabithia* (Paterson) *Baby* (MacLachlan)
13	*Missing May* (Rylant) *Where the Red Fern Grows* (Rawls)
14	*A Day No Pigs Would Die* (Peck) *Scorpions* (Myers)
15	*The Golden Compass* (Pullman) *The Dark Is Rising* (Cooper) *A Wizard of Earthsea* (Le Guin)

Descriptions of Text Levels One Through Seven

TEXT LEVEL ONE

This level roughly corresponds to the following levels in other systems:

Reading Recovery© (RR) Levels 1–2
Developmental Reading Assessment (DRA) Levels A–2

Text Characteristics for TC Level One

- The font is large, clear, and is usually printed in black on a white background.

- There is exaggerated spacing between words and letters. (In some books, publishers have enlarged the print but have not adjusted the spacing which can create difficulties for readers.)

- There is usually a single word, phrase, or simple sentence on a page, and the text is patterned and predictable. For example, in the book *I Can Read*, once a child knows the title (which is ideally read to a Level One reader) it is not hard for the child to read "I can read the newspaper," "I can read the cereal box." These readers are regarded as "preconventional" because they rely on the illustrations (that support the meaning) and the sounds of language (or syntax) and not on graphophonics or word/letter cues to read a sentence such as, "I can read the newspaper."

- Usually each page contains two or three sight words. A Level One book *may* contain one illustrated word on a page (such as "Mom," "Dad," "sister," "cat") but it's just as easy for a child to read "I see my mom. I see my Dad. I see my sister. I see my cat." because the sight words give the child a way into the text.

- The words are highly supported by illustrations. No one would expect a Level One reader to solve the word "newspaper." We would, however, expect a child at this level to look at the picture and at the text and to read the word "newspaper."

- Words are consistently placed in the same area of each page, preferably top left or bottom left.

Characteristics of the Reader

Readers in this group will demonstrate most of these behaviors.

- Remember the pattern in a predictable text
- Use picture cues

- Use left to right directionality to read one or two lines of print

- Work on matching spoken words with printed words and self-correcting when these don't "come out even"

- Rely on the spaces between words to signify the end of one word and the beginning of another. These readers read the spaces as well as the words, as the words are at first black blobs on white paper

- Locate one or two known words on a page

Benchmarks

The following titles are representative of the kinds of books found in this grouping.

A Birthday Cake, Joy Cowley
Cat on the Mat, Brian Wildsmith
The Farm, Literacy 2000/Stage 1
Growing Colors, Bruce McMillan
I Can Write, Rozanne Williams
Time for Dinner, PM Starters

Assessment

The following titles can be used to determine if a reader is ready to move on to the next grouping of books. This type of assessment is most effective if the text is unfamiliar to the reader. If these titles will be used as assessment texts, they should *not* be part of the classroom library.

My Home, Story Box
The Tree Stump, Little Celebrations
DRA Assessments A–2

We move children from Level One to Level Two books when they are consistently able to match one spoken word with one word written on the page. This means that they can point under words in a Level One book as they read and know when they haven't matched a spoken word to a written word by noticing that, at the end of the line, they still have words left on the page or they've run out of words. When children read multisyllabic words and compound words and point to multiple, instead of one, word on the page, we consider this a successful one-to-one match.

TEXT LEVEL TWO

This level roughly corresponds to the following levels in other systems:

Reading Recovery© (RR) Levels 3–4
Developmental Reading Assessment (DRA) Levels 3–4

Text Characteristics of TC Level Two

- There are usually two lines of print on at least some of the pages in these books, and sometimes there are three. This means readers will become accustomed to making the return sweep to the beginning of a new line.

- The texts are still patterned and predictable, but now the patterns tend to switch at intervals. Almost always, the pattern changes at the end of the book. The repeating unit may be as long as two sentences in length.

- The font continues to be large and clear. The letters might not, however, be black against white although this is generally the case.

- Children still rely on the picture but the pictures tend to give readers more to deal with; children need to search more in the picture to find help in reading the words.

- High frequency words are still helpful and important. The sentences in Level One books tend to begin with 2 to 3 high frequency words, for example, "I like to run. I like to jump." At this level, the pages are more apt to begin with a single high frequency word and then include words that require picture support and attention to first letters, for example, "A mouse has a long tail. A bear has a short tail."

- Sentences are more varied, resulting in texts that include a full range of punctuation.

Characteristics of the Reader

Readers in this group will demonstrate most of these behaviors.

- Get the mouth ready for the initial sound of a word

- Use left to right directionality as well as a return sweep to another line of print

- Locate one or two known words on a page

- Monitor for meaning: check to make sure it makes sense

Benchmarks

The following titles are representative of the kinds of books found in this grouping.

All Fall Down, Brian Wildsmith
I Went Walking, Sue Williams
Rain, Robert Kalan
Shoo, Sunshine

Assessment

The following titles can be used to determine if a reader is ready to move on to the next grouping. This type of assessment is most effective if the text is unfamiliar to a reader. If these titles will be used as assessment texts, they should *not* be part of the classroom library.

The Bus Ride, Little Celebrations, DRA 3
Fox on the Box, School Zone, DRA 4

We generally move children from Level Two to Level Three texts when they know how to use the pictures and the syntax to generate possibilities for the next word, when they attend to the first letters of unknown words. These readers will also read and rely on high frequency words such as *I*, *the*, *a*, *to*, *me*, *mom*, *the child's name*, *like*, *love*, *go*, and *and*.

TEXT LEVEL THREE

This level roughly corresponds to the following levels in other systems:

Reading Recovery© (RR) Levels 5–8
Developmental Reading Assessment (DRA) Levels 6–8

Text Characteristics of TC Level Three

It is important to note that this grouping includes a wide range of levels. This was done deliberately because at this level, readers should be able to select "just right" books for themselves and be able to monitor their own reading.

- Sentences are longer and readers will need to put their words together in order to take in more of the sentence at a time. When they are stuck, it's often helpful to nudge them to reread and try again.

- The pictures are not as supportive as they've been. It's still helpful for children to do picture walks prior to reading an unfamiliar text, but now the goal is less about surmising what words the page contains and more about seeing an overview of the narrative.

- Readers must rely on graphophonics across the whole word. If readers hit a wall at this level, it's often because they're accustomed to predicting words based on a dominant pattern and using the initial letters (only) to confirm their predictions. It takes readers a while to begin checking the print closely enough to adjust their expectations.

- Children will need to use sight words to help with unknown words, using parts of these familiar words as analogies, helping them unlock the unfamiliar words.

- The font size and spacing are less important now.

- Words in the text begin to include contractions. We can help children read these by urging them to look all the way across a word.

Characteristics of the Reader

Readers in this group will demonstrate most of these behaviors.

- Reread and self-correct

- Read with some fluency

- Cross check one cue against another

- Monitor for meaning: check to make sure what has been read makes sense and sounds right

- Recognize common chunks of words

Benchmarks

The following titles are representative of the kinds of books found in this grouping.

Bears in the Night Stan and Jan, Berenstain
The Chick and the Duckling, Ginsburg
It Looked Like Spilt Milk, Charles G. Shaw
Mrs. Wishy-Washy, Joy Cowley

Assessment

The following titles can be used to determine if a reader is ready to move on to the next grouping. This type of assessment is most effective if the text is unfamiliar to a reader. If these titles will be used as assessment texts, they should *not* be part of the classroom library.

Bread, Story Box, DRA 6
Get Lost Becka, School Zone, DRA 8

We move a child to Level Four books if that child can pick up an unfamiliar book like *Bread* or *It Looked Like Spilt Milk* and read it with a little difficulty, but with a lot of independence and with strategies. This reader should know to reread when she is stuck, to use the initial sounds in a word, to chunk word families within a word, and so on.

TEXT LEVEL FOUR

This level roughly corresponds to the following levels in other systems:

Reading Recovery© (RR) Levels 9–12
Developmental Reading Assessment (DRA) Levels 10–12

Text Characteristics of TC Level Four

- In general, the child who is reading Level Four books is able to do more of the same reading work he could do with texts at the previous level. This child reads texts that contain more words, lines, pages, and more challenging vocabulary.

- These texts contain even less picture support than earlier levels.

- Fluency and phrasing are very important for the Level Four reader. If children don't begin to read quickly enough, they won't be able to carry the syntax of the sentence along well enough to comprehend what they are reading.

- These books use brief bits of literary language. That is, in these books the mother may turn to her child and say, "We shall be rich."
- These books are more apt to have a plot (with characters, setting, problem, solution) and they tend to be less patterned than they were at the previous level.

Characteristics of the Reader

Readers in this group will demonstrate most of these behaviors.

- Reread and self-correct
- Read with fluency
- Integrate cues from meaning, structure, and visual sources
- Monitor for meaning: check to make sure what has been read makes sense, sounds right, and looks right
- Make some analogies from known words to figure out unknown words
- Read increasingly difficult chunks within words

Benchmarks

The following titles are representative of the kinds of books found in this grouping.

> *The Carrot Seed*, Ruth Krauss
> *Cookie's Week*, Cindy Ward
> *Rosie's Walk*, Pat Hutchins
> *Titch*, Pat Hutchins

Assessment

The following titles can be used to determine if a reader is ready to move on to the next grouping. This type of assessment is most effective if the text is unfamiliar to a reader. If these titles will be used as assessment texts, they should *not* be part of the classroom library.

> *Are You There Bear?*, Ron Maris, DRA 10
> *The House in the Tree*, Rigby PM Story Books
> *Nicky Upstairs and Downstairs*, Harriet Ziefert
> *William's Skateboard*, Sunshine, DRA 12

We move a child to Level Five books if that reader can independently use a variety of strategies to work through difficult words or parts of a text. The reader must be reading fluently enough to reread quickly, when necessary, so as to keep the flow of the story going. If a reader is reading very slowly, taking too much time to work through the hard parts, then this reader may not be ready to move on to the longer, more challenging texts in Level Five.

TEXT LEVEL FIVE

This level roughly corresponds to the following levels in other systems:

Reading Recovery© (RR) Levels 13–15
Developmental Reading Assessment (DRA) Level 14

Text Characteristics

- Sentences in Level Five books tend to be longer, more varied, and more complex than they were in previous levels.

- Many of the stories are retold folktales or fantasy-like stories that use literary or story language, such as: "Once upon a time, there once lived, a long, long time ago. . . . "

- Many books may be in a cumulative form in which text is added to each page, requiring the reader to read more and more text as the story unfolds, adding a new line with every page turn.

- The illustrations tend to be a representation of just a slice of what is happening in the text. For example, the text may tell of a long journey that a character has taken over time, but the picture may represent just the character reaching his destination.

- There will be more unfamiliar and sometimes complex vocabulary.

Characteristics of the Reader

Readers in this group will demonstrate most of these behaviors.

- Reread and self-correct regularly

- Read with fluency

- Integrate a balance of cues

- Monitor for meaning: check to make sure what has been read makes sense, sounds right, and looks right

- Demonstrate fluent phrasing of longer passages

- Use a repertoire of graphophonic strategies to problem solve through text

Benchmarks

The following titles are representative of the kinds of books found in this grouping.

George Shrinks, William Joyce
Goodnight Moon, Margaret Wise Brown
Hattie and the Fox, Mem Fox
Little Red Hen, Parkes

Assessment

The following titles can be used to determine if a reader is ready to move on to the next grouping. This type of assessment is most effective if the text is unfamiliar to a reader. If these titles will be used as assessment texts, they should *not* be part of the classroom library.

> *The Old Man's Mitten,* Bookshop, Mondo
> *Who Took the Farmer's Hat?,* Joan Nodset, DRA 14

We move children from Level Five to Level Six texts when they are consistently able to use a multitude of strategies to work through challenges quickly and efficiently. These challenges may be brought on by unfamiliar settings, unfamiliar language structures, unfamiliar words, and increased text length. The amount of text on a page and the length of a book should not be a hindrance to the reader who is moving on to Level Six. The reader who is ready to move on is also adept at consistently choosing appropriate books that will make her a stronger reader.

TEXT LEVEL SIX

This level roughly corresponds to the following levels in other systems:

> Reading Recovery© (RR) Levels 16–18
> Developmental Reading Assessment (DRA) Level 16

Text Characteristics of TC Level Six

- The focus of the book is evident at its start

- Descriptive language is used more frequently than before

- Dialogue often tells a large part of the story

- Texts may include traditional retellings of fairy tales and folktales

- Stories are frequently humorous

- Considerable amount of text is found on each page. A book in this grouping may be a picture book, or a simple chapter book. These books offer extended stretches of text.

- Texts are often simple chapter books, and often have episodic chapters in which each chapter stands as a story on its own

- Texts often center around just two or three main characters who tend to be markedly different from each other (a boy and a girl, a child and a parent)

- There is limited support from the pictures

- Texts includes challenging vocabulary

Characteristics of the Reader

Readers in this group will demonstrate most of these behaviors.

- Reread and self-correct regularly

- Read with fluency

- Integrate a balance of cues

- Demonstrate fluent phrasing of longer passages

- Use a repertoire of graphophonic strategies to problem solve through text

Benchmarks

The following titles are representative of the kinds of books found in this grouping.

Danny and the Dinosaur, Syd Hoff
The Doorbell Rang, Pat Hutchins
Henry and Mudge, Cynthia Rylant
The Very Hungry Caterpillar, Eric Carle

Assessment

The following titles can be used to determine if a reader is ready to move on to the next grouping. This type of assessment is most effective if the text is unfamiliar to a reader. If these titles will be used as assessment texts, they should *not* be part of the classroom library.

Bear Shadow, Frank Asch, DRA 16
Jimmy Lee Did It, Pat Cummings, DRA 18

TEXT LEVEL SEVEN

This level roughly corresponds to the following levels in other systems:

Reading Recovery© (RR) Levels 19–20
Developmental Reading Assessment (DRA) Level 20

Text Characteristics of TC Level Seven

- Dialogue is used frequently to move the story along

- Texts often have 2 to 3 characters. (They tend to have distinctive personalities and usually don't change across a book or series.)

- Texts may include extended description. (The language may set a mood, and may be quite poetic or colorful.)

- Some books have episodic chapters. (In other books, each chapter contributes to the understanding of the entire book and the reader must carry the story line along.)

- There is limited picture support

- Plots are usually linear without large time-gaps

- Texts tend to have larger print and double spacing between lines of print

Characteristics of the Reader

Readers in this group will demonstrate most of these behaviors.

- Reread and self-correct regularly
- Read with fluency, intonation, and phrasing
- Demonstrate the existence of a self-extending (self-improving) system for reading
- Use an increasingly more challenging repertoire of graphophonic strategies to problem solve through text
- Solve unknown words with relative ease

Benchmarks

The following titles are representative of the kinds of books found in this grouping.

A Baby Sister for Frances, Russell Hoban
Meet M&M, Pat Ross
Nate the Great, Marjorie Sharmat
Poppleton, Cynthia Rylant

Asessment

The following titles can be used to determine if a reader is ready to move on to the next grouping. This type of assessment is most effective if the text is unfamiliar to a reader. If these titles will be used as assessment texts, they should *not* be part of the classroom library.

Peter's Pockets, Eve Rice, DRA 20
Uncle Elephant, Arnold Lobel

More Information to Help You Choose the Library That is Best for Your Readers

Library A

Library A is appropriate if your children enter kindergarten in October as very emergent readers with limited experiences hearing books read aloud. Use the following chart to help determine if Library A is about right for your class.

Approximate Distribution of Reading Levels of a Class Matched to Library A		
Benchmark Book	*Reading Level*	*Percentage of the Class Reading at about This Level*
The Cat on the Mat, by Wildsmith	TC Level 1	45%
Fox on the Box, by Gregorich	TC Level 2	30%
Mrs. Wishy-Washy, by Cowley	TC Level 3	25%

Library B

Library B is appropriate for a class of children if, in October, they are reading books like *I Went Walking*. Use the following chart to help determine if Library B is about right for your class. (Note to New York City teachers: Many of your students would score a 3 on the ECLAS correlated with titles such as, *Things I Like to Do* and *My Shadow*.)

Approximate Distribution of Reading Levels of a Class Matched to Library B		
Benchmark Book	*Reading Level*	*Percentage of the Class Reading at about This Level*
The Cat on the Mat, by Wildsmith	TC Level 1	10%
Fox on the Box, by Gregorich	TC Level 2	10%
Mrs. Wishy-Washy, by Cowley	TC Level 3	30%
The Carrot Seed, by Krauss	TC Level 4	25%
Goodnight Moon, by Brown	TC Level 5	15%
Henry and Mudge, by Rylant	TC Level 6	5%
Nate the Great, by Sharmat	TC Level 7	5%

Library C

Library C is appropriate for a class of children if, in October, many of your students are approaching reading books like *Mrs. Wishy-Washy* and *Bears in the Night*. (Note to New York City teachers: Many of your students would be approaching a 4 on the ECLAS that would be correlated with *Baby Bear's Present* and *No Where and Nothing*.)

Approximate Distribution of Reading Levels of a Class Matched to Library C		
Benchmark Book	*Reading Level*	*Percentage of the Class Reading at about This Level*
Fox on the Box, by Gregorich	TC Level 2	8%
Mrs. Wishy-Washy, by Cowley	TC Level 3	8%
The Carrot Seed, by Krauss	TC Level 4	20%
Goodnight Moon, by Brown	TC Level 5	20%
Henry and Mudge, by Carle	TC Level 6	20%
Nate the Great, by Sharmat	TC Level 7	15%
Pinky and Rex, by Howe	TC Level 8	5%
Ramona Quimby, by Cleary	TC Level 9	2%
James and the Giant Peach, by Dahl	TC Level 10	2%

Library D

Use the following chart to help determine if Library D is right for your class.

Approximate Distribution of Reading Levels of a Class Matched to Library D		
Benchmark Book	*Reading Level*	*Percentage of the Class Reading at about This Level*
Good Night Moon, by Brown	Level 5	8%
Henry and Mudge, by Rylant	Level 6	20%
Nate the Great, by Sharmat	Level 7	25%
Pinky and Rex, by Howe	Level 8	30%
Ramona Quimby, by Cleary	Level 9	10%
James and the Giant Peach, by Dahl	Level 10	2%

Library E

Library E is appropriate for a class of children if, in October, a readers list tends to look approximately like the following chart.

Approximate Distribution of Reading Levels of a Class Matched to Library E		
Benchmark Book	*Reading Level*	*Percentage of the Class Reading at about This Level*
Nate the Great, by Sharmat	Level 7	10%
Pinky and Rex, by Howe	Level 8	25%
Ramona Quimby, by Cleary	Level 9	30%
James and the Giant Peach, by Dahl	Level 10	22%
Shiloh, by Naylor	Level 11	5%
Baby, by MacLachlan	Level 12	5%
Missing May, by Rylant	Level 13	2%
Scorpions, by Myers	Level 14	1%

Library F

Library F is appropriate for a class of children if, in October, a readers list tends to look approximately like the following chart.

Approximate Distribution of Reading Levels of a Class Matched to Library F		
Benchmark Book	*Reading Level*	*Percentage of the Class Reading at about This Level*
Pinky and Rex, by Howe	Level 8	2%
Ramona Quimby, by Cleary	Level 9	20%
James and the Giant Peach, by Dahl	Level 10	25%
Shiloh, by Naylor	Level 11	30%
Baby, by MacLachlan	Level 12	20%
Missing May, by Rylant	Level 13	2%
Scorpions, by Myers	Level 14	1%

Library G

Library G is appropriate for a class of children if, in October, a readers list tends to look approximately like the following chart.

Approximate Distribution of Reading Levels of a Class Matched to Library G		
Benchmark Book	*Reading Level*	*Percentage of the Class Reading at about This Level*
James and the Giant Peach, by Dahl	Level 10	10%
Shiloh, by Naylor	Level 11	10%
Baby, by MacLachlan	Level 12	30%
Missing May, by Rylant	Level 13	30%
Scorpions, by Myer	Level 14	20%

About the Guides

Soon we'd begun not only accumulating titles and honing arrangements for dream libraries, but also writing teaching advice to go with the chosen books. Our advice to the contributors was, "Write a letter from you to others who'll use this book with children. Tell folks what you notice in the book, and advise them on teaching opportunities you see. Think about advice you would give a teacher just coming to know the book." The insights, experience, and folk wisdom poured in and onto the pages of the guides.

A written guide accompanies many of the books in the libraries. These guides are not meant to be prescriptions for how a teacher or child should use a book. Instead they are intended to be resources, and we hope thoughtful teachers will tap into particular sections of a guide when it seems fit to do so. For example, a teaching guide might suggest six possible minilessons a teacher could do with a book. Of course, a teacher would never try to do all six of these! Instead we expect one of these minilessons will seem helpful to the teacher, and another minilesson to another teacher. The teaching guides illustrate the following few principles that are important to us.

Teaching One Text Intensely in Order to Learn About Many Texts

When you take a walk in the woods, it can happen that all the trees look the same, that they are just a monotony of foliage and trunks. It is only when you stop to learn about a particular tree, about its special leaf structure and the odd thickness of its bark, about the creatures that inhabit it and the seeds it lets fall, that you begin to see that particular kind of tree among the thickets. It is when you enter a forest knowing something about kinds of trees that you begin to truly see the multiplicity of trees in a forest and the particular attributes and mysteries of each one. Learning about the particulars of one tree leads you to thinking about all of the trees, each in its individuality, each with its unique deep structure, each with its own offerings.

The same is true of texts. The study of one can reveal not just the hidden intricacies of that story, but also the ways in which truths and puzzles can be structured in other writings as well. When one book holds a message in the way a chapter ends, it gives the reader the idea that any book may hold a message in the structure of its chapter's conclusions. When one book is revealed to make a sense that is unintended by the author, we look for unintended sense in other books we read. Within these guides, then, we hope that readers like you will find truths about the particular books they are written about, but more, we hope that you find pathways into all the books you read. By showing some lengthy thinking and meditations on one book, we hope to offer you paths toward thinking about each and every book that crosses your desk and crosses your mind.

Suggesting Classroom Library Arrangements

Many the attributes of a book, detailed in a guide, can become a category in a classroom library. If a group of students in a class seems particularly energized by the Harry Potter books, for example, the guide can be used to help determine which books could be in a bin in the library marked, "If You Like *Harry Potter*—Try These." The similarity between the *Harry Potter* books and the other books in this group may be not only in difficulty gradient, but also in content, story structure, popularity, or genre. That is, a class of children that like *Harry Potter* might benefit from a bin of books on fantasy, or from a collection of best-selling children's books, or from a bin of "Long-Books-You-Can't-Put-Down," or from stories set in imagined places. As you browse through the guides that accompany the books you have chosen, the connections will pop out at you.

Sometimes, the guides will help you determine a new or more interesting placement for a book. Perhaps you have regarded a book as historical fiction, but now you realize it could alternatively be shelved in a collection of books that offer children examples of "Great Leads to Imitate in Your Own Writing." Or, perhaps the guides will suggest entirely new categories that will appeal to your class in ways you and your students haven't yet imagined. Perhaps the guides will help you imagine a "Books That Make You Want to Change the World" category. Or maybe you'll decide to create a shelf in your library titled, "Books with Odd Techniques That Make You Wonder What the Author Is Trying To Do."

Aiding in Conferring

Teachers' knowledge of what to ask and what to teach a reader who says, "this book is boring" comes not only from their knowledge of particular students but also from their knowledge of the text they are talking about. Does "boring" mean that the book is too easy for the reader? Perhaps it means instead that the beginning few chapters of the book are hard to read—confusing because of a series of flashbacks. A guide might explain that the book under discussion has mostly internal, emotional action, and, if the reader is accustomed to avalanche-and-rattlesnake action in books, she may need some time to warm up to this unfamiliar kind of "quiet" action. The guide can point out the kinds of reactions, or troubles, other readers have had with particular books. With the guides at our fingertips, we can more easily determine which questions to ask students, or which pages to turn to, in order to get to the heart of the conference.

Providing a Resource for Curriculum Planning

One Friday, say, we leave the classroom knowing that our students' writing shows that they are thirsting for deeper, more complicated characters to study and imitate. As we plan lessons, we can page through the guides that correspond with some of the books in our library, finding, or remembering, books that students can study that depict fascinating characters.

On the other hand, perhaps we need a book to read aloud to the class, or perhaps we need to recommend a book to a particular struggling reader.

Maybe a reader has finished a book he loves and has turned to you to help him plan his reading for the next weeks. When designing an author study or an inquiry into punctuation and its effects on meaning, it also helps to have the guides with you to point out books that may be helpful in those areas. In each of these cases, and many more, the guides can be a planning aid for you.

Reminding Us, or Teaching Us, About Particular Book Basics

No teacher can read, let alone recall in detail, every book that every child will pick up in the classroom. Of course, we read many of them and learn about many more from our colleagues, but there are far too many books in the world for us to be knowledgeable about them all. Sometimes, the guides will be a reminder of what you have read many years ago. Sometimes, they will provide a framework for you to question or direct your students more effectively than you could if you knew nothing at all about the book. "Probably, you will have to take some time to understand the setting before you can really get a handle on this book, why don't you turn to the picture atlas?" you might say after consulting the guide, or "Sharlene is reading another book that is similar to this one in so many ways! Why don't you go pair up with her to talk." You might learn to ask, "What do you think of Freddy?" in order to learn if the student is catching on to the tone of the narrator, or you might learn you could hint, "Did you get to chapter three yet? Because I bet you won't be bored any more when you get there. . . ." The guides provide a bit of what time constraints deny us: thoughtful insights about the content or unusual features of a given book.

Showcasing Literary Intricacies in Order to Suggest a Reader's Thinking

Sometimes, when we read a book, our idea of the author's message is in our minds before we even finish the story. Because we are experienced readers, much of our inferring and interpreting, our understanding of symbols and contexts, can come to us effortlessly. In the guides, we have tried to slow down some of that thinking so that we can all see it more easily. We have tried to lay out some of the steps young readers may have to go through in order to come to a cohesive idea of what the story is about, or a clear understanding of why a character behaved the way she did. As experienced readers, we may not even realize that our readers are confused by the unorthodox use of italics to show us who is speaking, for example. We may not remember the days when we were confused by changing narrators, the days when it took us a few chapters to figure out a character wasn't to be believed. In these guides, we have tried to go back to those days when we were more naïve readers, and have tried to fill in those thoughts and processes we are now able to skip over so easily.

By bringing forth the noteworthy features of the text, features experienced readers may not even notice, we are reminded of the thinking that our students need to go through in order to make sense of their reading. It gives us an idea of where to offer pointers, of where readers may have gone off in an unhelpful direction, or of where their thinking may need to go instead of where it has gone. By highlighting literary intricacies, we may remember that every bit about the construction of texts is a navigation point for students, and every bit is something we may be able to help students in learning.

Providing a Community of Readers and Teachers

The guides are also intended to help teachers learn from the community of other teachers and readers who have used particular texts already. They make available some of the stories and experiences other teachers have had, in order that we might stand on their shoulders and take our teaching even higher than they could reach. These guides are intended to give you some thinking to go with the books in your classroom library, thinking you can mix with your own ideas.

In the end, we don't all have a community of other teachers with whom we can talk about children's literature. The guides are meant not to stand in for that community, but instead to provide a taste, an appetizer, of the world of supportive professional communities. We hope that by reading these guides and feeling the companionship, guidance and insight they offer, teachers will be nudged to recreate that experience for the other books that have no guides, and that they will ask their colleagues, librarians, and the parents of their students to talk with them about children's literature and young readers. Then, when teachers are creating these guides for themselves, on paper or in their minds' eyes, we will know this project has done the work for which it was created.

Bibliography

Atwell, Nancie. 1987. *In the Middle: Writing, Reading, and Learning with Adolescents.* Portsmouth, NH: Boynton/Cook.

Calkins, Lucy. 2001. *The Art of Teaching Reading.* New York: Addison-Wesley Educational Publishers, Inc.

Cambourne, Brian. 1993. *The Whole Story: Natural Learning and the Acquisition of Literacy in the Classroom.* Auckland, NZ: Ashton Scholastic.

Krashen, Stephen. 1993. *The Power of Reading: Insights from the Research.* Englewood, CO: Libraries Unlimited.

Meek, Margaret. 1988. *How Texts Teach What Readers Learn.* Thimble Press.

Smith, Frank. 1985. *Reading Without Nonsense.* 2nd ed. New York: TC Press.

A Field Guide to the Classroom Library Ⓒ

26 Fairmount Avenue
Tomie dePaola

Book Summary

This is a memoir of the life of the famous writer Tomie dePaola. It begins in 1938 when he is five and there is a hurricane. The story moves quickly from this adventure to the joy of his first family home being built, to his love of his two great grandmothers. His many uncles, aunts, cousins, and friends continue with him through the other adventures of his young life in Meriden, Connecticut.

Basic Book Information

This Newbery Honor (2000) chapter book is the first in a series of memoirs. The series includes two other texts of the same length and style, *Here We All Are* and *On My Way*. The book's 56 pages include nine chapters. In this text, readers meet 16 characters that play an important part in Tomie's early life. Readers are also introduced to many characters that appear in the author's picture books.

Noteworthy Features

This is a story that many children will understand and relate to. It is written clearly in the voice of a quite young Tomie dePaola, making it simple to read. Included are pictures of family members (drawn by dePaola) and maps of the house at 26 Fairmount Avenue. There is very little dialogue in this text, but when dialogue is present, it is clear who is speaking to whom.

The vocabulary and style of this text are very much what readers of Tomie dePaola have come to expect. Narrated in the author's first person voice, this book will feel familiar to those who have read other works by dePaola. At the end of the text is "A Note from the Author" that will give both teacher and students additional information about how and why Tomie dePaola wrote this memoir.

Teaching Ideas

This book can be included in any memoir stack. As a read aloud in the primary grades, *26 Fairmount Avenue* can help students get the sound of memoir into their heads. Later, students can reread the text focusing on dePaola's craft and the characteristics of memoir. Teachers might point out how much of the author's life has been omitted; he has clearly chosen only particular memories to highlight for his readers. This book provides a good opportunity to discuss how memoir is not a comprehensive autobiography, but a detailed recounting of selected events (or moments, or people). For example, this book, like so many memoirs, is built out of tiny life moments, told in exquisite detail.

Series

Tomie dePaola memoir trilogy

Illustrator

Tomie dePaola

Publisher

Putnam Publishing, 1999

ISBN

0698118642

TC Level

9

What the author does choose to include is described in great detail. Students can benefit as writers from thinking about how dePaola stretches out specific moments in time. How does he make whole chapters out of what probably began as tiny notebook entries? In fact, in the author's note, dePaola says that the challenge of this book was exactly this issue. Because he writes brief picture books, learning to use a lot of words to describe a single event in his life was a new challenge for him. Students may identify with this struggle.

Whenever an author decides to focus in on particular moments, that author has to deal with the issue of how to move through time, skipping past large sections. Teachers might ask students to pay close attention to the way dePaola's text moves through time and consider where he places emphasis as well as what remains untold. A useful exercise might be for students to make timelines of Tomie dePaola's memoir in order to highlight how much time goes by without an anecdote. Teachers might also want readers to think of this text as a series of vignettes (like Eric Carle's *Flor and Tiger* or Bessie Nickens' *Walking the Log*), discussing why dePaola may have chosen to tell his tale in chapters.

Students could spend some time considering how the chapters work. What similarities do the chapters share, and how do they connect with each other? Tomie helps us follow this lengthy tale by beginning each chapter with words that clearly mark time (e.g., "Right after the Christmas of 1938..." "In the fall of 1939, almost one year after the Hurricane of 1938..."). Students will benefit as both readers and writers from paying close attention to these markers of time and from making sure that they have similar markers in their own writing.

Teachers might even choose to put the beginning of the text on an overhead and help readers to notice that this book doesn't begin with Tomie dePaola's birth. As a writer of memoir he had to make a decision about where to begin, and so will they. The beginning of this book is almost identical to the beginning of *House on Mango Street* by Sandra Cisneros, a book that many teachers use to illustrate techniques for crafting one's memories. The fact that both texts have a house as their focal point also makes for easy comparison.

As a read aloud, this book can be used when teachers want to begin to launch partner talk. When reading to students, teachers can ask them to turn to each other to discuss their reactions to the text or analyze specific questions. At first, teachers can model for children the kinds of questions that can lead to good discussions, and then the teachers can prompt the children to come up with questions of their own. One class listened to *26 Fairmont Avenue* and suggested these topics for conversation: (1) Tomie lived in a big family. Why was he so happy about it? (2) What was Connecticut like back then? (3) Why did Tomie's mother let him draw on the walls? (Is this how he became such a good artist?)

This book can inform a realistic fiction study. Though this is memoir, when readers line this text alongside dePaola's fiction, they'll see that this writer has used the stories of his life as material for his fiction. Students familiar with *26 Fairmount Avenue* will be able to see that *Nana Upstairs, Nana Downstairs* has its roots in Tomie dePaola's early life. The pictures young Tomie chalks onto the wall of his unfinished house on Fairmount Avenue may suggest to children how dePaola's developed the visual style they can see in his picture books.

26 Fairmount Avenue, along with the other two books in this memoir series, would make excellent additions to an author study of Tomie dePaola. Whenever students decide to look closely at the work of a particular author, it is wise for them to search for a memoir or biography of the author. Some questions that drive author studies are, "How did the author's life feed and nurture his (or her) writing? What sections of his or her books seem to be based on the author's true experiences?" After reading this memoir, children will appreciate dePaola books such as *Nana Upstairs and Nana Downstairs* in new ways. *The Art Lesson* is probably drawn from dePaola's love of drawing. *Now One Foot, Now the Other Foot* is clearly drawn from dePaola's memories of his relationship with his grandfather. Such comparisons can also inform a realistic fiction study.

Book Connections

This is a memoir and as such could be studied alongside other memoir including *Shortcut* by Donald Crews and *When I Was Young in the Mountains* by Cynthia Rylant. Because it is dePaola's memoir, it can be set alongside his other books, particularly *The Art Lesson* and *Now One Foot, Now the Other Foot.*

Genre
Chapter Book; Memoir

Teaching Uses
Read Aloud; Teaching Writing; Independent Reading; Author Study

A Kiss For Little Bear
Else Holmelund Minarik

Book Summary

Little Bear sends a picture to his grandmother, and she, in return, sends a kiss. The thank-you kiss passes from friend to friend until it finally finds him, but not without some humorous results. The charming but never mushy story and drawings will please readers of the *Little Bear* series.

One theme of *A Kiss For Little Bear* is that affection multiplies. Little Bear's gift to his grandmother brings his friends together in a variety of ways, and results in the marriage of the skunks. In the final pages of the story, the marriage itself brings the friends together again. Another theme involves the work that is done for friends. Although Hen is inconvenienced, Frog gets pecked and Cat gets wet, their love for Little Bear makes the work worthwhile.

Basic Book Information

A Kiss For Little Bear, an *I Can Read Book*, is one of several books about the title character. Maurice Sendak is the illustrator of many classic books for children, including *Where The Wild Things Are*, winner of the Caldecott Medal. Although the books in the series stand alone, the first book, *Little Bear*, is a good place to start.

Noteworthy Features

A Kiss For Little Bear is a gracefully written story that, like all the *Little Bear* books, artfully combines simple vocabulary and short-but-varied sentence structure. Most of the text consists of one-syllable words, with a few repeated exceptions: "little," "Grandmother," "another," "kissing." The book has a cozy, humorous air that does not condescend to its readers. Much of the book consists of dialogue, and dialogue tags make it clear to the reader who is speaking. The text often changes from present to past tense, using common, simple verbs such as *is, are, was,* and *have*.

The characterizations of Little Bear and his friends are subtle, thanks to the detailed drawings. The costumes are old-fashioned and set the story in the general past. The portrayal of woods and ponds has a naturalistic precision, and the characters' coloration and texture are carefully evoked. Sendak manages to make Hen scowl and Frog wave while still making them look more realistic.

Teaching Ideas

A Kiss For Little Bear is appropriate for independent reading. In addition, readers might practice expressive reading in pairs or small groups, focusing on the dialogue.

Series
Little Bear

Illustrator
Maurice Sendak

Publisher
Harper Collins, 1998

ISBN
0064440508

TC Level
5

A Field Guide to the Classroom Library, Lucy Calkins and the Teachers College Reading and Writing Project, Heinemann, ©2002 Teachers College, Columbia University; http://www.heinemann.com/fieldguides

Readers can use text and illustrations to discuss what they know about different characters, and how those characters feel at different points in the story. The illustrations give a lot of information not present in the text. For example, Cat eyes a bird while Frog waves from the pond (page 13). What does that tell the reader about Cat?

Students could use what they know about friendship to help discuss the friendship of these animals. What do they get out of friendship? What do they do for their friends, and what do their friends do for them? It's important to help children process their reading through talk. *A Kiss For Little Bear* can get a bit confusing. Having children stop and talk is one way to prevent confusion.

Book Connections

This book is the first in the *Little Bear* series. Other books that follow in the series are *Father Bear Comes Home* and *Little Bear's Visit*.

Genre
Picture Book

Teaching Uses
Independent Reading; Partnerships

Able's Moon

Shirley Hughes

Book Summary

Adam's father Able travels far and wide in his work, and spends long stretches of time away from his family. When he comes home to their happy, noisy clutter, they rejoice and listen to his stories. When he goes away again, he leaves behind the stories he has written down and the table he had moved into the garden to write on. The children play with the table and make adventures of their own to tell their father when he returns. They know the same moon that shines on him shines on them as well.

Basic Book Information

In this 28-page picture book, much of the details of the story are told visually; every page contains water-colored art, but author and illustrator Shirley Hughes places text on only three-quarters of the pages. The length and placement of text on the page varies considerably. There are no page numbers.

Noteworthy Features

This book is unusual and unpredictable in many subtle ways, making it surprisingly challenging and complicated for readers. The happy scene on the cover, warm colors of the artwork, and romantic title suggest an up-beat book. After the first two sentences reveal a man named "Able Grable" with wife named "Mable," the reader might anticipate a funny, light story. Since the story begins from Able's point of view as he returns home and gets started writing, and since Able lends his name to both the title and the opening of the book, readers will probably expect that the story will revolve around him. Expectations built from any of these cues will not be completely fulfilled, so some predictions may need to be put aside before a real understanding of the book can be built. Some readers find this putting aside of subconscious expectations to be difficult and oddly confusing and may give up on book early on.

   On the other hand, some less experienced readers may not pick up on any of these cues to begin with, and therefore will not experience the double work of building, unbuilding, and then rebuilding expectations.

Teaching Ideas

A character study of the father Abel and of his oldest son Adam usually yields especially fruitful understandings of the text, and will feel rewarding to the children because there is much to uncover about the two. On a quick read, most readers assume that Able is a model father. But if a teacher nudged a child dig deeper, it would be fairly easy for that child to collect

Illustrator
Shirley Hughes

Publisher
DK Publishing, 1999

ISBN
0789446014

A Field Guide to the Classroom Library, Lucy Calkins and the Teachers College Reading and Writing Project, Heinemann, ©2002 Teachers College, Columbia University; http://www.heinemann.com/fieldguides

evidence from the text to support theories that Able may be a flawed parent. He clearly doesn't spend much time at home. When he is at home, he wants the rest of the family to be quiet so he can write about himself. The children sit and listen to his stories, saying nothing for themselves, and when he writes to them, they feel they have nothing to say back. He doesn't pick up the table after himself, leaving it for someone else to take care of. He tells Adam that the moon is a cold place, even as Adam wants to romanticize the moon and make it a bond between them. The reader doesn't even know when and if Able will return home. Perhaps, if students only find what is nice about Able, teachers could challenge a few of their ideas and let them explore other possibilities about his character.

If students uncover some of Able's shortcomings, they may also scrutinize how his sons feel about him, and how their relationship to him appears to change. Adam and Noah seem at first to have put their father on a pedestal, using their dramatic play to mimic the adventures their father has told them about. In writing, they feel like they have nothing worth saying compared to him. Then a switch happens, and the boys get an idea of their own, not of their father's, for how to play. They make a moon machine out of the table. Adam feels bigger, closer to the moon, and dreams of going himself to wherever his father is, instead of waiting for his father to come home to him. He also thinks of how, this time, he will have the stories to tell while it is his father who listens and asks for more. This may be the reason why the story starts out being framed by the father and ends up being framed by the son, as mentioned before. This change in the boy as he grows up can be very hard to see, but with study, children often find it.

Book Connections

The content of this book is rather parallel to the content in several other books in this library. Children might compare *Able's Moon* to dePaola's *The Art Lesson*, Podoshen's *The Artist* and Rylant's *All I See*.

Genre
Picture Book

Teaching Uses
Read Aloud; Independent Reading; Interpretation; Critique; Character Study

Abuela

Arthur Dorros

Book Summary

A little girl goes with her grandmother to the park. While there, she imagines taking a flying trip around the city with her grandmother. The girl talks about all the places they would see and all the relatives they would visit, imagining all the conversations they would have. The girl remembers she is still in the park with her *abuela*, whom she loves greatly. The two go for a boat ride together.

Basic Book Information

Abuela has 34 unnumbered pages with large illustrations accompanying each page's text. While the narration is in English, there is simple, referenced, italicized dialogue in Spanish throughout this imaginative story. More complicated phrases are first quoted and/or italicized in Spanish and then paraphrased in English as the girl, who narrates the story, reflects on what her grandmother says. Usually, the context provides clues about how to translate the Spanish (e.g., "'Mira,' Abuela would say, pointing. And I'd look ..."). For students who do not speak Spanish or cannot translate it in context, there is a glossary, which also provides tips on pronunciation.

Noteworthy Features

Most people love the colorful, detailed, and playful illustrations in the story. Children are often enthralled with the picture in which the girl and her grandmother are soaring over the bustling, happy city. The book's multiple Spanish phrases mixed with the English story bring to print the bilingual experience many students have.

Every Spanish phrase the grandmother speaks is translated by her granddaughter in the phrases just following it, either directly, or via the girl's replies. Readers who need the glossary should get into the habit of checking in the back of a book for a glossary whenever they are reading a book that contains foreign words that they don't understand and feel uncomfortable skipping.

Teaching Ideas

The Spanish words in the text present engaging possibilities for practicing how to use context clues to figure out unknown vocabulary. Those students who do not already read Spanish should see the ways in which the little girl repeats her grandmother's words in English, and then uses the English words to understand the Spanish. Students who don't speak Spanish can use the glossary to see if they are getting the gist of the Spanish words. Students can apply this skill of informed, contextualized guessing to any unfamiliar

Illustrator
Elisa Kleven

Publisher
Trumpet, 1991

ISBN
0140562257

TC Level
8

A Field Guide to the Classroom Library, Lucy Calkins and the Teachers College Reading and Writing Project, Heinemann, ©2002 Teachers College, Columbia University; http://www.heinemann.com/fieldguides

words they encounter while reading - even to words already in English.

The trickiest part of this story could be understanding the time in which things happen, and managing the tenses of the story. The structure of time in the book is not at all simple, and following it takes quite a bit of skill. The book starts out in the present tense, with the girl and her grandmother going to the park. Once she imagines flying, the tense changes. The girl speaks in the future conditional tense about what *would* happen first and then what *would* happen next. After her lengthy daydream, the girl remembers she is in the park, and switches back to the present tense. From there, she and Abuela go on a real, present-tense adventure in a boat. The illustrations for both reality and daydream are in the same style. Thus, catching the switch from reality to fantasy and back to reality can be tricky, as only the tense shifts provide cues. If such a misunderstanding occurs, however, it might be a perfect time to intervene and explain about "would" and what the word suggests.

In the writing workshop, this book can be set alongside other books, such as *Jamaica's Find*, or *Tar Beach* to show that the story, and the plot, does not always revolve around external events. Sometimes the important events during a day in the park (or any other day) are the *internal* events and sometimes they are the *interpersonal* events. This can be a significant lesson for young writers who tend to retell what they did and to overlook all mention of what they thought or imagined or wished they had done.

Book Connections

Gary Soto has written several books that mix Spanish with English, including *Chato's Kitchen*. *Tar Beach* is a bit similar to this book in content and illustrations. Interesting conversations could result from comparing and contrasting the messages, content and structure of these two books. *Grandma's Cookie Jar* by Louise Dundas and *Knots on a Counting Rope* by Bill Martin Jr. and John Archambault have similar themes of grandchildren and grandparents telling stories. Readers who want to read more by Arthur Dorros will probably enjoy *Alligator Shoes*.

Genre
Picture Book

Teaching Uses
Teaching Writing; Language Conventions; Read Aloud; Partnerships

All About You

Catherine Anholt; Laurence Anholt

Book Summary

This book is a series of questions to the reader about his or her daily life and preferences. For example, one page asks, "Are you feeling hungry? What do you like?" and then gives the reader twenty-one labeled pictures from which to choose. There are questions about the reader's friends, what the reader sees outside his or her window, where the reader likes to go, and so on.

Basic Book Information

This picture book has about 20 pages. Excluding the opening and closing of the book, which have four-line rhymes about people's differences, each double-page spread has a sentence, usually a question, and many small pictures labeled with one word-each a possible answer to the question. This format ends up being similar to a picture dictionary, with lots of small pictures of objects and activities labeled with one word each. The serif text is very large, about an inch per letter. The questions are of all types and do not follow a particular pattern or start with the same opening word.

Noteworthy Features

The structure of this book is unusual. Like books with flaps (such as *Where's Spot?*), this book was designed so that readers will probably end up interacting with the text. One can imagine a partnership of two readers taking these questions quite seriously, and wavering over whether their favorite food is cake or hot dogs. Children who rely largely on illustrations to help them word-solve will certainly not be able to ascertain that the word under the boy who is reading books is "quiet" or that the word under the girl with her tongue sticking out is "fight." Still, the book is not written in sentences, so 90 to 95 percent accuracy is not necessary for comprehension.

The opening verse is written on the same page as the dedication and copyright information, and for this reason, many readers skip it. Missing these lines should not interfere with students' understanding or enjoyment of the book. The same is true of the closing verse on the final page.

In fact, many children enjoy browsing through the pages and reading the labeled pictures without really being able to decipher the questions on each page.

Teaching Ideas

This book will stand out in a library for beginning readers both because of its size and shape (it doesn't look as if it belongs in a kit) and because of its structure. Children won't get lost in this story, but they will read the book as older readers read many nonfiction texts-skimming, talking back to the text,

Illustrators

Catherine Anholt;
Laurence Anholt

Publisher

Scholastic, 1991

ISBN

0590469886

TC Level

4

using the text as the grounds for conversation, and so on.

Because of its unusual, questioning structure, the book can suggest to children a new format for their own writing. It also can function almost as a picture dictionary, and spark conversations about words. And because of all the labeled pictures, this book is also a good resource for students for whom English is a foreign language.

If children read the book much like a picture dictionary, they certainly won't do any interpretation work. However, if they read all the questions and think through their own answers to those questions, they will have accumulated a bit of information about themselves, and perhaps also about their reading partners. By bringing all of this information together as a whole, readers can consider what kinds of things tend to be true about the person. In order to make the book amount to anything more than just a list, students might be prompted to ask, "What does all this information tell you about yourself or reading partner?"

Children will often write lists and read lists as well, and often it will seem at first glance that there is not particular order to the items on a list. This book is, on careful inspection, quite structured. The first question is about waking up. The last question is about going to bed. Children will want to look at other texts to see if there is a hidden logic to the sequence of items in other lists.

Book Connections

Peter Spier has written a book called *People* that is similar, yet more complicated and detailed. It, too, pictures people all over the world in different houses and doing different activities, yet without the personal note found in this book.

Any picture dictionary will also have a structure similar to this one, with lots of labeled images that make it easy to read.

Genre
Picture Book

Teaching Uses
Independent Reading; Teaching Writing

A Field Guide to the Classroom Library, Lucy Calkins and the Teachers College Reading and Writing Project, Heinemann, ©2002 Teachers College, Columbia University; http://www.heinemann.com/fieldguides

All Along the River

Allan Fowler

Book Summary

All Along the River is a nonfiction book that relates simplified information about what rivers are, where they come from, and how people use them. Introduced in the book are some different parts of rivers (such as waterfalls and dams), the effects of rivers (such as floods and deltas), and the many ways people use rivers (such as river-rafting and farming).

Basic Book Information

This nonfiction book is 29 pages long. There is a section at the end called *"Words You Know"* that repeats vocabulary from the book in one-to-one correspondence with matching photographs. There is also a fairly thorough index. The book begins by asking the question, "Where do rivers begin?" The rest of the text is the answer. The text is at the top and bottom of the brightly colored photographs. Some pages are all text and some are a full-page photograph. There are one to three sentences per page and frequently there is one long sentence that is stretched over two pages. Although there is not a lot of text in the whole book and the text is written in a straightforward way, the vocabulary and concepts are quite difficult. The majority of the text is made up of words that are not easily decoded, and are not necessarily easily gleaned from the photographs or the context.

Noteworthy Features

There are many books in this series that are much easier than this one (e.g., they are written with a simple pattern), although they have the same format and style as this book. Readers may make the mistake of choosing this as an appropriate nonfiction book to read independently, when in fact this book is a lot more difficult than the other books in the series, and probably is best read in partnerships. On almost every page, there is a concept that is likely to be unfamiliar to some readers who are at this level. Many pages introduce a concept, but do not explain or give background information that is necessary for the reader to gain a general understanding of the concept. Further complicating matters, the text sometimes presents pictures that do not illustrate the content of the text on nearby pages. For example, on page 4 the text states: "Some rivers begin as springs rising out of the ground." The concept of "springs" is not explained in the text and the corresponding photograph looks like a big slab of rock with a crack in it. (The "springing" water is not recognizable as water.) There are many places like this in the book.

Teachers may initially believe the book covers simple concepts but on further reflection may realize that the concepts only seem simple because they are already familiar to most adults. One example of this is on page 13.

Series
Rookie Read about Science

Publisher
Children's Press, 1994

ISBN
0516460196

TC Level
5

The text states: "People build large dams to hold back the water. Some dams use the rushing water of rivers to produce electricity." After reading this, one teacher asked (with students in mind): What is a dam? Hold back the water from what? How does it hold it back? How are dams built? How does the rushing water make electricity? Where is the river in the photograph? All of these questions are hard to answer for most readers of texts at this level.

The format of the book is enticing and intriguing. The photographs are bright and informational. The book starts with a question for the reader that could act as a hook to get the reader involved, and the book is small (in size) and short.

There is a well laid out "glossary" of photos and words, and a detailed, yet simple index in the book as well. These are both accessible to the early reader and will work nicely as an introduction to these nonfiction features for the reader who is unfamiliar with them.

Teaching Ideas

This book can be used for several different reading experiences. *All Along the River* can be used as part of a genre study of nonfiction. Teachers may use this book to show how to an index works, what a glossary is, and that format and/or layout of the book is similar to others in the series.

Teachers may model for children how to read nonfiction. Readers can practice reading in smaller chunks, rather than start to finish. Readers can practice generating a list of questions based on the title, skimming of the book, or a small chunk they've read. Then they can try reading for informational answers to their specific questions.

This book can be used to develop the nonfiction reading skill of formulating hypotheses *after* reading. This will lead them to do more research, either by rereading this text or finding other texts like it for further research.

All Along the River can be used in a reading center as one of a group of books about rivers (or water, or dams or canyons, etc.) for readers to compare and contrast. As readers become more familiar with the topic, they may want to do some very simple cross-referencing to discover what books about rivers (or water or dams or canyons, etc.) have in common, or what this particular book lacks or adds to their study of the topic.

As readers become more familiar with their research topic, they may use this book as a model for writing their own book about rivers. They may write a simple "research report" about what they've learned. They may also want to write a book based on the questions, hypotheses, and so on that lead their research and information-gathering. Writers may want to try including a simple index or glossary in their books.

As is the case with most nonfiction, this book presents many opportunities for relevant, meaningful discussion (including all the places of difficulty mentioned in the above "Noteworthy Features"). Readers will need ample time to discuss their questions; their hypotheses based on questions they have, or information they've gathered; and their speculation about the topic. These discussions will enable readers to understand more of what they read as well as possibly introducing them to a topic that might excite them.

A Field Guide to the Classroom Library, Lucy Calkins and the Teachers College Reading and Writing Project, Heinemann, ©2002 Teachers College, Columbia University; http://www.heinemann.com/fieldguides

Book Connections

This book can be used in conjunction with other books from the *Rookie Read About Science* series as part of a nonfiction study. It can also be used in conjunction with other books about rivers and other topics covered in this book at this level. Other series at this level include *TWIG Books* and early readers in *The Wright Group*.

Genre
Picture Book; Nonfiction

Teaching Uses
Content Area Study; Partnerships; Teaching Writing

A Field Guide to the Classroom Library, Lucy Calkins and the Teachers College Reading and Writing Project, Heinemann, ©2002 Teachers College, Columbia University; http://www.heinemann.com/fieldguides

Amelia Bedelia Helps Out

Peggy Parish

Book Summary

Amelia is a housemaid who has responsibilities such as cleaning the house and preparing and cooking dinner for her employers, Mr. and Mrs. Rogers. Amelia is hard working and well meaning, but easily confused. In this story, the reader is introduced to Amelia Bedelia's niece, Effie Lou, and a friend of the Rogers, Miss Emma. Amelia Bedelia and Effie Lou set out to help Miss Emma get her house ready for her garden club's afternoon tea party, but Amelia Bedelia is comically baffled by the jobs on her list. In the end, Amelia's baking skills save the day.

Basic Book Information

Amelia Bedelia Helps Out is one continuous story without chapters. There are supportive, humorous pictures on every page that help readers understand Amelia Bedelia's unusual work habits.

Both children and adults laugh aloud as they read these funny books. Usually, Amelia is given instructions that she tries to follow *exactly*, but she confuses homophones and ends up creating giant fiascoes everywhere she goes. The *Amelia Bedelia* books do not need to be read in any particular order. However, the initial book in the series, *Amelia Bedelia*, introduces the recurring characters of Amelia, Mr. Rogers and Mrs. Rogers, so it may help to read this book first.

Noteworthy Features

Amelia Bedelia books are much more difficult than they at first appear. The text has many features that make texts accessible for students beginning work with longer books, such as referenced dialogue, linear plot structures, a large and well-spaced typeface, and illustrations that match the text on each page. However, some students may struggle to understand the humor of these books. Often, Peggy Parish uses terms with which students may not be familiar. *In Amelia Bedelia Helps Out*, for example, Mrs. Rogers asks Amelia to "sow" grass seeds and "stake" green beans. Students who have little experience gardening may not understand how 'sowing' seeds relates to planting, or that 'staking' vines involves training them up along a vertical structure. Thus, students can find themselves in the embarrassing position of no less confused than a character they know tends to be dizzy and befuddled.

Amelia Bedelia is nonetheless a humorous and lovable character. After reading a couple of books in this series, readers grow to expect silly things from Amelia's well-intentioned work habits. Young readers may not know what Mr. and Mrs. Rogers have in mind when they give their maid orders, but they will likely develop a sense that another disaster is coming up and

Series
Amelia Bedelia books

Illustrator
Lynn Sweat

Publisher
Harper Trophy, 1979

ISBN
0380534053

TC Level
8

that it will be something involving a humorous play on words.

The setting in this book is different from the others in the series. Although Amelia says good-bye to Mr. Rogers on the first page when he drops her off at Miss Emma's house, she still works for Mr. and Mrs. Rogers as their housekeeper. Readers may be confused by this, not realizing that Amelia works occasionally for other people as well as for the Rogers.

Teaching Ideas

In a conference with one or more children who are reading *Amelia Bedelia*, a teacher may want to talk about the concept of homonyms, words that look alike and sound alike but have different meanings. Homonyms are fundamental to the humor in this book. The same problem could be approached through a discussion of literal versus figurative meanings. Whether or not the term "homonym" is used in teaching, even young children should be able to grasp the concept, which has probably caused similar misunderstandings in their interactions with other people and with books. (Indeed, many children's jokes are based on words or phrases that have multiple meanings). English language learners may be even more tuned in to this communicative challenge and could benefit from a discussion of homonyms.

Some children who can produce a word-perfect performance of these books still may not get the jokes because the books require a rarified vocabulary. If readers don't know what it means to "dress the turkey," to "write bread-and-butter letters," or to "stake the string beans," they will run into some difficulties with these books. That can be half the fun of it, but only if readers understand puns and figurative language enough to comprehend at least a fair percentage of this book. A picture walk through the text may help the reader envision just what kinds of tasks Amelia is asked to perform.

Reading easier books filled with puns can be a good preface to the *Amelia Bedelia* series. Readers can develop finesse by reading Fred Gwynne's *A Chocolate Moose for Dinner* and *The King Who Rained*.

Children who are just beginning to read chapter books will often find themselves reading either mystery books (such as the *Boxcar Children*, *Nate the Great*, and *Cam Jansen*) or else humorous books (such as the *Wayside School* or *Joshua Adams* books). It might be reasonable, therefore, for teachers to do some whole-class work with humorous books. The whole class might listen to a read aloud of an *Amelia Bedelia* book and talk about the special kind of work that readers of this book (and perhaps other humorous books) need to do. Teachers may ask their classes to choose their independent books from a collection of humorous books.

During a read aloud discussion or mini-lesson, children might notice that when they read (or listen to) *Amelia Bedelia*, they are leaning forward to co-author the funny parts. The text says that Amelia is to "stake the string beans;" as good readers, they get pleasure out of being one step ahead of the text, imagining what Amelia will do. After a mini-lesson explaining how readers of humor try to beat the author to the punch line, it will be time for independent reading. Teachers may preface independent reading by saying, "Today, when you are reading your independent books, keep an eye out for sections of the text that you expect will turn out to be funny, and see if you can predict what the punch lines will be."

   Of course, there are a host of other things readers will notice as they read *Amelia Bedelia*, including the fact that from time to time something funny in the text will fly right over their heads. They should be encouraged to reread to see if on closer inspection they can "get the joke."

Book Connections

Amelia Bedelia Helps Out is similar in difficulty to *Cam Jansen* by David Adler, *Pinky and Rex* by James Howe, and *The Golly Sisters* series by Betsy Byars. It is more difficult than *Frog and Toad* by Arnold Lobel and the *Fox* series by Edward Marshall. Once children can successfully read *Amelia Bedelia* and other books of similar difficulty, they may find themselves well prepared to read the *Horrible Harry* series by Suzy Kline, *The Zack Files* series by Dan Greenburg, and *Freckle Juice* by Judy Blume.

Genre
Short Chapter Book; Picture Book

Teaching Uses
Independent Reading; Language Conventions; Character Study; Small Group Strategy Instruction

An Angel for Solomon Singer

Cynthia Rylant

Book Summary

In this gentle, resonant picture book the author recounts the story of Solomon Singer, who resides in a hotel for men in New York City. Lonely and friendless, depressed by his drab room, Solomon wanders the city at night, dreaming of his boyhood home in Indiana. One evening he chances upon the Westway Café and a friendly waiter named Angel. The cozy café becomes a regular destination, and the warm welcome Solomon finds there satisfies his painful yearnings and alters his view of the city.

Basic Book Information

This 28-page picture book is an ALA Notable Book, an NCSS-CBC Notable Children's Trade Book in Social Studies, and a Child Study Association Book of the Year. Cynthia Rylant is the 1993 Newbery medalist for *Missing May* and the author of many highly regarded picture books (*When I was Young in the Mountains* among others) and books for older readers. The rhythmic prose and poetic language of this story make it a fine choice for a read-aloud session.

Catalanotto's rich-hued watercolor illustrations provide a dream-like complement to the author's memorable text. In the opening spread, for example, Solomon Singer's elongated body and face are seen in an image reflected in a steaming teakettle. Later his reflection appears, upside down, in a puddle. Other illustrations mingle Solomon's wishes and memories with the real-life details of his present surroundings, blending, for example, a view of a city street by night with an image of Solomon's boyhood home in Indiana. Sharp-eyed readers will point out that the tiger cat following Solomon on the street in the beginning of the story looks like the cat Solomon is holding on the final page of the book, after the story's conclusion.

Noteworthy Features

Children will enjoy focusing on the vivid details the author uses to make Solomon believable. Solomon dreams of a balcony, a fireplace, a porch swing, and a picture window for watching the birds. He wishes the walls of his room were yellow or purple. In the café he orders two biscuits, some bacon, and a large glass of grapefruit juice. Also noteworthy is Rylant's command of prose style. For example, she uses many long, rhythmic sentences with repeated grammatical elements, sometimes followed by a very short sentence (*The menus told him how much hamburgers and bowls of soup and pieces of pie and other things cost. But it didn't put a price on dreams.*)

Illustrator
Peter Catalanotto

Publisher
Orchard Books, 1992

ISBN
0531070824

TC Level
9

A Field Guide to the Classroom Library, Lucy Calkins and the Teachers College Reading and Writing Project, Heinemann, ©2002 Teachers College, Columbia University; http://www.heinemann.com/fieldguides

Teaching Ideas

Teachers in the Teachers College Reading and Writing Project community often regard this as one of Cynthia Rylant's best pieces of fiction, and it is often used as a touchstone text in Writing Workshops. For example, children who are trying to write short fiction have studied the craft in this book to learn strategies they too can use in their own stories. It helps that *An Angel for Solomon Singer* is a short story and that it is written in third person like the stories students write. Children (and teachers) especially notice that Rylant's book moves through time beautifully. Like many other favorite books, it has just a bit of magic in the text.

The setting of this text is New York City and this is valuable to us because there aren't many stories written about the city that students can enjoy. A teacher may want to help readers understand the implications of living in this kind of residential hotel for men. This can become a grand lesson on how a writer takes from the real (characters based on real people) and creates fiction.

Each of the story elements in this book is clear and easy to follow and find. A teacher could help students to think about the following things in this book:

How do stories begin (this one begins by describing the character)

How a story must, at some point, move from "everyday" to the "one day." In this book, it's "One evening..."

How to use parenthesis to create an aside

The name of the character is really a part of the story (Angel, the waiter's name is significant.)

How to include a list inside a story

How to move from writing that stretches time out making it move slowly (each night he visits the restaurant), to writing that shrinks time ("For many, many nights Solomon Singer made his way west, carrying...")

How to show the change that the character is undergoing

Although this book is perfect for craft studies within the writing workshop, a teacher could also spend an equal amount of time focusing on the story and its message.

An Angel for Solomon Singer also lends itself to work with the story elements, and would provide for an interesting study of character. While students often get to know characters through dialogue with others, we get to know Solomon through his dreams. These dreams provide rich opportunities for making inferences about Solomon's character. The story tells readers that Solomon was a wanderer by nature. How might Solomon's wandering have influenced the course of his life-the jobs he took, the places he lived, and the relationships he formed or didn't form? For what reasons might Solomon have landed in New York City-far, in many ways, from his boyhood home in Indiana? Some students may have connections to people who live alone, and seem to have no friends or relatives, like Solomon. Knowledge of such people may contribute to their understanding of Solomon.

Children may be coached to notice that Rylant's spare portrait of Solomon omits a great deal. Rylant gives no explanation for how he came to reside in the hotel in New York City or how he supports himself. The story tells readers only that Solomon was a wanderer by nature. Teachers could use this as an opportunity to encourage thinking outside of the text to seek answers to unresolved questions. What are *some* of the reasons that may lead a person to live in a hotel? What are *some* of the ways Solomon may be supporting himself? Students can use their knowledge of the world to infer possible explanations.

In reviewing the book, a teacher might think that there are several aspects that might cause challenges for students, and when she talks with children who read the book, she may want to dig a bit to see if these parts were in fact confusing. One thing that can confuse readers is the references to Indiana. Students may not know what Indiana is like (or know the term *Midwest*). The teacher might start off by talking about Solomon's boyhood home in Indiana, far different in many ways from New York City. This can help students understand why Solomon Singer is lonely in New York City. Students might also get confused with the parenthesis that appear sporadically. It might be helpful if the teacher talked with a reader about the text that sometimes appears in parenthesis. Finally students may find trouble with Rylant's use of the word *dreams*. Solomon Singer carries "a dream in his head, each night ordering it up with his supper." Teachers may want to talk about the fact that not everything is meant to be taken literally.

Readers may also be interested in discussing the role that Angel plays in the story. While he is not the central character, Solomon is changed by his interactions with Angel. Authors include minor characters for a reason. Why did Rylant choose to make a waiter Solomon's Angel? What can Angel's impact on Solomon tell us about the role minor players can play in our own lives?

One teacher decided to have a small group of students read this book on their own. She decided to introduce the book to help them have a fluent and meaningful first read of it. She said to the small group, "Today you're going to have the chance to read a book by Cynthia Rylant, *An Angel for Solomon Singer*. It is a book about an older man named Solomon Singer. Solomon Singer lives in a hotel here in New York City but he doesn't like where he lives and he is lonely. He is sad and misses where he grew up. If you look on page 4, we learn he is from Indiana-which is a state where there are lots of fields and trees. It's a good place to walk around-to wander. One day when Solomon Singer is in New York City, he comes to a café. It reminds him of being in Indiana. This makes him feel good so he eats and dreams. Do some of you have dreams? Do you ever dream of a place you want to go or what you want to be when you grow up? That's what Solomon Singer does in this book while he is eating. The café makes him happy and reminds him of home. Today you can read this wonderful book all the way through by yourself. If you finish the book, read it again and mark bits that you notice. Then we'll talk a lot about it."

Book Connections

Students who liked this book might want to read other books that Cynthia Rylant and Peter Catalanotto worked together on, *All I See* and *Soda Jerk*.

For a different take on a person who spent much of her life wandering and who has wound up living alone, try *Miss Rumphius* by Barbara Cooney.

Genre
Picture Book

Teaching Uses
Author Study; Teaching Writing; Interpretation

A Field Guide to the Classroom Library, Lucy Calkins and the Teachers College Reading and Writing Project, Heinemann, ©2002 Teachers College, Columbia University; http://www.heinemann.com/fieldguides

And I Mean It, Stanley

Crosby Bonsall

Book Summary

This book opens with a little girl peering through the crack under the fence and talking to Stanley (we're not sure who Stanley is) saying "Listen, Stanley, I know you are there, I know you are in the back of the fence. But I don't care, Stanley. I don't want to play with you. . . ." The girl continues protesting that she absolutely has no use for Stanley; she doesn't care that he's not there; she's having a lot of fun and she's making a contraption out of junk. Stanley finally appears-he is a bounding, licking dog-and the book ends in a companionable chaos.

Basic Book Information

This is part of the *I Can Read* series from Harper Trophy. Other books in this series include *Little Bear* and *Danny and the Dinosaur*. Although these are listed as Level 1 in this series, they probably won't be first-level books for most children.

Noteworthy Features

The text of this story is a one-way conversation that the girl is carrying on with Stanley as she builds the "thing." Stanley does not appear until the last three pages. The reader will be delighted and a little surprised at Stanley's appearance, and at the discovery that Stanley is a dog.

Teaching Ideas

It will not be the words themselves which make this book challenging. Instead, the difficult thing for readers is that the book has been written to be puzzling. Readers are not expected to understand what's going on. The little girl is talking to *someone* but we have no clue who the missing Stanley is. And we're supposed to just "get it" that the girl doesn't mean what she's saying one bit. When she tells Stanley, "I don't need you, Stanley. And I mean it, Stanley," she of course means exactly the opposite of what she is saying.

What a lesson this can give to readers! This book is a perfect text for using in mini-lessons or strategy lessons designed to teach readers that sometimes, especially at the start of a book, we're *supposed* to read and think, "Huh?" and we read on expecting clarity-which eventually comes in this book. Then, too, sometimes characters in books say something and just because they say it and the words are printed in a book, this doesn't mean that readers must take everything a character says at face value. Well known examples are: The fox tells the Gingerbread Boy, "Get on my nose and I'll take you safely across the river." The reader should be suspicious. The witch

Series
I Can Read

Illustrator
Crosby Bonsall

Publisher
Harper Collins, 1974

ISBN
006444046X

TC Level
4

says, "Come closer that I may feel your cheeks," and the reader should think, "Stay away, stay away, she's not to be trusted." Similarly, in this book, the character keeps saying she doesn't want Stanley's companionship, but she means exactly the opposite of what she says. Readers would profit from being aware that this happens in books, and the class could keep an eye open for examples.

There are many opportunities in the text for the teacher to observe the orchestration of the strategies and cues needed to read this text. For example, if on page 9 the reader reads "I don't car (care)," the teacher would point out that the word "car" *looks* right, but does it make sense? Another example could be if the reader reads "This stuff (thing) I am making is really neat," (on page 22), the teacher would point out that "stuff" makes sense, but does it look right? If the reader becomes stymied by particular words, the teacher will want to notice whether the reader looks all the way across words (rather than just looking at the initial letters.) If a child is stopped by the word *thing*, for example, looking across the word and asking, "Have I seen any part of this word before?" will pay off because the child will probably recognize the *-ing* in *thing*.

The engaging illustrations, the surprise ending, and the plot offer many opportunities for comprehension discussions. The construction of the "truly great thing" and the conversation with Stanley can lead to a discussion of which is more important to the little girl-the thing or having Stanley to play with. The illustrations on the last three pages answer this question. In a conference, a teacher might nudge a reader to infer why the girl might be making the "thing."

Book Connections

The tone in this book resembles the tone in many of Judith Viorst's books, including *Alexander and the Terrible, Horrible, No Good, Very Bad Day* and, especially, *Earrings.* Readers may also want to read *Who's Afraid of the Dark?* also by Crosby Bonsall.

Genre
Picture Book

Teaching Uses
Independent Reading; Whole Group Instruction

Ant Cities

Arthur Dorros

Book Summary

This book describes the activities of harvester ants in particular and many other kinds of ants in general. First the reader learns about ant nests, what they look like and how they are made. Readers learn about the various jobs ants have, from feeding and caring for the larvae to husking seeds, removing garbage, and digging dirt. Readers learn about how ants sense the world, how they defend themselves, and what they like to eat. The book even describes what some common ant houses look like so that readers can find them in the woods.

Basic Book Information

This book is a continuous description of harvester ants, with about three simple sentences on each of 30 pages. Every page contains a large illustration, many of which have labels on them. These labels are in extremely small font, and some children will have difficulty deciphering them. Some pages have several illustrations showing different kinds of ants.

There is no index or table of contents and there are no text dividers like subheadings. At the end of the text, there is a boxed-in page describing how to make your own ant farm, and some tips for making it a healthy one.

Noteworthy Features

This book starts wisely with what children may already have noticed about ants-the large mounds some kinds of ants make for homes. These early pages also tell about sidewalk ants so every child will probably feel as if they have prior experiences with the topic of this book. By starting with children's own experiences, the book may draw readers in more easily than other books that begin right away describing the physical features of the insects or some other equally unfamiliar aspect of their existence.

Although there are no subheadings or other such dividers, nor is there any other overt organizing principle, the text is still fairly easy to follow. This may be because the sentences are structured in simple ways.

At several points in the text there are comparisons that make the information easier to understand. For example, the text says that if humans could lift as much as ants can lift in proportion to their body weight, we would be able to lift cars. These comparisons can help children make sense of raw data.

Teaching Ideas

This would be an excellent book to accompany children outside, alongside an anthill. Although it is not designed for easy reference, it could be read

Illustrator
Arthur Dorros

Publisher
Harper Trophy, 1998

ISBN
0064450791

TC Level
8

A Field Guide to the Classroom Library, Lucy Calkins and the Teachers College Reading and Writing Project, Heinemann, ©2002 Teachers College, Columbia University; http://www.heinemann.com/fieldguides

cover to cover after an intense ant-watching experience. It would also make an excellent companion to a classroom or home ant farm.

The directions for assembling an ant farm that come at the end of the book may well be enough for children to create their own ant farm. However, the book cautions that readers will have to include the queen ant in order to have the other ants survive, and it does not explain how to make sure you have the queen, where to find her, or what she looks like. (Some of this information can be found elsewhere in the book, but not all of it can.) The book also cautions in its earlier pages that some ants bite or sting, but it does not explain which ones do this. These could be sticking points for readers who have no other resources to depend on in creating their own ant farm.

One first grade teacher used this book to help in a whole-class study of insects. The class pets were some giant cockroaches (!) and during the whole class read-aloud, this teacher read several books about cockroaches. She proceeded to model for children, through the whole-class study of cockroaches, how to study any insect (or truthfully, any nonfiction topic). One day the teacher read aloud about cockroach homes and the class then drew and labeled a diagram to illustrate what they had learned. In small groups then, everyone in the class studied and made illustrations of the homes of the insects their group had chosen to study, all benefiting from the whole-class study of cockroaches. The class studied the body parts of insects in the ensuing days, then the life cycle of the cockroach and then of their insects, and so on.

Genre
Nonfiction; Picture Book

Teaching Uses
Content Area Study; Independent Reading; Partnerships

Arthur's Birthday Party

Lillian Hoban

Book Summary

When Arthur (a chimp) decides to have "gymnastics party" for his birthday, he is sure he will win the prize for all-around best gymnast. As his sister Violet, and friends practice their gymnastics, Arthur boasts. At the party, Violet and her friend, Wilma "wow" the rest of them with the routine they have been practicing all along. At first, Arthur is jealous, but then Violet points out that each kid deserves a prize for his or her own specific skill. Arthur agrees, and wins the "best all-around gymnast" prize after all.

Basic Book Information

Arthur's Birthday Party is a 64 page *I Can Read Book*. Each page is brightly illustrated. All of the dialogue is referenced.

Noteworthy Features

Arthur's Birthday Party captures Arthur's desire to be the best as well as his feelings of jealousy and pride. The dialogue between Arthur and Violet is also quite authentic, and children will recognize their relationships with their own siblings in this (and other) stories about Arthur and Violet.

There are some sentences in the story where the author uses italics or capital letters for emphasis. Readers at this level may be unfamiliar with this writing device.

There is quite a bit of gymnastics-related vocabulary throughout the text, which may be difficult for early readers to decode or glean from the context. These words include *trampoline, gymnast, gymnastics, tumbling, balancing, balanced, twirled, backwards, arched, somersaulted,* and *cartwheeled.*

Teaching Ideas

This book, as well as the other *Arthur* books (not to be confused with Arthur the Aardvark from the popular *Marc Brown* series) is a great book to use for teaching readers how to feel personal connection to the characters and the story. The plot of the *Arthur* books is usually written around a universal experience of childhood, which many children will readily relate to. Teachers may want to lead the discussion by saying, "I know exactly how Arthur feels when Violet does such an amazing job with Wilma in their gymnastics routine. I have a little sister too. I love her, but I used to feel jealous when she would get a lot of attention. I was especially jealous when she could do something that I could do. And if she was better than me, I would feel bad because she was younger than me!"

Children who are ready to read this book and others like it will have enough sight words and enough word-solving skills to be able to figure out

Series
Arthur books

Illustrator
Lillian Hoban

Publisher
Harper and Row, 1984

ISBN
0064442802

TC Level
7

A Field Guide to the Classroom Library, Lucy Calkins and the Teachers College Reading and Writing Project, Heinemann, ©2002 Teachers College, Columbia University; http://www.heinemann.com/fieldguides

most of this story. They may, however, be quite stymied by the gymnastic-related terms. In a strategy lesson with one reader, a small group of readers, or the whole class, a teacher might say that she's noticed that many children no longer do a picture walk to orient themselves to books. "That makes sense in a way, because the pictures no longer tell the whole story in these books," the teacher might say. "But there is a reason to glance over the books, and I want to show it to you." Then the teacher could take this book, scan through it, and mutter (as if to herself), "So this has a lot to do with gymnastics. Hmmm. That makes me think that if I *do* get to hard words, they might be gymnastic-words. I'll see if they say *cartwheels* or *somersaults* or *balance* or words like that."

Then the teacher could tell students that many books are linked to a topic and contain the words of that topic. When *Poppleton* goes to the library, readers should expect library words. When Arthur celebrates Halloween, the book is dotted with Halloween words. "Sometimes it helps to talk over Halloween, or the library, or gymnastics if that's what the book is about," the teacher might say before sending children off to see if any of their books have a topical focus.

Book Connections

Arthur's Birthday Party is one of several books about the same main characters. Other titles include *Arthur's Loose Tooth, Arthur's Pen Pal, Arthur's Christmas Cookies,* and *Arthur's Prize Reader.*

Genre
Picture Book

Teaching Uses
Independent Reading; Partnerships

Arthur's Halloween Costume

Lillian Hoban

Book Summary

Arthur's Halloween Costume is about Arthur (a chimp), his sister, Violet, and his regular group of friends. Arthur is dismayed to find out that on Halloween, he will not be the only ghost in his school. His morning gets worse when he spills ketchup on his ghost sheet, when there's no chicken left for his sandwich, when he loses his homework notebook, and when he argues with his friend Norman. Finally, when Arthur decides to be a warrior-with some help from the garbage-everyone mistakes his costume for something other than what it is. By the time he gets to school, with a cat perched on his head, a trash can lid in his hand and a ketchup-stained sheet, his sister Violet dubs him "The Spirit of Halloween." Arthur is satisfied that he now has the most original costume in school.

Basic Book Information

This *I Can Read Book* or Arthur series is 64 pages, with no chapters. There are several sentences per page.

Noteworthy Features

Arthur's Halloween Costume captures Arthur's excitement and frustration in his quest for "the most original Halloween costume."

There are some sentences in the story in which the author uses italics or capital letters for emphasis. Readers at this level may be unfamiliar with this writing device.

There is some vocabulary that is specific to Halloween and Halloween costumes that may be unfamiliar and hard for early readers to glean from context. Some of these words include *warrior, vampire, sword, shield, Pied Piper, shrunken, trainer, enemy, battle,* and *tramp.*

Although the story is pretty simple, it can be a little hard to follow at times. The main plotline involves Arthur's quest for an original Halloween costume. But during his quest, he searches for a missing homework book, bickers with his sister and his friend, and is continuously mistaken for other Halloween characters. There is a lot of action and several changes of setting. Because of these things, the main plotline may be hard for early readers to follow. This may be particularly hard for readers who are reading this book in conjunction with other *Arthur* books, which tend to be more clearly written.

Teaching Ideas

This book can also be used for readers who are just beginning to read books that have a fair amount of dialogue. The dialogue in *Arthur's Halloween*

Series
Arthur books

Illustrator
Lillian Hoban

Publisher
Harper Collins, 1984

ISBN
0064441016

TC Level
7

A Field Guide to the Classroom Library, Lucy Calkins and the Teachers College Reading and Writing Project, Heinemann, ©2002 Teachers College, Columbia University; http://www.heinemann.com/fieldguides

Costume is straightforward. It is always referenced; it is usually contained on one page; there are no ellipses or dashes; and it is not the main portion of the text. Still, there is enough dialogue in the text to make it important and meaningful for teachers to do several strategy or mini-lessons on reading dialogue.

This is a great book for readers to use in a study of Arthur. In it Arthur reveals a lot of the traits of his personality that recur from book to book.

Book Connections

Arthur's Halloween Costume is one of several books about the same main characters. Other titles include *Arthur's Loose Tooth, Arthur's Pen Pal, Arthur's Christmas Cookies,* and *Arthur's Prize Reader.* Arthur at one point seems to be having the type of day that Alexander tells of in Viorst's book, *Alexander and the Terrible, Horrible, No Good, Very Bad Day.*

Genre
Picture Book

Teaching Uses
Independent Reading; Partnerships

A Field Guide to the Classroom Library, Lucy Calkins and the Teachers College Reading and Writing Project, Heinemann, ©2002 Teachers College, Columbia University; http://www.heinemann.com/fieldguides

Arthur's Honey Bear

Lillian Hoban

Book Summary

Arthur's Honey Bear is about a chimp named Arthur and his sister, Violet. Arthur decides that he is going to go through his old toys and games and have a tag sale. As he puts tags on all his items and sets them up for the sale, he resists putting his old "Honey Bear" up front. Several children come to the sale and find nothing they like. Finally, their friend Wilma arrives and asks about Arthur's Honey Bear. Arthur talks her out of buying the Honey Bear and then very reluctantly sells the bear to Violet, who proceeds to dress him up and play with him. Arthur struggles with his sadness about losing Honey Bear until he realizes that he is, in fact, Honey Bear's uncle. From then on, he and Violet happily share Honey Bear.

Basic Book Information

Arthur's Honey Bear is 64 pages long and does not contain chapters. Although most books of this level contain four or five self-contained chapters, this book contains one story that spans from cover to cover. This *I Can Read* book is part of a series involving Arthur the chimp. It is at a similar difficulty level as short chapter books of this length.

Noteworthy Features

Arthur's Honey Bear is warmly written and really captures Arthur's conflicted feelings about letting go of a toy from earlier in his childhood. The dialogue between Arthur and his sister, Violet, can feel quite real; children may recognize their relationships with their own siblings in this and other stories about Arthur and Violet.

Some of the text is broken into two, three or four words on a line, with four or five lines going together to make a completed sentence. For some readers, this layout may help them progress bit by bit through long lists of items in a sentence, but for many readers, it can be difficult to hold onto the words in one line as their eyes travel to another line, another, and another.

There are several sentences in the story in which the author uses italics for emphasis. Readers at this level may be unfamiliar with this writing device. Page 17 contains a 'hand-painted' sign for the tag sale that, because it is not in typed text, may be a little difficult for early readers to decode.

Teaching Ideas

As a read aloud, a teacher may do a short mini-lesson or strategy lesson on how readers use their voices (aloud or in their heads) appropriately when text is italicized. A teacher may show part of the text on an overhead projector or photocopies of the pages where text is italicized, so that many

Series
Arthur books

Publisher
Harper Collins, 1974

ISBN
0064440338

TC Level
7

A Field Guide to the Classroom Library, Lucy Calkins and the Teachers College Reading and Writing Project, Heinemann, ©2002 Teachers College, Columbia University; http://www.heinemann.com/fieldguides

readers can follow along. The teacher can read the text and ask children to describe how their voice changed when they came to the italicized parts.

This book can also be used for strategy lessons to help readers who are just beginning to read books that have more dialogue in them. The dialogue in *Arthur's Honey Bear* is fairly straightforward. It is always referenced, contained on one page and contextualized by narration. The dialogue never employs ellipses or dashes. Readers will not be overwhelmed by the amount of dialogue, but there is enough to make it important and meaningful for teachers to do several strategy lessons.

This dialogue study might include an emphasis on making a movie in one's mind so one already knows Violet is talking even before the text says, "said Violet." It could also include a pointer or two on intonation, although it is not helpful to push readers to read as if they were actors on a stage.

Because some readers read chapter books as if the challenge is simply to get through so many words and lines, it's helpful to encourage readers to stop often to talk about the text. One way to do this is look over a book (or section of a book) prior to reading it, and putting Post-It s in that will signal, "Stop-and-Talk." Because this book is quite long and is not separated into stories or chapters, assigning oneself some "stop and reflect places" can be especially useful. These stopping points can be used to reflect, retell, and reread and maybe to discuss the text with a partner or group.

Teachers may use *Arthur's Honey Bear* as a starting point on studying what it means to read books within a series. The *Arthur* books retain the same main characters, the same level of vocabulary, and similarities in the context across the entire series. Readers can read, write and discuss ways in which the books are similar and different, how the author's voice is consistent from book to book and whether the characters grow and change.

Book Connections

Arthur's Honey Bear is one of several books about the same main characters. Other titles include *Arthur's Loose Tooth, Arthur's Pen Pal, Arthur's Christmas Cookies* and *Arthur's Prize Reader.* Similar in level, Jean Van Leeuwen's *Oliver Pig* is also built on the true-life dramas of growing up and of living with siblings. Children could profit from looking at and comparing these series. How are they similar? How are they different?

Genre
Short Chapter Book

Teaching Uses
Independent Reading; Small Group Strategy Instruction; Character Study

A Field Guide to the Classroom Library, Lucy Calkins and the Teachers College Reading and Writing Project, Heinemann, ©2002 Teachers College, Columbia University; http://www.heinemann.com/fieldguides

Baby Hippo
Beverley Randell

Book Summary

This book begins, "The hippos are asleep down in the river. Can you see Baby Hippo?" Baby Hippo is sleeping on Mother Hippo's back as a group of hippos swim and doze in the sun. "He is safe," the book says. The lions are also sleeping in the sun, not too far away. When Baby Hippo wakes up he goes for a walk. The lions wake up and see Baby Hippo. Fortunately, Mother Hippo wakes up and sees the lions. She's too big for the lions and they run away. Mother Hippo takes Baby Hippo back into the water where he is safe.

Basic Book Information

The Rigby PM series was developed by Beverley Randell who continues-at age 70-to be a primary author of these books today. She began to write the books after ten years as a New Zealand classroom teacher. The PM readers always rely on a traditional story structure which, in Randell's mind, includes having a central character that has a problem; a climax or pivotal moment in which readers worry whether the problem be solved; and the resolution, when the problem is solved. Randell claims that because she also values meaning and wants to teach youngsters to monitor for sense, "you will find no traces of mad fantasy, certainly no hint of the supernatural, and the very minimum of surprise twists in plots." She feels that books about witches and ghosts or books full of playful nonsense don't teach kids the habit of expecting sense and of self-correcting when a book does not make sense.

Noteworthy Features

The book includes many high frequency words including *in*, *the*, *can*, *see*, *on*, *is*, *like*, *are*, *going*, *and*, *up*, *looking*, *come*, and *here*. The repetition of these sight words will give readers a way into the new content on each page. That is, because the book isn't repetitive, readers will need to rely on known sight words, on the moderately supportive pictures, and on their own word-work in order to find meaning. The print is large and well-spaced. Text varies between one to five lines on a page. Most sentences are short, but there are two sentences that have twelve words.

Teaching Ideas

If a teacher wants to do a book introduction to help an individual reader (or a partnership or a small group of readers) with this book, the teacher might invite readers to look at the cover page and she might say, "Baby Hippo is safe asleep on Mother Hippo's back. While Mother is still sleeping, he wakes up and takes a walk. I hope he doesn't run into any danger!" The children

Series
Rigby PM

Illustrator
Elizabeth Russell-Arnot

Publisher
Rigby, 1997

ISBN
0763515124

TC Level
4

could look at the cover and predict from the picture that the lion would come. "Let's turn the pages and see what happens."

Another teacher, however, might worry that such an introduction would leave the child with lots of word work to do on his or her own, but with very little comprehension work to do. This teacher might instead take note of what a child does on his or her own to get ready to read. If the child simply begins pointing at words and moving through the print, the teacher might say, "I find it helps to glance over the book before I read to see if I can get an idea of how the story might go. Can I watch you do that?" Then the teacher might stop the child after a few pages of looking at the pictures. "If this is a story, it'll usually start by showing us who the story is about. Who will this story be about?" If the reader doesn't know the name for hippo or the lion, the teacher can give these names to the child. "Hmm," the teacher could then say. "So there is a baby hippo and some lions-I wonder what will happen?"

The child who can successfully read this book will be quite proficient at pointing under the words. There are more words on a page than some children will have encountered often, so pointing under the words may still pose some challenges for a reader. As always, if the child errs and doesn't notice that he's done so and therefore doesn't correct himself, it's best to let the child continue reading until he reaches something that gives him the feedback necessary to lead him to see the problem and to self-correct by going back and rereading the line. Teachers might in the end need to prompt this self-correcting by asking, "Did it match?" or "Does that look right?" but once children are reading well enough to be working with books of this difficulty level, most of them are quite proficient at one-to-one matching.

By now, when children *do* see that they are pointing incorrectly, this information won't necessarily come from the fact that the one-to-one pointing "didn't come out even." Now children will be noticing some of the letters in words, and expecting known sight words to be spelled in the conventional way. "Wait! That's not *look*," the child will say and in this way, the letters nudge the child to go back and try reading and pointing again.

In order to nudge students to use more sight words and to attend to the letters in words, teachers might help a child with a word or two and then say, for example, "Can you find the word *walk* on page 9? What letter would you expect *walk* to start with?"

When children "get stuck" on words, teachers may want to resist the temptation to jump right in to help. The important thing is for a reader to be active, using strategies he or she has for dealing with difficulty. Teachers can see these strategies only when children encounter difficulties before their eyes. Hopefully when readers do run into hard parts, they will back up and reread, "turning their brains on more to think 'What *could* go here?'"

If a reader has no difficulty pointing at the words while reading, teachers may want to suggest that the child reread it without pointing. "Just bring your finger out when you run into trouble and need it," the teacher might say to some children who are reading books of this difficulty level.

Teachers will also find the opportunity to teach other early reading behaviors such as prompting the child to look at the picture and to get ready for the first sound. Also, once a child generates a possibility for the word in question, the teacher might want to often ask, "Does that make sense?"

A Field Guide to the Classroom Library, Lucy Calkins and the Teachers College Reading and Writing Project, Heinemann, ©2002 Teachers College, Columbia University; http://www.heinemann.com/fieldguides

Teachers can anticipate that a child may encounter difficulty with *river* on page 4 and watch the child's work with that page, expecting to learn about the strategies the child tends to use. For example, did the children check the word *river* on page 4 with the picture? Did the child look at the letters to know this wasn't a stream, a swamp or a lake? On page 16, the children may have difficulty with the word *back*. Does the child read the sentence, getting his or her mouth ready to make the /*b*/ sound?

The child may or may not figure out *back* on her own. If she seems stuck even after rereading the sentence, it can help (oddly enough) to copy the letters b-a-c-k slowly on paper, seeing if the child can say and blend the sounds.

Genre
Picture Book; Nonfiction

Teaching Uses
Small Group Strategy Instruction; Partnerships; Content Area Study

Beaver at Long Pond

William T. George; Linsay Barrett George

Book Summary

This is a captivating story of a beaver's nocturnal work. First, the animal checks for danger by sniffing the night air. Then he feels the rushing current with his whiskers and knows there is a break in the dam. He must next set about making repairs with mud and sticks and stones. Finally, he has time to eat in the forest. When he stays out too late past sunrise munching on a tree he has felled, he is frightened back to his lodge by a boy out fishing with his dog. Finally he swims into his home to sleep for the day.

Basic Book Information

This twenty-page-long nonfiction book is a continuous tale of one beaver at work at night. Information about this creature is imparted both in the telling of the tale and in the realistic illustrations. The book is formatted and reads like a fictional story but it is, in fact, nonfiction.

Noteworthy Features

Not only is this book packed with information about beavers, it is a well-told, suspenseful account of a beaver's night. The language is carefully chosen to create a mood and to try to make the reader feel the world from the beaver's point of view. Meanwhile, the book also contains precise information about the beaver.

Teaching Ideas

This book goes well with the book entitled *Beavers* published by Mondo; however, this *Beavers* lacks plot and is instead a book of organized facts. Nonetheless, this book contains facts and details omitted from the other book, as well as diagrams and explanations that add background to this story. Some questions may arise from the comparing of the two. For example, if beavers work at night, why are they pictured in the daylight in the *Beavers* book?

In style, tone, and format, this book is similar to a book about a sea turtle entitled *Into the Sea*. Both follow one creature through typical activities and tell the story with mood and a sense of place. Both have the air of fiction while relating detailed information about a little-known creature.

Some children might find it strange to be trying to glean facts or knowledge from a book that feels like a fictional story. They may be caught in the flow of the tale and not recognize a fact for a fact the first time they hear it. Teachers usually find students more able to take note of bits of information if they are talking back to the text. Teachers may suggest readers pause after every few pages to say, "The thing that surprises me here

A Field Guide to the Classroom Library, Lucy Calkins and the Teachers College Reading and Writing Project, Heinemann, ©2002 Teachers College, Columbia University; http://www.heinemann.com/fieldguides

Sidebar

Illustrator
Linsay Barrett George

Publisher
Harper Trophy, 1988

ISBN
0688175198

TC Level
7

is. . . ." Piaget says that we learn by assimilating new information with our existing ideas, or by accommodating (or revising) our initial ideas to make way for information that *doesn't fit* into what we thought we knew. Talking about surprising new information is one of the easiest ways to help readers do the important work of changing their ideas in the light of new information. Sometimes readers benefit from having a particular question they are trying to answer as they read. Searching for an answer to a question changes the way a reader reads or listens to a text-and this can be for the good and for the bad. The stance makes readers more active, but it can also encourage them to overlook everything that doesn't exactly fit into their questions. It may be that the reader is better off not trying to find the answer until the second read, that way the reader can experience the story itself before it becomes a collection of facts.

In a similar way, readers may hesitate before drawing conclusions from this text, and rightly so. Just because a beaver smacks his tail against the water once when he is in danger doesn't mean that he will do that every time he is in danger. Other books that simply state this fact, instead of implying it, are easier to trust.

Book Connections

Many children have found it useful to compare this book and the Mondo book, *Beavers* by Helen Moore. This book can also be compared to others by the Georges featuring *Long Pond*, *Box Turtle at Long Pond*, *Christmas at Long Pond*, and *Fishing at Long Pond*.

Genre
Nonfiction; Picture Book

Teaching Uses
Content Area Study; Reading and Writing Nonfiction

Blackberries

Beverley Randell

Book Summary

The book begins, "Father Bear and Mother Bear and Baby Bear went to look for blackberries." They each carry a basket to put their blackberries into. While Mother and Father Bear are filling up their baskets, Baby Bear is eating all the blackberries. Mother and Father Bear get a little anxious when they realize Baby Bear is not with them. When they find him he has an empty basket!

Basic Book Information

The PM Readers is a series published by Rigby. The PM Readers tend to come in kits in which every book is packaged like every other book. Some people think this is less than ideal because at every level, a library should be full of books, each with its own individuality. On the other hand, the PM Readers are an important resource for teachers because first, there are many at the early reading levels and second, the PM Readers recognize the supports that readers need and try to offer them. Many researchers feel that the PM Readers are especially good at providing a lot of easy text, full of high frequency words. That is, instead of saying: *the cow/ the pig/* a PM Reader is apt to say: *I see the cow./ I see the pig./* Also, the PM Readers are special because a great many of even the earliest books are stories. Other early books tend to be label-books, organized in a repetitive list structure, and it's nice to be able to also give beginning readers the opportunity to read stories that have not only problems and resolutions, but also characters. The PM Readers contain many books about Ben, many books about Sally, and so on. That is, just as more sophisticated books may feature the Boxcar Children across a series of tales, PM Readers feature Ben or Sally, or other characters, across a series of books.

Noteworthy Features

One sentence in *Blackberries* has as many as thirteen words, but most sentences are short and all contain many high frequency words. Most pages have about four lines of text.

Father Bear wears spectacles. Mother bear wears a floral scarf and a watch, and carries a basket that's substantially smaller than her spouse's basket. Other than this, there aren't many details in the illustrations of the story.

Teaching Ideas

One teacher decided to give a child an introduction to this book, and did so by saying: "Baby Bear is going to look for blackberries with Mother and

A Field Guide to the Classroom Library, Lucy Calkins and the Teachers College Reading and Writing Project, Heinemann, ©2002 Teachers College, Columbia University; http://www.heinemann.com/fieldguides

Series
PM Readers

Illustrator
Isabel Lowe

Publisher
Rigby, 1996

ISBN
0435049186

TC Level
3

Father Bear. How many of you have eaten blackberries?" After talking briefly about blackberries, she said, "We'll have to see if the bears find blackberries and what they do with them. Can I watch you look over this book and get ready to read it?" While looking over the book, the reader may point to the cover photo as if to say, "The bears *do* find blackberries."

Of course, some children will not need an introduction, benefiting more from the opportunity to do some good work when they encounter difficulties. Whether or not the teacher decides that a child needs the help of an introduction, it is important to observe the ways in which readers use the pictures and the print, cross-checking their information. For example, there is a picture of a basket on page 5. The teacher might observe whether the child uses the picture as a source of information and then checks it against the letters *basket*. If the child doesn't seem to check the print, the teacher might say, "Does it say *basket*?" The child may say, "yes?" as if the teacher is the final source of assurance. "How do you know?" the teacher can then ask, redirecting the child's focus back to the print.

The teacher can also help readers with new words by asking the reader to find these unknown words. For example, a teacher might say to the child before he or she reads, "This book has a word in it you'll want to know. It's *where*. (The teacher writes it.) What do you notice about the word? (They discuss it.)" Then the teacher might say, "Can you find the word *where* on page 9? What letters would you expect *where* to start with?" Teachers will also find the opportunity to teach other early reading behaviors such as prompting children to reread, to look at the picture, and to get their mouths ready for the first sound.

The teacher can also help the children practice the process of using information while reading on the run. For example, on page 5, if the children have difficulty with the word *went*, the teacher might take that word out of the sentence and write it. Teachers should write out each letter in the word while slowly modeling how the sounds are blended together.

The teacher will use what she observes about the children's knowledge of letters, words, and strategies to teach. For example, the word *shouted* is used on page 15. If the teacher expects that for this reader, *out* is a known word but doesn't notice the reader using this knowledge, the teacher can call attention to this chunk and ask the student, " Do you know anything about this word that will help you figure it out?" Let the children know that they can solve a new word by thinking about another word or chunk that they know.

Book Connections

Blackberries is part of a series written by Beverly Randell. Other books in the series include *Father Bear Goes Fishing, Baby Bear Goes Fishing, Baby Bear's Present, Honey for Baby Bear, Baby Bear Climbs A Tree, Baby Bear's Hiding Place, House Hunting,* and *Father Bear's Surprise*.

Teachers may want to tell readers that many books revisit the same motifs. If the children have read *Father Bear Goes Fishing*, the teacher and students can discuss and compare the two books about the Bear Family. This book also resembles the folktale, *The Three Bears* in some places (such as page 5 when we see Father Bear's basket, Mother Bear's basket, and Baby Bear's basket.) It is most similar to McClosky's *Blueberries for Sal.*

A Field Guide to the Classroom Library, Lucy Calkins and the Teachers College Reading and Writing Project, Heinemann, ©2002 Teachers College, Columbia University; http://www.heinemann.com/fieldguides

Genre
Picture Book

Teaching Uses
Independent Reading

Blueberries for Sal

Robert McCloskey

Book Summary

Little Sal and her mother go to Blueberry Hill to pick blueberries. At the same time, Little Bear and his mother are eating blueberries on Blueberry Hill. Little Sal gets caught up in the eating of the berries and gets way behind her mother. The same happens to Little Bear. Before long, both are lost. As they search for their mothers, the two get mixed up. Soon, Little Sal is following Little Bear's Mother and Little Bear is following Little Sal's mother. Both mothers quickly discover the mix-up, and after backing away from the children, find their own little ones. Then they all go home with their respective stores of blueberries.

Basic Book Information

This book is a Caldecott Honor book for 1948. It is 55 pages long and has about four lines of large print on every page. There is direct speech on many of the pages, and the speaker is always named near the quotation.

Noteworthy Features

This old classic is happily still on the shelves of many classrooms. Perhaps because of its three-toned cover and navy and white ink illustrations, *Blueberries for Sal* doesn't often get taken off the library shelves by students who don't already know the story. Once they know the story, however, it is chosen again and again, living up to its reputation as a great work of literature for children. Usually, the book benefits from a promotion-either a tantalizing talk from someone who has read it, or simply a bit of reading it aloud.

Some of the situations in *Blueberries for Sal* aren't familiar to children and can make following the story, with mental images, a little harder than some stories. Some children don't know what canning is, and some have only gotten blueberries from a store. If this seems to be interfering with readers' ability to get connected to the story, a little pause to help readers picture berries that one can eat growing on bushes sometimes helps.

Understanding the humor, or even the literal actions, of Little Sal, takes some skill in picturing. The author describes, step by step, what Little Sal is doing with her blueberries, and the reader has to picture it carefully and thoroughly. The picture is a still shot, and it is the little girl's actions that are funny. No one in the text or in the pictures laughs or says that anything is funny; the funniness has to come from the moving picture of what Little Sal is doing in the reader's mind. In the end, however, there is a lot to enjoy in the story even if the humor is lost on the reader.

Some editions of *Blueberries for Sal* may be a bit difficult for some readers. The text is justified both right and left margins in a way that is

A Field Guide to the Classroom Library, Lucy Calkins and the Teachers College Reading and Writing Project, Heinemann, ©2002 Teachers College, Columbia University; http://www.heinemann.com/fieldguides

somewhat unusual for picture books. This means that the spacing between words and letters is irregular, and at times, a bit cramped. This can be frustrating for a reader who is already struggling.

The vocabulary is varied in this book, although the story line is kept simple. Words like "hustle," "struggle," "tramping," partridge," spot the text, but always have plenty of contextual clues for deciphering their general meanings.

Teaching Ideas

Students sometimes don't feel immediately connected to the story because by the time they are old enough to read the book, Little Sal is much younger than they are, and a protagonist who is younger than the reader is a turn-off for some children. However, if the readers or listeners realize how funny Little Sal's behavior is, eating and picking and eating until she doesn't have any berries in her bucket at all, then they can enjoy laughing at her, the way they laugh at the funny antics of a beloved little sibling who doesn't know any better. This transfer of the kind of identification the reader makes with the main character isn't necessarily easy. Some readers go into every book expecting to relate to the main character as if the character were just like themselves. Learning to change this can be the opening of a very large door in the reader's reading life. Talking to students about the main character, Sal, in this book may allow teachers to see which students are able to find ways to relate to Little Sal and which aren't. Teachers can then help bring the strategies of those who can relate to those who can't.

Some teachers use this book in small group strategy lessons. One teacher, for example, pulled together a small group of readers. She said, "Readers, I got this group of us together because I have found a great book that might help us become better readers. You guys could use some help in figuring out books that have two stories occurring at the same time. The independent books that you are reading all have a story in which two smaller stories are happening within the text. The author goes back and forth from one to the other and it is confusing sometimes to keep track of this. The book that I have here, *Blueberries for Sal*, has the same feature. Let me show how the author of this book gives you clues throughout the text when he changes from one mini-story to the other." At this point, the teacher went to sections of the text including for example, the one that said, "On the other side of Blueberry Hill, Little Bear came with his mother to eat blueberries." She told the students, "These are different supports that the author gives you to keep up with him. Now, I want you to read this book independently and place a Post-It note every time you see a change from one story line to the next. I'll be conferring with some of you to see how it's going."

The idea of parallel story lines and the theme of mistaken identity switches among pairs of people come up often in literature, even in Shakespeare. Children will begin to learn how these kinds of stories tend to flow with this early example. They may even notice, or be asked to notice other examples in their own reading history.

Book Connections

The PM Story *Blackberries* is strikingly similar to this book.

A Field Guide to the Classroom Library, Lucy Calkins and the Teachers College Reading and Writing Project, Heinemann, ©2002 Teachers College, Columbia University; http://www.heinemann.com/fieldguides

Genre
Picture Book

Teaching Uses
Independent Reading; Read Aloud; Small Group Strategy Instruction

Bread, Bread, Bread

Ann Morris

Book Summary

Bread, Bread, Bread is a "round-the-world" tour of different kinds of bread: making bread, bread being bought and sold, and bread being used as part of a religious ceremony. People of all ages, from around the world, are shown eating loaves, rolls, pretzels, pizza, challah, and pita.

Basic Book Information

Bread, Bread, Bread is a picture book. There are 28 pages and the text begins on page 5. There are pages with no text, pages with one sentence, and pages with a few words from a long sentence that spans two to three pages. There are brightly colored photographs on each page. Some pages are a full-page photograph, some have a photograph with the text at the bottom or top, some have a photograph with the text on the side and some have three to four photographs with the text under each photograph. Each photograph supports the text in some way, usually in direct correspondence with some part of the text. But, the photographs have a lot of information that can be "read" besides the information that matches the text. (For example, on page 24, the text states: "Bread for sale!" The photograph is of an Israeli man selling a large loaf of multigrain bread with a hole in the middle, from a small stand on the street.) Much of the text is made up of high frequency words such as *people, all, the, eat, there, are, many, to, your, up, and, they, head, too, helps,* and *good.*

The font is large and well-spaced. There is an "index " at the back of the book, which describes the type of bread, culture and/or nationality of the people in the photograph, the country where the photograph has been taken, and the way in which the bread is being shown that corresponds to each page in the book. The photographs represent Israel, the United States, Indonesia, Peru, Guatemala, Italy, Sicily, Ecuador, Germany, Ghana, England, France, India, Mexico, Portugal, Hong Kong, and Greece. This index is written in language that is more complex and the font is quite small. Early readers may need help with this section of the book.

Noteworthy Features

This book is beautifully photographed and fascinating to read. The variety of types and uses of bread is well represented, yet simply and succinctly explained. The inclusion of people from around the world going about their daily business as they deal with bread is lovely and remarkable. Each page lends itself to long discussions about various aspects of what is represented in the individual photograph. The index, also, is well stocked with even more detailed and equally interesting information about culture, tradition, and types of bread. The book inevitably makes everyone hungry!

Series
Around the World

Illustrator
Ken Heyman

Publisher
William Morrow, 1993

ISBN
0688122752

TC Level
4

A Field Guide to the Classroom Library, Lucy Calkins and the Teachers College Reading and Writing Project, Heinemann, ©2002 Teachers College, Columbia University; http://www.heinemann.com/fieldguides

Although the book is large (in size), the font is large, there are a lot of high frequency words, and there is very little text overall, it still could be challenging for early readers. There are ellipses, sentences that stretch over two-three pages, and some vocabulary that is not easily decoded or gleaned from the context (e.g., *soak, basket,* and *market*).

Teaching Ideas

If a teacher wanted to provide more support for readers of this text, she might give a book introduction saying, "This is a book by Ann Morris called *Bread, Bread, Bread*. And it's all about...(you guessed it)... Bread! It says people eat bread all over the world. It talks about all the kinds, shapes, and sizes of bread: skinny, fat, round, flat, and even bread with a hole, crunchy, pizza, pretzels, and bread meant to soak up an egg. If you turn to page 15 you can even see bread on a table and bread on your head. The book gets a little tricky on page 22. Can everyone open up to that page? In the beginning of the book, Ann Morris is giving us lots of information about bread but now the book becomes like more of a story. 'Fill up the basket... off to the market. Bread for sale.'"

A teacher might also give a strategy lesson on the nonfiction elements of this book. She might say, "I chose to show you this book because it has an index at the end of the book. You'll be seeing many indexes as we read more nonfiction books. If you turn to the second to last page you'll find the word 'index.' The index tells us the country that this particular bread is from. As a reader of nonfiction, I like to always look over an index such as this after I read a book because it gives me additional facts. Today I'm hoping you'll even read this book and when you finish reading it, I'm going to admire the way you turn to read the index to find out additional facts."

Bread, Bread, Bread can be used part of an author study of Ann Morris books (particularly those photographed by Ken Heyman). Many of her books have a similar format, a simple premise and photographs from around the world that support the premise. Readers may find similarities and differences in all the Ann Morris books.

Bread, Bread, Bread, is also available as a "big book" and so may be used in several different ways by teachers, with a small group or the whole class, to support early reading behaviors. This book lends itself to doing word work because there are a lot of high frequency words, as well as words that are unfamiliar and will be challenging for the early reader. Teachers may use this book to support lessons on one-to-one matching of the words to the picture, "getting your mouth ready" for an upcoming word, predicting or figuring out text from looking at the picture, asking yourself, "What would make sense here?" Young readers may memorize the text through repeated readings, and then may work with the big book in small groups or reading partnerships to practice all of the above early reading strategies.

Bread, Bread, Bread may be used as part of a reading center that is organized around several different principles. In fact, one great exercise for young readers is to build their own centers with a handful of books and to define the organizing principle themselves. (Although young readers often need help with choosing reading center books that belong together. Their topics may be too broad, too vague or too esoteric to do good reading center work.) This book may be in a center about bread, bakeries, books about things that cultures share, or books by Ann Morris.

This book may also be used as part of a study of the genre of nonfiction. Teachers may model for the children how nonfiction is read differently from fiction. Readers can practice reading smaller chunks, rather than straight through from start to finish. Teachers may model for children the many opportunities for, and the necessity of, frequent and interesting discussions that nonfiction text presents to the reader. While reading to a group, the teacher can make frequent stops at relevant sections and encourage the children to "say something" to someone about the text read.

Bread, Bread, Bread may be used to support other areas of the curriculum, particularly Social Studies and Science. Many teachers in early grades do whole class studies of bread or bakeries or the similarities and differences of cultures around the world. This book may be used as a rich and valuable source of information about any of these topics. Teachers may show readers how to use this book as a "reference" for their studies.

As readers become more familiar with the text, they may use *Bread, Bread, Bread* as a "touchstone text" to help them write their own simple nonfiction books. Readers may choose a small topic (which ultimately expands into something much larger, like "bread") and write their own nonfiction books in a similar format to this one. They may use *Bread, Bread, Bread* to guide them with their own writing.

Book Connections

There are several other books written by Ann Morris and photographed by Ken Heyman that follow a similar format to *Bread, Bread, Bread*. One is *Hats, Hats, Hats*. There are also many other books at this level about bread. One similar book is *Different Kinds of Bread*, published by the Wright Group.

Genre
Nonfiction; Picture Book

Teaching Uses
Reading and Writing Nonfiction; Content Area Study; Author Study; Independent Reading; Teaching Writing

Buffy's Tricks

Lucy Lawrence

Book Summary

Buffy is Lucy's "ordinary" dog who likes to do everyday, regular things. One day, Lucy decided that she would make Buffy more than just an ordinary dog by teaching him some fancy tricks. Lucy tries to teach Buffy how to jump though hoops, fetch the newspaper, and balance a ball on his nose. Each time Lucy tries to teach Buffy a new trick he always foils her plan. Buffy always has a "better idea" than doing the trick; for example, he rips the hoop apart with his teeth. In the end, Buffy wins the battle of wills, and Lucy and he play an ordinary game of fetch.

Basic Book Information

Buffy's Tricks is a 16-page book with approximately 98 words. Much of the vocabulary consists of high frequency words. There are one to three sentences per page, some of which wrap-around. The text is printed clearly on the top of each page against a white background. Below the text, on each page, are colorful, cartoonish illustrations that are moderately supportive of the text.

Noteworthy Features

Buffy's Tricks contains the traditional elements of the story characters, plot, time, problem, and resolution. The story contains repetitive elements, but does not follow a consistent pattern throughout. In the beginning of the story, there is a pattern as the book explains all of the ordinary things that Buffy likes to do. On three consecutive pages, the text reads, "He liked. . . [e.g., chasing cats]." Later, the story takes on another pattern, as Lucy tries to teach Buffy new tricks. Each time Lucy tires to teach Buffy, she says, "Come on Buffy, . . .[e.g., jump through the hoop]" Then, on the next page it reads, "Buffy had a better idea."

The repetitive text creates a singsong rhythm to the book that will help to engage young readers. It is important to note, however, that the repetitive elements will foster the memorization of the text. As a teacher, it is essential to discover if the students are chanting what they have memorized, instead of actively processing the text.

One of the challenging aspects of the text is time. The book is written entirely in the past tense. At the start of the book, the author develops the character of Buffy by explaining all of the ordinary things that he likes to do on a regular basis. It may be confusing for readers to realize that these are activities that Buffy partakes in all of the time. Then, the story moves forward in time, as noted by, "One day Lucy had an idea." The book then explains all of the tricks that Lucy tries to teach Buffy.

Other noteworthy features of the book, besides time, include the heavy

Illustrator
Lucinda Hunnum

Publisher
Rigby, Literacy 200 Series, 1989

ISBN
0732700698

TC Level
5

A Field Guide to the Classroom Library, Lucy Calkins and the Teachers College Reading and Writing Project, Heinemann, ©2002 Teachers College, Columbia University; http://www.heinemann.com/fieldguides

use of dialogue, commas, and exclamation points.

Teaching Ideas

If a teacher decided that a reader needed a whole lot of support with this text, the teacher might give a book introduction that could begin, "Buffy is an ordinary dog who likes to do ordinary things. One day Lucy tries to teach Buffy some new tricks, but Buffy has a better idea each time. Let's read to find out Buffy does." During a picture walk the teacher might check to see if the reader is familiar with the things dogs are said to do-bury, chase, fetch. The teacher might show the reader a couple of unknown words. For example the word "listen" (on page 6) is important since it starts a new sentence.

This book is appropriate for the reader who has early reading behaviors at his command. The illustrations will enable the reader to hypothesize what the words probably say, such as on page 7 where the text says, "jump through the hoop," but the reader will need to check this against the visual information. On page 9, if the reader predicts that the text is "Come on, Buffy throw the ball," when the text uses the word "balance" the teacher might prompt the reader to make sure that what makes sense also matches the illustration.

In addition if the reader is stuck on a word such as "ordinary," "inside," or "win," the teacher has an opportunity to model looking for known chunks to get to unknown words. The teacher would have the reader locate the chunk "in" and then add the "w." The same could be done with the "or" in "ordinary" and the "in" in "inside."

This book lends itself to a discussion comparing what Lucy would like Buffy to learn and what Buffy decides to do. The engaging illustrations carry a great deal of the story and should be used to extend the text's meaning.

This book is geared to students who have already mastered many early reading behaviors since it is somewhat challenging. The illustrations do not provide clear textual support. For instance, on page 2 it reads, "Buffy was an ordinary dog, and he liked doing ordinary things," and shows a picture of Buffy scratching his ear. Readers will need to rely on more than the graphophonic information in order to gain meaning from the text. It is important for teachers to remind students to check for meaning and context when they miscue, for example, "Does that make sense?" "Does that word fit?" Teachers should also encourage students to self-correct when the miscue.

Self-correction is a reading behavior that students should become adept at during this early stage of reading. When students do not read the text correctly, teachers should urge them to give it another try by looking at the picture and getting their mouths ready. This device will help students use multiple cueing systems to process the text.

Although, the text contains some difficult vocabulary, sentences usually begin with high-frequency words (e.g., He liked . . .) that will allow readers to gain some confidence and fluency before tackling some of the more difficult words.

One-to-one matching is another reading behavior that *Buffy's Tricks* can be used to develop. Young readers who are appropriately matched to this text may need to be instructed on how to crisply point under each word as they read. It is important for teachers to monitor whether students are pointing succinctly. If they are not, teachers can ask students to self-correct and say something like, "When you came to the end of the line, you had extra words. Let's try again and make sure that we point clearly under each word as we say it." By pointing to each word in turn, students can do focused word work. There are high frequency words contained in the text that can act as anchors for their one-to-one matching.

In *Buffy's Tricks* there is heavy use of quotation marks, exclamation marks, and commas. Teachers may use this book as a way to illustrate how punctuation affects the way that a book is read. *Buffy's Tricks* could be used as an illustrative tool in a reading workshop mini-lesson on such a topic.

It is important for teachers to remember that even in these early reading stages, children should be critically analyzing the story and forming viewpoints. This book provides many opportunities for discussion in reading partnerships or in whole class formats. A discussion may revolve around why Lucy wasn't content with Buffy just the way he was, or why did she feel the need to teach him different tricks than the ones that he already knew? Another point of discussion could be centered on what makes something ordinary and another thing extraordinary. Finally, children may delight at speculating on the reason why Buffy "wins" in the end and convinces Lucy that he does not need to learn any new tricks. Reading should not feel like a chore. Young children are at the beginning of their journey to becoming lifelong fans of reading.

Buffy's Tricks is a wonderful introduction to the kind of joy that can be gained from reading. The illustrations and story line are humorous. Young readers will probably delight in the funny ways that Buffy thwarts Lucy's plans. Children may close the book realizing that Buffy was no ordinary dog after all.

Genre
Picture Book

Teaching Uses
Independent Reading; Language Conventions

A Field Guide to the Classroom Library, Lucy Calkins and the Teachers College Reading and Writing Project, Heinemann, ©2002 Teachers College, Columbia University; http://www.heinemann.com/fieldguides

Captain Cat

Syd Hoff

Book Summary

A cat joins the army by walking past the guards and onto an army base. Because the cat is striped, the soldiers name him "Captain Cat." He marches with the soldiers and becomes friends with one of them-Pete. Because Pete plays with the cat instead of "soldiering," he is given kitchen duty. Captain Cat keeps him company while he peels potatoes. When the soldiers go out into the field, crawling through mud and hiking through rain and sleet, Captain Cat lets them go. He chases birds and sleeps on Pete's bed. Tired from all the marching, Pete sleeps and dreams of his friend Captain Cat. Captain Cat also sleeps and dreams of his friend Pete.

Basic Book Information

With 39 pages of text, this is a book beginning readers can read and enjoy. Sentences average in length between five and seven words. The syntax is simple and should be easy for beginning readers to comprehend. The cartoon-like illustrations are humorous depictions of the soldiers and their comings and goings. They follow the story and, to some extent, assist readers with certain concepts-kitchen duty, for example. Rather than a plot with a problem/resolution format, this story is a list of things that Captain Cat does at the army base. The humorous antics of Captain Cat, both in the illustrations and the story, should entertain the young reader.

Noteworthy Features

The story is told in the third person. Most of the sentences are simple subject/predicate in format with one or two complex sentences.

Teaching Ideas

If the teacher were with a child as he or she got ready to read this story, it might be useful to have students study the title and cover illustration. Students can predict some things they think might happen in this story by looking at the illustrations. What do they already know about learning to be a soldier? A teacher then might introduce the book by saying, "This is a book called *Captain Cat* by Syd Hoff. Just by looking at the picture on the cover I see people in uniform and the word Captain makes me think of the army. I'm reading the summary on the back now to familiarize myself with the story. 'Guess who has joined the army! Captain Cat, that's who. He has whiskers and paws, and more stripes than the soldiers have ever seen. But most important, he has a best friend who can make an army barracks feel like home.' So Captain Cat is in the army. When I'm reading a book about a specific subject it helps to brainstorm words that might go with that subject

Publisher
Harper Collins, 1993

ISBN
0064441768

TC Level
5

so my brain is ready for them when I read. For example in a book like this about the army, I'm thinking there may be army words like *weapons, general, corporal, sergeant, guard duty,* and *mess hall.*"

A teacher may notice some students encountering difficulty because some sentences wrap around to the next line rather than finishing at the end of the line. A student may for a minute or two practice reading aloud a sentence that is carried over to a second line or to the next page.

If the class can read the book, then they can get together with a partner and retell the text afterward. This is something children could do with this book without much teacher support. A reader could retell the story focusing on Cat's actions-he joined the army, marched with the soldiers, and so on. With nudging from a teacher, a child could make a timeline of the action-sequence in the book and then go back over each point on the timeline and also describe the cat's feelings at that time. Some of these feelings will need to be inferred from the pictures.

Often, beginning readers are so intent on identifying words they fail to make inferences and miss meaning in a story. This is especially true with humorous situations. To avoid this, a partnership may look back over the book to find parts that made them laugh.

They could also talk over pages that have "big meanings" and tell each other how they knew what the writer meant. This would be helpful because there are a number of places in the story that require inference. For instance, why did the soldiers decided to name the cat Captain? Some alert students might notice that captains are not, in fact, identified as having more stripes than others. Why did the sergeant call him "sir"? Why did Pete get "kitchen duty" for playing with Captain Cat? What made Captain Cat go "the other way" when the soldiers marched to the general's command? Sometimes writers don't tell us exactly what they mean, and the reader has to make inferences based on information "in their heads" and in other parts of the story.

Book Connections

Students might enjoy reading other Syd Hoff stories-*Mrs. Brice's Mice, Oliver,* and *The Lighthouse Children,* for example.

Genre
Picture Book

Teaching Uses
Independent Reading; Partnerships

A Field Guide to the Classroom Library, Lucy Calkins and the Teachers College Reading and Writing Project, Heinemann, ©2002 Teachers College, Columbia University; http://www.heinemann.com/fieldguides

Commander Toad and the Big Black Hole

Jane Yolen

Book Summary

The crewmembers of the spaceship Star Warts gather at a meal, commenting on how their food always looks the same. Commander Toad mentions that his mother always tells him not to talk with his mouth full, which becomes an important concept, key to the resolution of the problem in the story. In the midst of this meal, the crew notices a black hole, which sparks a conversation about black holes as places where creatures live. Commander Toad then reminisces about his home life on Earth, and recalls singing. To the misfortune of his crew, he sings. They cover their ears. During an argument on whether toads can sing (and a near mutiny), the crew feels a huge bump. They are now stuck on what they discover to be a gigantic tongue of the E.T.T. (extra-terrestrial toad). Every crewmember uses his or her specialty to release the Star Warts from the tongue, to no avail. In the end, Commander Toad uses his ingenuity to solve the problem. He sings and thus is released by the E.T.T., who clears his throat to sing along. This solution directly refers back to Commander Toad's mother and her advice (mentioned earlier during the meal) not to talk with one's mouth full.

Basic Book Information

Jane Yolen, the author of this series is also the author of the beloved picture book, *Owl Moon* and of the popular *Devil's Arithmetic*, as well as about 200 other widely diverse books. *Commander Toad in Space* won the 1980 Garden State Children's Book Award and was a Junior Literary Guild Book.

The book is one of seven (with an eighth on its way) in the *Commander Toad* series. Yolen begins this book, as well as the others in the series, with an introduction to the setting and repeating characters. Because of this feature, the series does not need to be read in chronological order. A major component of the *Commander Toad* series is the use of puns and play on words, which occur with high frequency. Readers may need to be keyed in on the frequent puns to appreciate the humor. Jane Yolen is a high caliber author who uses puns and humor to satirize pop culture fantasies such as *Star Wars*.

Noteworthy Features

The combination of picture and text look similar to the *Fox* books by Edward Marshall. This story, however, is much more difficult. Readers must be able to construct a coherent story out of fragments that involve different

Series
Commander Toad

Illustrator
Bruce Degen

Publisher
Paper Star, 1996

ISBN
0698114035

TC Level
8

scenes.

Jane Yolen crafts a beautiful story, one in which all the parts are connected. It is important for the reader to pay attention to all parts of the story to fully appreciate the way the whole story works as a unified text. Readers will need to realize this isn't the realistic fiction they tend to expect but instead fantasy, written in the language of a science fiction story such as *Star Wars*.

Jane Yolen uses plays on words and ideas from popular culture (i.e., Star Warts, Jake Skyjumper, E.T.T., hip hop, toad-al, and Doc Peeper) to create a humorous tale. The one word that may be difficult for readers and yet is important to the text is the word *mutiny*. Due to the play on words, the humor can be quite sophisticated. Readers who can decode this text may still rely on the pictures to support their comprehension. Jane Yolen also tends to use more literary language than students reading this level of book will have encountered.

Teaching Ideas

Teachers can also use this book to study the use of italics and all capital letter words. It's also a great book to introduce the use of dialogue. Partnerships might reread parts of the dialogue taking on different characters. Teachers can also use this book to show how a character refers to the past. The author uses words to clue the reader into the shift like, "On Earth my mother and I had..." and "I remembered back to my tadpole days. . . ."

Several books from this series could make up a character reading center for strong readers. The center could keep track of places in the various books where the characters act in particular ways.

Book Connections

In addition to the rest of this series of *Commander Toad*, readers may enjoy the *Pinky and Rex* series written by James Howe.

Genre
Picture Book; Fantasy

Teaching Uses
Independent Reading; Character Study; Language Conventions

A Field Guide to the Classroom Library, Lucy Calkins and the Teachers College Reading and Writing Project, Heinemann, ©2002 Teachers College, Columbia University; http://www.heinemann.com/fieldguides

Days with Frog and Toad
Arnold Lobel

Book Summary

Frog and Toad are a quirky pair who sometimes help each other and sometimes play tricks on each other, but remain best friends. Frog cheers up Toad when he is feeling down in the dumps; they struggle together to make a kite fly; Frog tells a scary story; Toad thinks big thoughts to make his head grow; and then Frog goes off-temporarily-to be by himself.

Basic Book Information

Days with Frog and Toad is 64 pages long with five chapters divided into approximately twelve pages each, exactly like the other titles in the series. The sentence structure is simple yet has some complex structures scattered throughout. Dialogue is clearly referenced. There are supportive pictures on every other page or every page. The pictures are detailed and reflect the characters' mood and the setting. Arnold Lobel is consistent in portraying the characters in the series.

Day with Frog and Toad by Arnold Lobel is one of four in the series of *Frog and Toad* books. Frog and Toad are the best of friends. They have distinctive personalities, which unfold as the reader journeys though the episodic chapters. The friends have many adventures in this book together. Readers will find they remain friends, always. Frog is always responsible, reasonable, looks for solutions when there is a problem, and doesn't get ruffled very easily. Toad is more nervous, demanding, impatient, and easily discouraged in situations. Often he gives up quickly and doesn't seem to have a very strong work ethic.

Noteworthy Features

Although *Days With Frog and Toad* is simply written, the gently ironic humor will please more sophisticated readers. Because the characters remain consistent throughout the series, the reader can make easy predictions as to how Frog or Toad might respond in any given situation.

Frog and Toad have distinct characteristics, with Frog established as the cleverer one, and Toad the more earnest and effusive. The characters' moods are varied, ranging from morose to exuberant. Readers will enjoy the comedy in Frog's and Toad's dramatic reactions to nearly everything. Illustrations support the humorous situations and the sense of camaraderie between Frog and Toad.

Themes and big ideas are easy to pick out in this series. Arnold Lobel has chosen numerous adventures for Frog and Toad that match situations human beings deal with. For example, the message of the first chapter seems to be "Don't put off something you can do today until tomorrow."

Friendship is another theme of all the *Frog and Toad* books. Many of the

Series
Frog and Toad books

Illustrator
Arnold Lobel

Publisher
Harper Trophy, 1984

ISBN
0064440583

TC Level
6

chapters in *Days With Frog and Toad* involve the tests of friendship, for example, how Toad feels and reacts when Frog goes off to be by himself. Because of their differences, Frog and Toad have misunderstandings and conflicts, but they never let those differences interfere with their friendship. Other chapters involve the benefits of friendship, for example, how ghost stories are enjoyable when you have company, or how it is easier to get a kite off the ground when you have help and encouragement from a friend.

Teaching Ideas

Frog helps Toad out of many situations throughout the book. In Chapter One, "Tomorrow," Toad plays a trick on himself without knowing that he is doing it. His house is messy and in great need of a cleaning but he doesn't want to do it until tomorrow. Frog is a very tidy character and reminds Toad of all the things he already set aside to do tomorrow, which upsets Toad. He can't stop thinking about tomorrow. Eventually, Toad starts doing his chores today because he doesn't want tomorrow to be spoiled.

Readers can compare Frog and Toad, gathering clues from the reading and illustrations. They can follow each character through the adventures taking note of individual strengths and weaknesses. Also, the reader can put Post-It notes in places where they find similarities and differences in the characters. They may place Post-Its on the places where the characters act according to their character and the places where they act out of character. The students can keep a chart of their observations in order to compare the results. Either a t-chart or a Venn diagram would suit these findings.

Book Connections

If a child enjoyed *Sammy The Seal* by Syd Hoff, *Joe and Betsy the Dinosaur* by Lillian Hoban, *and No More Monsters for Me* by Peggy Parish, the child will probably find the *Frog and Toad* series to be a great next read. Children who can successfully read this book will also find that *Tales of Oliver Pig* by Jean Van Leeuwen and the *Henry and Mudge* series by Cynthia Rylant are just right for them. Once children have read the *Frog and Toad* series and perhaps others of similar difficulty, they will probably be ready to take on *Pinky and Rex* by James Howe and *Commander Toad* by Jane Yolen.

Genre
Picture Book

Teaching Uses
Independent Reading; Interpretation; Character Study

A Field Guide to the Classroom Library, Lucy Calkins and the Teachers College Reading and Writing Project, Heinemann, ©2002 Teachers College, Columbia University; http://www.heinemann.com/fieldguides

Dear Zoo
Rod Campbell

Book Summary

The child in this story is writing to the zoo for a pet. The zoo sends him a series of zoo animals (elephant, giraffe, lion, camel, snake, monkey, frog). Since each animal is inappropriate as a pet, the child sends each back. This continues as each new pet arrives until the zoo takes time to think. Then the zoo sends the child a puppy. Of course the puppy is perfect, and the child keeps him.

Basic Book Information

This book contains 115 words over 18 unnumbered pages. The size and spacing of the print is appropriate for a reader who understands the left to right directionality of print, the return sweep necessary to read a second line, and one-to-one matching of words spoken with words on the page. The print appears on each left page and under the illustrations on the right page. The reader reads the left page and then lifts the flap on the right page to discover which animal the zoo has sent. The animal's name never appears in print, only in the illustration. So the reader reads "So they sent me a" and lifts the flap on the opposite page. There are many high frequency words.

Noteworthy Features

The colorful illustrations with the interactive flaps will probably keep the reader engaged and motivated. The illustrations do not contain any details of the story. Therefore, the reader is going to have to infer from his knowledge of the animal why this animal may be inappropriate as a pet.

The repetitive pattern is "So they sent me a. . . . He was too_____! I sent him back." The use of the repetitive pattern will enable the reader to use meaning to predict the text and to practice fluent reading. The pattern changes on page 2 and on the last two pages.

Teaching Ideas

Children will have a great time reading this book "as best they can" without needing much support from a teacher or a partner. They'll encounter difficulties, but should be able to use sight word knowledge, phonics, and a focus on meaning to construct a good deal of the text.

If a child has done some independent work and is still needing more support, instead of helping with one hard word, then the next, a teacher might say, "Can we look over the whole book together" and use this as a time to do a belated book introduction. The teacher might say, "The child went to the zoo, didn't he, asking for a pet? But the animals weren't right, were they?" Then turning the pages to the different animals, teachers might

Illustrator
Rod Campbell

Publisher
Penguin Putnam Books, 1982

ISBN
0317621807

TC Level
4

want to use-in a conversational way-some of the words they anticipate will be especially tough (*fierce, naughty*). Teachers may want to also teach children a few words they may not know and may not have ready access to, including *thought*. By the time a child can read a book like this one, the child should not read, "He was too big (tall)" on page 5 and not realize that he has made a mistake. The teacher needs to acknowledge that the prediction made sense, but prompt and/or model monitoring and cross-checking a prediction with the letter cues a word offers. The teacher would ask the reader to predict what he would expect to see at the beginning of the word "big" and then check it against the print. In addition the teacher may ask what chunk the reader knows in the word "tall."

The use of a repetitive pattern will offer the teacher an opportunity to model and/or prompt a student for fluent reading.

The change in the repetitive pattern on the last two pages and page 2 will require the reader to do more visual searching than on the patterned pages.

Book Connections

If the reader enjoys the lift-the-flap books some others at this level are *Where is Spot?* and *Here Comes the Bus*.

Genre
Picture Book

Teaching Uses
Independent Reading

A Field Guide to the Classroom Library, Lucy Calkins and the Teachers College Reading and Writing Project, Heinemann, ©2002 Teachers College, Columbia University; http://www.heinemann.com/fieldguides

Don't Forget to Write
Martina Selway

Book Summary

In this picture book, the author/illustrator, Martina Selway, captures the gradual, emotional changes of a young girl placed in an unfamiliar setting. Reluctantly sent to her Grandfather's farm for a two-week visit, Rosie dutifully remembers her mother's parting words, "Don't forget to write." The events that bring about her change of heart are chronicled in the continuing letters she writes home.

Basic Book Information

Don't Forget to Write marks Martina Selway's debut into the United States children's book market. Prior to this, she had written and illustrated over 50 early education titles that were published in England.

Noteworthy Features

The letter format of this text has the feel of a daily journal. It is strongly supported by the illustrations. The structure of the text follows Rosie's daily experiences. Selway describes Aunty Mabel's actions to build her character. In addition, Selway uses Grandfather's words throughout the text to develop his character and to show his wonderful sense of humor. Looking carefully at the incidental illustrations will enrich this story for listeners and readers alike.

This 26-page book will stir the memories of children who have warily entered a new situation and learned through positive experiences that it is a great place to be. It is an excellent choice for a read aloud and children will also love reading the book independently.

Teaching Ideas

If a teacher felt children's reading of this book needed the support of an introduction, the teacher could prepare those children by discussing situations they might have faced-new school, a new class, a new neighborhood, a visit away from home-that made them feel apprehensive. The teacher might ask the students how they felt about these new experiences and how the initial reluctance and feelings changed over time. "You might find that happens to Rosie in this book, too," the teacher could say. Later, this teacher might want to encourage students to wonder whether their fears were the same kind of fear of the unknown that Rosie experiences, or were they different in some ways. How so? Were they-like Rosie-encouraged by a family member to try something new? Were they proud of themselves as they learned to enjoy the new experience? How does their recollection of their own feelings change how they understand Rosie?

Illustrator
Martina Selway

Publisher
Ideals Children's Books, 1994

ISBN
0824986369

How does Rosie's experience change their ideas about their own?

This line of questioning should help a child make personal connections to this text in ways which are much more helpful than the common practice of simply noting ways a child's life and the text are the same. "We have a blue car like that," a reader might say, and some children have been taught that any "text-to-self" connection represents good reading work. It's much more helpful to show children that reading involves thinking back and forth between the text and the reader's own life. By examining the two almost as if they were two texts set alongside each other, readers can come to new discoveries about the text and their lives.

This book offers a wonderful example of written communication. It can be referred to when the whole class enters a letter-writing unit of study within the writing workshop or when an individual child initiates letter writing. Children can learn from this book about how friendly letters tend to go.

The farm life described in this book is very different from the daily life of many city children. Children unfamiliar with the setting might generate a lively discussion about what to expect from a visit to a farm.

Book Connections

Another engaging story told in letter form is *The Gardener* by Sarah Stewart. Young Lydia Grace Finch moves from the country to the city because her family cannot afford to take care of her. In this story, the reader learns how she copes in her new situation with the help of a loving grandmother.

Genre
Picture Book

Teaching Uses
Independent Reading; Teaching Writing

A Field Guide to the Classroom Library, Lucy Calkins and the Teachers College Reading and Writing Project, Heinemann, ©2002 Teachers College, Columbia University; http://www.heinemann.com/fieldguides

Fish Is Fish
Leo Lionni

Book Summary

A tadpole and a minnow are best friends. One day, the tadpole grows legs and tells the minnow he is going to be a frog. They argue about how such a thing is possible, and finally the tadpole declares, "Frogs are frogs and fish is fish." Eventually, the tadpole becomes a frog and climbs out of the pond. While he is gone, the fish wonders where his friend is. One day, the frog comes back into the pond. He tells the fish about the wonderful things he has seen on land: birds, cows, and people. The fish pictures them all as marvelous, fish-like creatures. After the frog has left, the fish decides to go on land to see them himself. He leaps out of water and lies on the bank flapping until his friend pushes him back in the water. Relieved, he decides his friend is right: frogs are frogs and fish is fish.

Basic Book Information

This is a picture book, with Leo Lionni's characteristic illustrations-watercolors, stamping, and cut paper. Lionni is an award-winning author, and has written many well-known and well-loved books for children including *Swimmy* and *Alexander and the Wind-Up Mouse.*

Noteworthy Features

Readers who don't know tadpoles become frogs and minnows become fish will be at a disadvantage reading this book because they may wonder whether this is magic or whether the tadpole is wrong in thinking he will grow up to be a frog. On the other hand, readers who don't know this fact will learn it from this book, and will not necessarily enjoy or understand the story less.

Teaching Ideas

The images of birds, cows, and people in the fish's mind, depicted in the illustrations, often become a topic of conversation for children. At first, they tend to think the pictures of fish-cows and fish-kids are funny. Then, after the exclamations die down, readers tend to focus on why the fish imagines the animals in this way. Most come to the conclusion that all the beasts he knows are fish, so he imagines what he knows. Other readers point out that he knows what the frog looks like and what other underwater creatures look like, so he could well have pictured them that way. Then readers sometimes decide that since he thinks the creatures are so marvelous and wonderful, maybe he imagines them closest to the most wonderful-looking creature he knows: himself. Few readers think about how this corresponds to the way

Illustrator
Leo Lionni

Publisher
Knopf, 1987

ISBN
0590400061

TC Level
8

they use their own imaginations. A thought from the teacher here might help the conversation turn that corner, at least briefly.

There are many possible interpretations that children may puzzle over. Is the message of the story that if people tell you aren't suited to do something then you should believe them and not try to do it? Is the message that your world is undoubtedly the most beautiful, just because it is the world in which you are most comfortable and that is most familiar? Is the message that certain kinds of beings are suited best for certain kinds of things and not others and so everyone should stay in his or her place? Is the message that we should accept our limitations without fighting them? Maybe the message is that all people have things they can't do, and they have to accept that and not yearn for things they cannot have. Many children find it difficult to find a message in this book that they agree with and feel comfortable with. They might feel that people who accept the messages of the book wouldn't get very close to their dreams in life.

Some readers think that the fish would have been better off if he were not sitting around waiting for the frog to show up again and tell him about all the things he cannot see. Instead, he should have been off on his own exploring the deepest, most hidden parts of the pond, or watching the long and complicated life processes of the creatures and plants that live there. Why was he not focusing on what he could do well, and the powers he did have? From the beginning, the fish is focused on the frog and the changes happening in him, perhaps because they are more dramatic than his own changes. But still, the outward focus seems to lead him to dissatisfaction more than happiness. Usually, kids don't have much trouble seeing what kinds of messages this sends to human readers of the story about their own lives.

Book Connections

Leo Lionni has written and illustrated many books for children. Perhaps the book most similar to this one in style and content is *Swimmy*. Both books are partially about fish and both books have large segments in which the fish picture or encounter new things. Children might find interesting work in comparing and contrasting the two books.

Genre
Picture Book

Teaching Uses
Independent Reading; Partnerships; Interpretation; Critique

A Field Guide to the Classroom Library, Lucy Calkins and the Teachers College Reading and Writing Project, Heinemann, ©2002 Teachers College, Columbia University; http://www.heinemann.com/fieldguides

Flies

Cheryl Coughlan

Book Summary

The book gives illustrated information about flies. It opens by saying, "Flies have two wings," and showing a full-page color illustration. The next page says, "Flies have two halters that help them fly," and again this is illustrated. The text covers the flies' hair and eyes, that they spit on their food, and that they eat with a proboscis.

Basic Book Information

Flies is part of a series of books on insects that includes books on ants, beetles, crickets, and dragonflies. A note to parents and teachers says the *Insect* series shows insect features that help them live in different environments. The book is a small, square hardcover book, making it an appealing addition to a library of books for early readers. *Flies* contains a table of contents, a glossary of words, a list of suggested books, and Internet sites for further study.

Noteworthy Features

This book appears to be appropriate for very early readers but a closer look shows it contains a fair proportion of subject-specific words that will be very challenging to beginning readers, unless the words are introduced ahead of time.

The table of contents suggests the book is divided into three chapters: Body, Food, and Legs. However, when reading the book, each page proceeds without any demarcation that the reader has entered a new chapter. For example, the page that opens the food section simply says, "Flies spit on food to make it soft."

Teaching Ideas

This book could play a role in whole-class, small group, or reading center work on insects or flies, or it could fit under whole-class, small group, partnership, or individual work with nonfiction. Alternatively, it could simply be one child's choice during independent reading.

Some teachers have turned their science time into an opportunity to help children read nonfiction texts. A teacher might angle the independent reading work so that for a time children were each asked to choose books from a collection of nonfiction texts. Meanwhile, during mini-lessons, the teacher could highlight ways nonfiction is read differently than other types of books. Included in this would be lessons on studying the pictures, observing things, and generating questions. Also, it would be important to talk about how readers learn the new subject-specific words of a topic.

Publisher
Pebble Books, 2000

ISBN
0736802401

TC Level
4

Genre
Nonfiction; Picture Book

Teaching Uses
Independent Reading; Content Area Study; Partnerships; Small Group
Strategy Instruction; Reading and Writing Nonfiction

A Field Guide to the Classroom Library, Lucy Calkins and the Teachers College Reading and Writing Project, Heinemann, ©2002 Teachers
College, Columbia University; http://www.heinemann.com/fieldguides

Footprints in the Sand
Cynthia Benjamin

Book Summary

Footprints in the Sand is about nine desert animals and the way each gets back to its home. The text says: "Someone races home./ Someone flies home./ Someone darts home./ Someone creeps home." Finally, at the end of the book, a little girl walks home to her desert dwelling where she is warmly greeted by her mother, father, and sister.

Basic Book Information

This is a Scholastic *Hello Reader!* book. Immediately inside the front cover there are several pages of text written for a teacher or parent, including some information suggested by literacy expert Priscilla Lynch. There are 42 words and the book is twenty-nine pages long, with one to three words per page. In addition, the name of each animal is displayed in a box on the corner of each page that shows the animal in its home. The text begins and ends with: "Desert sun gleams. Desert sun glows." The rest of the text is the repeated, simple pattern: "Someone races home. Someone flies home," with only the verb changing. High frequency words are *someone* and *home*.

Noteworthy Features

This book provides a balance of supports and challenges for readers at this level. Looking over the book, a teacher sees that the supports include large and simple font, fairly large amounts of white space between words, and a large amount of patterned text in which the support the changing words.

An initial challenge of this book is that the title doesn't tell readers what the book will be about. In addition, there is text that is not supported by pictures. The good news is that these words-*someone, races, creeps*-are regularly spelled words that provide great opportunities for word work, including dividing unfamiliar words into recognizable chunks.

The book is also special because an observant and thoughtful reader can construct far more meaning from the text than is explicitly conveyed by the words alone. A study of the light in the illustration suggests that time passes from morning to evening throughout the book.

Teaching Ideas

It might be advisable for a teacher to use this book in a strategy lesson. Bringing together a partnership of two similar readers or a small group of four readers, the teacher could say, "In our word study time, we've been doing a lot of work with word chunks and you guys have gotten really good at taking words that seem new to you and finding, in them, chunks that you know. In this book, you are going to want to use those word-power muscles

Series
Hello Reader! Science Series

Illustrator
Jacqueline Rogers

Publisher
Scholastic, 1999

ISBN
059044087X

TC Level
3

to figure out the words. The pictures will help a bit, but you'll need to also take apart the words." The teacher might say, "Let's get our word power going in the title. Let's first look at the picture. . . .What do you see?" Readers will probably say they see a coyote, sand, and cacti. "In the books you have been reading, if you saw a *coyote*, this word [pointing to *footprints*] would say *coyote*? How can you tell that doesn't make sense?" Then we might say, "Would you work with your partner and see if you can do some word work on *footprints*?"

It will be important to get children rereading parts of the book smoothly (although the way sentences are stretched out across pages makes the book a poor choice for supporting fluency and phrasing). In this book, as in others, when children reread it individually, teachers can encourage them to use Post-It notes on intriguing parts and then to meet with partners for conversations. They'll probably notice the different animal homes; they'll certainly want to name what kind of animal is on each page. With encouragement, especially, they may study and compare footprints, which, after all, are supposed to be a big part of the message.

Book Connections

This book is organized like countless other early books, and young readers could gather books that follow a similar structure. How are they like and unlike each other? Many won't have the opening and closing pages organized in one pattern and the internal pages in another. Many won't have the repeating sentence divided across two pages. These books will tend to have a twist at the end of the list, but the ending twists will vary in interesting ways.

This book claims to be about *footprints* in the sand but it is also clearly about how animals move, about animal homes, and about how animals survive in the desert. It can be set alongside other books in any one of these topics.

This book follows the same sentence patterns and topics as the book *Footprints in the Snow*.

Genre
Nonfiction; Picture Book

Teaching Uses
Independent Reading; Small Group Strategy Instruction

Fox Be Nimble
Edward Marshall

Book Summary

In *Fox Be Nimble*, Fox is asked to baby-sit the Ling kids next door but doesn't want to because he's playing "rock star." He is not the most attentive caregiver and finds that the triplets have blown away because they were holding lots of balloons. Fox's next predicament comes when he trips on his skate and bangs his knee. Louise does the same thing, except Fox does all the complaining and moaning while little Louise says nothing about her pain. The doctor and Mom agree that Louise is brave. That's when Fox tells a white lie to the doctor and says that he is fine and does not like to make a fuss. Mom is silent. The next episode deals with Fox being a show-off and getting booted from a marching band. He meets up with Raisin, the cute little white fox, who is practicing baton twirling. Fox says it looks easy and tries it. He finds it's not so easy but gets the hang of it sooner than he thinks. He has a new part in the band . . . baton leader.

Basic Book Information

Fox Be Nimble is 48 pages long, divided into three chapters, each with supportive titles and relevant, humorous pictures on every page.

The *Fox* books do not need to be read in any particular order, but it's best to save *Fox Be Nimble* for the end of this series. Fox seems older and is more disrespectful toward his mother than he in the other books. Fox's mom is pregnant in three other books and in this book she is not pregnant, nor does she have twins. Fox's fear of heights is woven into several of *Fox* books including *Fox and His Friends* and *Fox on Wheels*.

Noteworthy Features

The *Fox* series is humorous, yet the reader needs to do some good thinking in order to understand the humor. The first two chapters titles are a play on words. Fox wants to be a rock star, and ends up on television-not because he's the hottest star, but because his fear of heights leads him to be rescued. "Fox the Brave" is a sarcastic title: Fox really isn't brave at all-it's Louise who is brave. The reader can find many examples of Fox being scared and Louise being quite the opposite.

Teaching Ideas

Seven characters are mentioned in the first two pages of this book alone. If children know the series, they'll know these characters, but otherwise they may want to jot a list of who's who, or to try to use the illustrations to identify the characters as they read.

When children read these books, they may put Post-It notes on parts that

Series
Fox books

Publisher
Puffin Books, 1990

ISBN
0140368426

TC Level
7

intrigue them and meet with a partner later to talk at length about them. In conferences with a reader or a partnership, teachers can help children see that their observations can be turned into inquiries that are worth pursuing across many pages and even many *Fox* books. With a teacher's help, a child can begin by placing Post-Its on weird/cool/odd sections of the text-whatever she decides-and end up researching and discussing larger themes such as any of these:

Times when Fox acts selfish and when he acts responsibly

Sections revealing Fox's character

Places that show Fox is brave and scared

Parts that show Louise is brave and Fox is not brave

Parts that seem fair to Fox and parts that seem unfair (Is Fox mistreated when he is asked to give up his time with his friends to do chores around the house while his Mom tends to the twins?)

Fox's fears

Places that show Fox as a show-off and talking about how the girls like to watch him

Parts that show his relationship with his Mom

Book Connections

Fox Be Nimble is similar in difficulty to *Frog and Toad* by Arnold Lobel, *Nate the Great* series by Marjorie Weinman Sharmat, and *The Little Bear* series by Else H. Minarik. *Fox Be Nimble* is harder than *Sammy the Seal* by Syd Hoff, *The Little Yellow Chicken* by Sunshine, and *When Will I Read?* by Miriam Cohen. Once children have read the *Fox* series, they may enjoy turning to the *One in the Middle is the Green Kangaroo* by Judy Blume, or to *Rollo and Tweedy* or to *The Ghosts at Dougal Castle* by Laura Jean Allen, or to the *Pinky and Rex* series by James Howe.

Genre
Picture Book

Teaching Uses
Character Study; Independent Reading

Frog and Toad Are Friends

Arnold Lobel

Book Summary

Frog and Toad Are Friends has two interesting characters, Frog and Toad. At first, Frog wakes up to a new Spring and does his best to get his good friend, Toad, to wake up and enjoy it with him. Some of the traits of Frog and Toad are scientific traits of frogs and toads in nature: their colors, some personality traits, and the fact that frogs are out first in the Spring before toads. Frog and Toad are great friends, yet very different in character. In the second chapter, "The Story," the reader will see how caring Toad can be when he wants to help Frog feel better. Frog asks him to tell a story but Toad cannot remember one to tell. He does everything he can to remember a story to tell Frog. Each chapter shows how caring, thoughtful, serious, and funny each character can be but also shows the differences between Frog and Toad. The author may want his readers to notice the differences between these two animals because many people confuse the two with one another. Frog and Toad act just like human beings. Sometimes they are happy, sometimes sad, angry or embarrassed. In the fourth chapter, "The Swim," Toad doesn't feel good wearing his bathing suit in front of people. The other animals wait for Toad to come out of the water to see how funny he looks, so Toad tries to stay in the water as long as he can. He gets so cold that he starts to shiver and sneeze. Toad does eventually get out, and finds that his friends-the snail, the snake, the turtles, and the lizards -are all having a good laugh at his expense.

Basic Book Information

Frog and Toad Are Friends is 64 pages long and divided into 5 chapters, each chapter approximately 12 pages in length. There are detailed supportive pictures on every other page. This book is a Caldecott Honor book. The chapter titles are not overly supportive due to their brevity, such as "Spring the Letter." The chapter titles are printed in green or brown, matching the color of the characters' (Frog and Toad's) bodies,and each chapter title's color matches the significant character in the spotlight. Of the four *Frog and Toad* books, this has the earliest copyright date and seems to be the first in the series.

Frog and Toad Are Friends by Arnold Lobel is a book in the four-book series *Frog and Toad*. Frog and Toad are the best of friends. They have distinctive personalities, which unfold as the reader journeys though the episodic chapters. Frog is always responsible, reasonable, looks for solutions when there is a problem, and doesn't get ruffled very easily. Toad is more nervous, demanding and impatient. He's easily discouraged and often gives up quickly. He doesn't seem to have a very strong work ethic. The friends have many adventures together and the reader will find that, no matter what, they remain forever friends.

Series
Frog and Toad books

Publisher
Harper Trophy, 1979

ISBN
0064440206

TC Level
6

Noteworthy Features

The main characters, Frog and Toad, are portrayed similarly in all of the titles in this series. A reader can count on the characters to act and react to situations accordingly. There are a few surprising moments in the book when Frog and Toad act out of character. For example, Toad is usually grumpy and a bit lazy. Yet, in Chapter 2, "The Story," Toad wants to make Frog feel better and puts forth great effort to remember a story to tell Frog.

Dialogue is used for each character. It is easy for readers to practice voice inflections with these characters as they each have very distinctive voices. The dialogue is always referenced.

The color-coded chapter titles clue the reader as to which character is going to be in the spotlight with a problem. The other character will be the one who tries to help him solve the dilemma, or just feel better.

The big idea in this series is always the same: good friends help each other all of the time. Sometimes they get mad at each other, but in the end they always make up.

At times, the vocabulary seems specialized when dealing with other characters, scenes, and settings. For example, in Chapter 3, "A Lost Button," Frog and Toad are walking in a meadow. They meet a sparrow and a raccoon that help look for Toad's lost button. Frog decides to sew many buttons onto a jacket for Toad. These days, sewing is not a part of most children's vocabulary or everyday life as much as a bathing suit or writing a letter, the subjects of two other chapters.

Teaching Ideas

Character development is a strong part of this text and series. It would be wise to follow each character and his actions and reactions to situations as a way of exploring different traits of each friend. It can be interesting to notice the similarities of each character to the scientific animal. Students may use Post-its to mark and discuss:

    *Places where they feel most like a certain character
    *Places where they disagree with the way a character responded
    *Parts that show friendship between Frog and Toad
    *Parts that support a theory the reader is developing about Frog or Toad. (For example, Frog is a responsible, neat, or obsessive character. Toad is a lazy, grumpy, or self-conscious character.)

Children who study and compare Frog and Toad will notice that Frog is the more proactive one in this book. When Frog gets sick, Toad is expected to rise to the occasion of being proactive. Frog asks for a story, and Toad feels the pressure mount and responds by doing a lot of silly things. He throws water on his face, bangs his head against the wall and so forth. In the end, Toad is in bed needing support and Frog, not surprisingly, meets this challenge and tells Toad a story.

Some teachers have found it powerful to use this book to teach children that it's important to make connections across the pages within a text or even within a chapter. Quite often children are taught instead to connect text to life or text to text. Sometimes the intra-text connections do the most for comprehension. One way to teach this is to pull readers together for a mini-lesson and to read the book aloud while showing pages on an overhead projector, or to distribute copies of the text for children to refer to.

On page 7, Frog pushes Toad out of bed, and out of the house. The children may conclude that Frog is being mean. Teachers could then ask, "Are there other places where you see this?" Soon students will find pages 12-14, where Frog is trying to trick his friend into not sleeping. Some children will say, "This isn't being mean. He's being a good friend and trying to wake Toad up to enjoy Spring." Students can celebrate this difference of opinion. As children look more closely to see if there is evidence that shows Frog's motivation, they'll cite page 12 where Frog admits that he wants Toad to wake up so that he (Frog) won't be lonely.

Book Connections

Frog and Toad Are Friends is similar in difficulty to *Tales of Amanda Pig* by Jean Van Leeuwen, *Bully Trouble* by Joanna Cole, *The Adventures of Benny and Watch*, created by Gertrude Chandler Warner and the Early Boxcar series. It is more difficult than *Sammy the Seal* by Syd Hoff, *Joe and Betsy the Dinosaur* by Lilian Hoban, and *No More Monsters for Me!* by Peggy Parish. Once children can successfully read *Frog and Toad Are Friends* and other books of comparable difficulty, they may find themselves well prepared to read *Pinky and Rex* by James Howe and *The One in the Middle Is the Green Kangaroo* by Judy Blume.

Genre
Chapter Book

Teaching Uses
Independent Reading; Character Study; Partnerships; Read Aloud

Frog and Toad Together

Arnold Lobel

Book Summary

In the first chapter, Toad writes a list of things to do, crossing off tasks he completes. When his list blows away, Toad becomes upset. Frog sits with him until it is late. They write, "Go to Sleep" in the sand, and after Toad crosses it out, they do. In the next chapter "The Garden," Toad plants seeds and assumes they are scared to grow immediately. Frog advises him to wait patiently, but Toad sits with them and tries to coax them to shoot upward. After a few days, Toad's garden begins to grow, and he is exhausted from the effort. In the third chapter, Frog and Toad worry that they are eating so many cookies they will soon become sick. Frog proposes several ways to hide the cookies, but Toad knows they will retrieve them anyway. Frog finally scatters the cookies for birds, and Toad goes home to bake a cake. In "Dragons and Giants," Frog and Toad dodge a snake, falling rocks, and a hawk that all threaten them. While they flee frantically, they tell themselves they are brave. Frog and Toad return to Toad's house and fall asleep, feeling brave indeed. In the final chapter, Toad dreams that he is on stage, expertly performing tricks for Frog. With each stunt, Frog shrinks until he eventually disappears. Toad realizes he will be lonely without Frog and desperately searches for him. Frog awakens Toad. They eat a big breakfast and spend a long day together.

Basic Book Information

Frog and Toad Together, a Newbery Honor Book, is 64 pages long with five chapters divided into approximately 12 pages each. The text has large print with large spacing between words and lines. The sentence structure is simple yet has some complex sentences scattered throughout. There are supportive pictures on almost every page. The pictures are detailed and reflect the character's mood and the setting.

There are four titles in the *Frog and Toad* series. Frog and Toad have many adventures and always remain the best of friends. They have distinct personalities that unfold through the episodic chapters. Frog is always responsible and reasonable. He looks for solutions when there is a problem, and does not get ruffled very easily. Toad is more nervous, demanding, impatient, and easily discouraged. His quirky vulnerability and needs propel these stories forward.

Noteworthy Features

The sentence structure in *Frog and Toad Together* is usually simple, though there are some complex sentences scattered throughout. Dialogue is clearly

Series
Frog and Toad books

Illustrator
Arnold Lobel

Publisher
Harper Trophy, 1972

ISBN
0064440214

TC Level
6

referenced, often in the middle of one character's speech. The pictures are detailed and reflect the character's mood and the setting. Vocabulary is generally less challenging than in other books at this level.

As with the other titles in this series, each chapter of this book can stand alone. The only two characters readers must remember are Frog and Toad themselves, whose personalities are consistent throughout this book and the other three. As a result, *Frog and Toad Together* works well for students who do not have much experience with chapter books because readers can start almost anywhere in the book and follow the story of a chapter.

Teaching Ideas

Because the characters behave consistently, this series makes for excellent character studies. Readers can jot on Post-its recurring characteristics of both Frog and Toad. They can discuss the main characters' general patterns of behavior - Toad's anxious fumbling and Frog's steady practicality - especially in the first three chapters. Since friendship is such an important theme in these books, students should think carefully about what the friendship between Frog and Toad is actually like. In teacher-student conferences or in partnership discussions between students reading together, students might discuss whether Frog balances out Toad, or whether this friendship is as uneven as the size of the two characters.

Once students have read the book several times and are familiar with the basic events of the plot, they might engage in some challenging discussions about the final two chapters. Careful readers may note that, when a hawk flies over their heads, both Toad *and* Frog seem to be scared. Students can infer why Frog suddenly becomes fearful, and speculate about why he changes. Are Frog and Toad actually brave? How do they seem once they return to Toad's house? "The Dream" also raises engaging issues. What does it say about Toad that he dreams, each time he succeeds with another trick, Frog shrinks some more? What does this dream say about their friendship? As a point of comparison, students may look at Henry's dream at the end of *Henry and Mudge: The First Book*. Both dreams are rich with possible metaphors.

Book Connections

Frog and Toad Together is similar in difficulty to *Tales of Amanda Pig* by Jean Van Leeuwen, and the series, *The Adventures of Benny and Watch*, created by Gertrude Chandler Warner. It is more difficult than *Sammy the Seal* by Syd Hoff, and *Joe and Betsy the Dinosaur* by Lillian Hoban. Once children have read *Frog and Toad Together* and other books of similar difficulty, they may find themselves well prepared to read books from the *Pinky and Rex* series by James Howe, and *The One in the Middle Is the Green Kangaroo* by Judy Blume.

Genre
Short Chapter Book

A Field Guide to the Classroom Library, Lucy Calkins and the Teachers College Reading and Writing Project, Heinemann, ©2002 Teachers College, Columbia University; http://www.heinemann.com/fieldguides

Teaching Uses
Interpretation; Independent Reading; Character Study

Good Work, Amelia Bedelia

Peggy Parish

Book Summary

In *Good Work, Amelia Bedelia*, Amelia is a housemaid with responsibilities such as cleaning the house and preparing dinner for Mr. and Mrs. Rogers. Amelia's specialty is baking pies that Mr. and Mrs. Rogers adore. Usually it's her pies that rescue her from losing her job, but in this story it is a butterscotch cake. Amelia Bedelia is baffled, as usual, by the jobs on her list. She makes the reader laugh as she carries out her duties in a most literal manner. For example, she is asked to pot the plants in the garden and bring them inside. She does this literally, getting all of the cooking pots from the kitchen and placing the plants in them. Mr. Rogers become upset with Amelia Bedelia when she serves him a raw egg instead of a cooked egg although she does this because he never instructed her to cook the egg. He responds, "Confound it, Amelia Bedelia!" He proceeds to tell Amelia to go fly a kite, which she does literally and happily.

Basic Book Information

Good Work, Amelia Bedelia is 56 pages long. The book has no chapters. There are supportive, humorous pictures on every page. This text has a simple sentence structure with referenced dialogue.

Both children and adults laugh aloud as they read these books. Usually, Amelia is given instructions that she tries to follow *exactly*, but she takes every word literally and ends up creating giant fiascos everywhere she goes. The *Amelia Bedelia* books do not need to be read in any particular order. However, there are advantages to reading *Amelia Bedelia* first as a way to introduce the characters of Amelia, Mr. Rogers, and Mrs. Rogers, who remain constant throughout the series.

Noteworthy Features

Because three main characters introduced in this text remain the same and are heard from consistently throughout the series, it is easy to follow the plot and character development. Amelia Bedelia is a humorous and lovable character. After reading a couple of books in this series the reader grows to expect silly things from Amelia's well-intentioned work habits.

The detailed pictures help the younger reader attain a better and clearer understanding of Amelia Bedelia's unusual work habits.

There is a similar pattern to all the books in this series. The stories have similar pictures that support a familiar point of view from Amelia Bedelia and the other characters. It is hard to find a moment when a character is acting out of character. A reader may suggest that Mr. Rogers is acting unlike himself at the end of the book due to his immense liking of Amelia's cakes and pies. However, a clever reader will notice the familiarity in the

Series
Amelia Bedelia

Illustrator
Lynn Sweat

Publisher
Camelot, 1996

ISBN
0380728311

TC Level
8

endings of all the books and decide that even here, Mr. Rogers is acting the way he usually does.

This text was written over ten years later than the original. Therefore, there are no "dated" words or meanings that the reader deals with as they do in some of the other texts in the series.

Teaching Ideas

Children will probably want to read many books in the series. If they do so, they may mark sections of the texts with Post-It notes and then meet with partners to discuss intriguing issues. For example, they may discuss any one of these topics, which tend to be of interest in any character study:

What sections of the text reveal the kind of character Amelia is? What is her true nature?

Why does Amelia act as she does? Is she lacking in intelligence?

Why do all the people in Amelia's life put up with her misunderstandings instead of correcting her and teaching her?

Is it predictable when she'll misinterpret the directions?

What do we not know about Amelia and her life and why didn't the author choose to tell us? How does this shape our ideas of her?

How is this book like and unlike those in the original series?

Book Connections

Amelia Bedelia Helps Out is similar in difficulty to *Cam Jansen* by David Adler, *Pinky and Rex* by Cynthia Rylant, and *The Golly Sisters* series by Betsy Byars. It is more difficult than *Frog and Toad* by Arnold Lobel and the *Fox* series by Edward Marshall. Once children can successfully read *Amelia Bedelia* and other books of similar difficulty, they may find themselves well prepared to read the *Horrible Harry* series by Suzy Kline, *The Zack Files* series by, and *Freckle Juice* by Judy Blume.

Genre
Picture Book

Teaching Uses
Partnerships; Character Study

Hairs/Pelitos

Sandra Cisneros

Book Summary

The narrator describes her family's hair poetically. Each member of the family has a different quality of hair, all appealing. But mother's is especially so, because of how it looks and how it smells. From a description of hair, the story becomes a memory of what her mother's hair smells like and what the feeling represents.

Basic Book Information

This picture book is an excerpt from Cisneros' *The House on Mango Street*, published in 1984. Liliana Valenzuela has translated it from the original English. Both English and Spanish appear on each page-English on top, Spanish below. Each page contains one sentence or one phrase, and all text is accompanied by rich and vibrant illustrations, which support the meaning of the text and amplify it.

Noteworthy Features

All sentences are simple, until the end when there is a very long sentence. Though it might be considered a run-on sentence, it allows the writer and the reader to linger on the nature and scent of the mother's hair and is very much entwined in the meaning of the text.

Teaching Ideas

This book is really an excerpt from *The House on Mango Street*, a book, which is often studied as an example of memoir writing. *Hairs/Pelitos* is an especially vivid example of the qualities of good writing one sees in all Cisneros's texts. *Hairs/Pelitos* can be used in primary classrooms as well as upper grade classes.

Writing teachers use this book to show youngsters how to linger on a subject, pulling the meaning out like taffy. "But my mother's hair, my mother's hair, like little rosettes, like little candy circles, all curly and pretty because she pinned it in pin curls all day, sweet to put your nose into when she is holding you, holding you and you feel safe, is the warm smell of bread before you bake it, is the smell when she makes room for you on her side of the bed still warm with her skin, and you sleep near her, the rain outside falling and Papa snoring." With each pull of the words, the meaning becomes more intense. Many times this is the hard part for writing students; it is hard for them to stay in one place and stretch out the meaning, creating more meaning as the writing happens. Cisneros can be an accessible mentor for all writers hoping to become more visual with their words.

Hairs/Pelitos can also be classified as a list book. Where many books

A Field Guide to the Classroom Library, Lucy Calkins and the Teachers College Reading and Writing Project, Heinemann, ©2002 Teachers College, Columbia University; http://www.heinemann.com/fieldguides

Illustrator
Terry Ybanez

Publisher
Dragonfly Books, 1997

ISBN
0679890076

TC Level
5

contain a story or narrative, there are many others that contain a list, or lists. *Hairs/Pelitos* is a list of all the kinds of hair the narrator's family has, from the father to the mother. Each family member's hair is described in one or two sentences. The first sentence about mother's hair is a list in itself, a list describing what her hair looks like, smells like, and what the smell reminds the narrator of. While studying list books is important to beginning writers, it is also an important structure for beginning readers to know about. If readers know that this is a list book, they will look for a pattern, which here is in the sentence structure.

One teacher decided to give *Hairs/Pelitos* a book introduction before she read it aloud to her second grade class. She began, "We've read this book before-I can't remember how many times. I've noticed so many things about it, and then just yesterday I was going through books looking for some that were list books. I realized that *Hairs/Pelitos* is a list book, too! I was amazed; I saw that I could figure out the order of the book, and I realized it goes from one person's hair to another person's hair. And at the end, it stays with the mother's hair. There's a little bit of a difference at the end." One student who had been reading Cindy Ward's *Cookie's Week* in her independent reading said, "Yeah! My book too does that! It's a list! Cookie goes from day to day and then on Sunday it's a little different. A lot of books do that!" This was a big discovery for this class, and they continued for the rest of the year with an awareness of texts that were structured like lists.

Genre
Picture Book; Memoir

Teaching Uses
Independent Reading; Teaching Writing; Read Aloud

Hattie and the Fox
Mem Fox

Book Summary

One morning, a big, black hen named Hattie looks up and discovers a frightful nose peering from a nearby bush. Her farm animal friends-goose, pig, sheep, horse and cow-remark uninterestedly as they continue their morning grazing and lazing in the sun. At the turn of each page, different body parts appear in the bushes: first the nose, then the eyes, next the ears, followed by two legs, and a long, furry tail. The farm animals continue to shrug off Hattie's nervousness in the repetitive text, saying such things as "Who cares?" and "So what?" Suspense builds until the final few pages when the creature jumps from the bushes and Hattie screams, "It's a fox! It's a fox!" All of the barnyard animals instantly react very differently than before and get very flustered. The animals lament and fret. With a resounding "MOOOOOOOO," only the cow takes action and chases the fox away, surprising the other animals and the reader.

Basic Book Information

Mem Fox is recognized around the world as a writer, storyteller, and an advocate of literacy teaching. Aside from *Hattie and the Fox*, Mem Fox has written over 25 books for children. Most popular are *Possum Magic, Koala Lou, Time for Bed,* and *Wombat Divine. Possum Magic* is the best-selling picture book in Australia. The idea for *Hattie and the Fox* came to Mem Fox after she attended a workshop about rhyming books. She began thinking of bouncy rhymes and wrote the first draft to *Hattie and the Fox* on the eve of the workshop. Mem Fox also based this book on the traditional hen-and-fox tales dating back to Aesop. She notes that *Hattie and the Fox* is structured somewhat like *The Little Red Hen*, and draws inspiration from Pat Hutchins' popular book, *Rosie's Walk*.

Patricia Mullins' illustrations are vividly painted in watercolor. She visited many local farms in Melbourne to take photographs and make sketches of animals in order to create the barnyard animals in this story. Mullins employed a collage technique using tissue paper and conte crayon to complete the beautiful illustrations for *Hattie and the Fox*.

Noteworthy Features

The typeface of the text is very clear and the words are well-spaced, allowing for one-to-one matching of spoken words to written ones. The engaging illustrations are supportive of the text. Readers continue to anticipate the ultimate outcome of the story due to Hattie's constant warnings to the other animals. For example, before the fox fully appears out of the bushes, Hattie says, "Goodness gracious me! I can see a nose, two eyes, two ears, two legs,

A Field Guide to the Classroom Library, Lucy Calkins and the Teachers College Reading and Writing Project, Heinemann, ©2002 Teachers College, Columbia University; http://www.heinemann.com/fieldguides

Illustrator
Patricia Mullins

Publisher
Bradbury Press, 1987

ISBN
0689716117

TC Level
5

and a body in the bushes!" This story also includes a great deal of repeating text. Hattie always exclaims what she sees in the bushes and says, "Goodness gracious me!" Each of the other characters, including, the goose, pig, sheep, horse, and cow repeatedly respond with the same dialogue until the end of the story. Their patterned response changes when the fox jumps out of the bushes.

The book includes many high frequency words. In fact, there are thirteen high frequency words on the first page alone. These include *was, a, big, one, she, up, and, said, me, can, see, in* and *the*. Children can use parts of these sight words as analogies to help them with unknown words.

Teaching Ideas

It is important for the students to be given ample opportunities to discuss and retell the story with a partner. A teacher might encourage the children to place Post-It notes on pages they find interesting or they have questions about. Later, the children could reread this part of the text with their reading partner and discuss the marked sections of the text.

If this book is a stretch for a reader, a teacher may give a book introduction. The teacher might introduce the title of the story first. Then the teacher and students could study the pictures on each of the pages and discuss the story elements.

There is a variety of punctuation used in *Hattie and the Fox*. Some teachers may decide to lead strategy lessons on using punctuation cues to read with phrasing and how authors sometimes use capital letters to emphasize and create a certain expression. The teacher might teach the students how authors sometimes choose to place quotation marks around a character's words to let you know he or she is speaking.

Hattie and the Fox contains a variety of exclamation points, question marks, commas, and periods. Each time Hattie talks about the fox, there is an exclamation point at the end of her sentence. For instance, "Goodness gracious me! I can see a nose in the bushes!" The goose and pig's responses throughout the story also end with an exclamation point. For example, "'Good grief!' said the goose. 'Well, well!' said the pig." The sheep, horse, and cow's responses often end with a question mark. For instance, "Who cares?" said the sheep. "So what?" said the horse. "What next?" said the cow. After the fox appears out of the bushes, all of the animals' responses end with an exclamation point. The cow's response is also in all capital letters to create a louder, more intense expression. A teacher might teach the children about the ways good readers notice punctuation to read with the appropriate phrasing. A teacher might also have the children practice rereading the story with a partner with the appropriate expressions based upon the punctuation.

A teacher might use this book to teach students to read with intonation. The teacher could say, "We have been noticing that many of the books in our classroom library include dialogue. I wanted to talk to you about how good readers sound as they read a book that has dialogue. I am going to read the story, *Hattie and the Fox* to the class and I want you to listen carefully to see if you notice anything about the way I read the story." Next, the teacher might read the story with a great deal of expression using a different character voice for each animal character. Then, the teacher would ask the children to brainstorm and share what they noticed about the way she read the story. After making a chart of their ideas, the teacher would send the children off with their reading partners to try to read the story with their own expressive voices.

In a conference with a child or with a small group of children, a teacher might focus on the beginning letters of words that have common chunks within the story. For example, the words, "gracious" and "grief" are found throughout the story. The teacher could call attention to the *gr* and help the student or students generate other words using *gr*.

Another teaching point that a teacher could make in a conference with a child or with a small group of children is to teach the children to recognize a larger or common chunk within a word. For example, the words, "nearby" and "anything" are found in the text. A teacher might teach the children to use a strategy to recognize the common chunks within these two words and refer the children to the class word wall to see if they can find words like "near," "by," "any," and "thing" in order to recognize the larger word.

Children invariably notice there's a pattern to the text. This book could be used in a mini-lesson designed to show children that sometimes readers pause in the midst of reading to note the pattern. A teacher, for example, could read a few pages of the book and then say, "Oh, look. Hattie keeps saying 'I can see a nose, two eyes. . . .' And then the animals say the same thing they said on the other page. I've noticed that sometimes in books, the author keeps repeating words. Let me keep reading and listening for the pattern." In this book, the pattern is cumulative. Every time Hattie sees another part of the fox hiding in the bushes she warns her friends. She begins by saying, "I can see a nose in the bushes!" Then she adds, "a nose and two eyes in the bushes!" Finally, she warns, "a nose, two eyes, two ears, a body, four legs, and a tail in the bushes!"

Book Connections

Hattie and the Fox could be added to a selection of books used for a Mem Fox author study in first or second grade. It could be compared across texts to *Rosie's Walk*, by Pat Hutchins, a similar hen-and-fox tale. This book's plot can be compared to *The Little Red Hen* in which the main character also tries to gain the attention (and help) of the other characters, but they don't listen-until it's too late!

Eric Carle's book, *Today is Monday* also includes engaging illustrations that are supportive of the text. Each successive page represents another day of the week and displays one more kind of food to be eaten by the children. The foods are clearly shown in the pictures and are accompanied with matching text. This is similar to how the illustrations in Mem Fox's *Hattie and the Fox* show more and more of the fox's body parts on each page as they are accompanied with matching text. Similarly, both books repeat part of the text.

The books, *Yo! Yes?* and *The Thingy Thing*, by Chris Raschka both provide similar opportunities to attend to punctuation. As in *Hattie and the Fox*, these books can be used to teach the strategy of how to use punctuation cues to read with phrasing.

A Field Guide to the Classroom Library, Lucy Calkins and the Teachers College Reading and Writing Project, Heinemann, ©2002 Teachers College, Columbia University; http://www.heinemann.com/fieldguides

Genre
Picture Book

Teaching Uses
Independent Reading; Author Study; Partnerships; Language Conventions; Small Group Strategy Instruction

Henry and Mudge and the Best Day of All

Cynthia Rylant

Book Summary

It is May 1st and it's the best day of all. It's Henry's birthday and he is having a birthday party. His dog Mudge is uninterested until Henry promises there will be crackers at the party. Soon balloons are all over Henry's house and Henry's father takes lots of pictures. After the pictures, it's time for Henry's favorite breakfast.

That afternoon, kids arrive and the party begins. The kids play ring-toss and go fishing, run potato-sack races, and try to crack open the piñata. Henry's birthday cake looks like his fish tank, which Mudge sniffs and sniffs. Henry gets great presents and when everyone goes home, he and his family rest.

Basic Book Information

This book is 40 pages long and the print size is large with spacing between words and lines. Most sentences are short and simple, but occasionally the sentences can be complex and very literary, especially for this level. There are lively pictures on every page, and they generally match and enhance the text.

This series focuses on the relationship between Henry and Mudge and their adventures together. The whole series does not have to be read in order, but it is suggested that readers begin with *Henry and Mudge: The First Book*. The books dealing with the character Annie, Henry's cousin, should be read in order because a story line develops over the course of the three *Annie* books. Many of the books in this series have short stories connected by a theme such as winter, moving, or a birthday.

Noteworthy Features

All the events in this story take place on May 1st, the day of Henry's birthday. The four chapters progress chronologically through the day, starting with waking up and ending with the family collapsed, resting at the end of a long and full day.

These titles do not serve as a mini-introduction to the chapters. Instead they function as labels or sub-heads. They are a bit artsy and their meaning is elusive, and therefore worth discussing.

A close reading of this text can yield lots of observations. It's interesting that most of the elements that become important in the final chapter of the book are present also in the first chapter. Notice the fish tank and the reference to Mudge's affection for crackers.

Series
Henry and Mudge

Illustrator
Sucie Stevenson

Publisher
Simon & Schuster, 1997

ISBN
0689813856

TC Level
6

A Field Guide to the Classroom Library, Lucy Calkins and the Teachers College Reading and Writing Project, Heinemann, ©2002 Teachers College, Columbia University; http://www.heinemann.com/fieldguides

Children may be puzzled with the line on page 15 that says the bookcase took a picture of the family, referring to a remote control camera.

Children may have some difficulties reading the names of the games children play at the party and the prizes they receive. For example, one sentence says, "The winners at ring toss got decoder rings."

Teaching Ideas

Like all the books in this series, this book deserves to be read and reread, studied and reread. A close reading will yield all sorts of grand conversations. Children may, with some encouragement, generate partnership conversations about topics of their choosing. Some kids have discussed these topics:

As they read the second chapter, many children will think that because this chapter begins with the balloons, and then has the father snapping photos and the birthday breakfast with more balloons and celebrating, that this *is* the party. Why does the author trick us? Why does Henry have two parties in one day?

The kids come to the party with their dogs in tow! The dogs have questionable manners. One chews on himself, and Mudge leers at a nearby dog. One dog slows down a child in the potato sack races.

At the party, Henry is given the chance to split open the piñata. His father first whispers something to him. What does he say?

On the final page of the book, a cat joins the family. There is no mention of the cat-he's just there. Where did he come from? A closer look suggests the cat was in a birthday gift box, along with a robot, an airplane, and a basketball. Perhaps the cat is what the text calls "a snow leopard."

When the party is over, Mudge finally gets a birthday hat. Why didn't he wear one sooner?

Many students will find this book easy to talk about because celebrating birthdays are familiar to most of them. Many students talk about the party and how much fun it is compared to parties they have been to themselves. Some students will vote on a scale of 1 to 10 the best things that happen on Henry's birthday. Many students will compare Mudge's behavior at the party with his behavior at grandma's house. Or compare various celebrations the family has like Henry's birthday to Christmas Eve in the *Henry and Mudge in the Sparkle Days*. Still others will sort out the endings of this series. Many books end with the family resting and Henry and Mudge hugging.

Book Connections

This book is similar in difficulty to the *Minnie and Moo* series by Denys Cazet, the *Little Bear* series by Else Holmelund Minarik, as well as the *Poppleton* and *Mr. Putter and Tabby* series, also by Cynthia Rylant.

Genre
Picture Book

A Field Guide to the Classroom Library, Lucy Calkins and the Teachers College Reading and Writing Project, Heinemann, ©2002 Teachers College, Columbia University; http://www.heinemann.com/fieldguides

Teaching Uses
Independent Reading; Partnerships

Hershel and the Hanukkah Goblins

Eric Kimmel

Book Summary

A small village is unable to celebrate Hanukkah because of some evil goblins in the haunted synagogue at the top of the hill. The only way to break the goblins' power is to stay in the synagogue for eight nights, lighting the candles of the menorah each night. On the last night, the goblin king himself must light the candles. Hershel of Ostropol volunteers to conquer the goblins. He goes to the old synagogue with some hard-boiled eggs and pickles for food. On each night Hershel tricks the goblins into letting the candles stay lit. On the eighth night, Hershel pretends he cannot see the goblin king, and the creature, in his hurry to strike fear into the heart of all who see him, willingly lights the candles so that Hershel may look upon him and tremble. This breaks the goblins' powers, and Hershel has freed the village to celebrate Hanukkah.

Basic Book Information

A noted storyteller, Dr. Kimmel has performed for children and adults throughout the United States. Many of his titles revolve around well-loved folktales and fairy tales from different cultures and nations. Of storytelling, Kimmel says, "You are not the same person you were yesterday. You are not the person you will be tomorrow. So it is with stories. They change each time they are told. They change with each teller. They change as they move across continents and generations. That is why I find being a teller of tales so exciting. It allows me to add something of myself to each story, just as each story adds something of itself to me." (Scholastics Online Authors Library, 2000)

Noteworthy Features

This is a Caldecott Honor book. Trina Schart Hyman's illustrations are beloved by many readers, especially those who know her artwork from *Cricket* magazine. The pictures alone, especially the goblins on the back cover, will draw readers to the book. Many teachers, however, do not keep the book on the library shelves, instead saving it for December to read alongside other holiday books.

Teaching Ideas

For some students, the vocabulary of Hanukkah will be new. For those who will be thrown off-track by the numerous holiday-related words, it would be helpful for them first to read the Author's Note at the end of the story. In it, there is a short history of Hanukkah, shorter descriptions of the objects used in the ceremony, and explanations of words used in the book that are

Illustrator
Trina Schart Hyman

Publisher
Caldeco, 1989

ISBN
0823411311

A Field Guide to the Classroom Library, Lucy Calkins and the Teachers College Reading and Writing Project, Heinemann, ©2002 Teachers College, Columbia University; http://www.heinemann.com/fieldguides

particular to Jewish culture. Since the typeface of the Author's Note is very small it might be helpful for the teacher to read this author's note to the children who need it.

For some listeners, the tricks that Hershel plays on the goblins will require pause. Listeners may well hear the things Hershel does with the goblins and not realize they are intended to trick the creatures. "Okay, Hershel squeezed an egg," one listener might say to herself, not realizing that the goblin thought it was a rock. For this kind of listener, it would help to have an opportunity to stop and talk at the end of each goblin encounter at the least. Perhaps it would also help to stop and talk before each goblin encounter. The last encounter, in which Hershel has the goblin king light the candles of the menorah, is less subtle and most listeners understand the trick without stopping for talk or thought.

If stopping to talk briefly isn't enough to help some readers understand what is going on between Hershel and the not-too-bright goblins, children could pause to act out the scenes for themselves. In this story as in many stories, the process of figuring out what to do in their acting forces children to decipher what is happening in the story. Pickles and hard-boiled eggs aren't necessary, only items to stand in for these things. Children can use standard dice if dreidels aren't available.

Book Connections

Some teachers like to read (or set out) this book in conjunction with other holiday books, like *'Twas the Night Before Christmas*. Books that describe Kwanzaa and Ramadan are usually also included, along with books that describe other religious and secular holidays. *The Legend of the Poinsettia* by Tomie dePaola is a book that tells the tale of the poinsettia plant and of Christmas in Mexico.

Genre
Picture Book; Fairy and Folk Tale

Teaching Uses
Read Aloud; Partnerships; Independent Reading; Interpretation

Honey, I Love

Eloise Greenfield

Book Summary

This poem was originally published in a collection of Greenfield's poems, then republished in this book by itself. Each five-line verse tells something the narrator loves: the way her cousin talks, the laughing sound she and her best friend make, the things she sees while riding in the family car and her mother's arm. The only thing the narrator does not love is going to sleep early. The poem ends with the line, "And honey, I love ME, too," a change from the original version, "And honey, I love you, too."

Basic Book Information

This 16-page poem has been a favorite since its initial publication. Each stanza has a five-line format, with the first and second lines and third and fourth lines rhyming. The stanzas are linked to one another by the word "and." The vocabulary is simple and easily understood by young children. Although the lines tend to be long-about twelve words -the syntax is not complex. Each stanza of the poem is given its own page on a reddish-brown background. The soft illustrations, with minimal detail, merge with each stanza and enhance the meaning. The fact that this poem, part of a collection of poems in the original printing, now has its own book allows the publisher to place each stanza on its own page. Gilchrist's illustrations, specific to the text, help young readers more easily comprehend the actions described. The placement of the text varies-stanzas appear at top left, others at bottom right. Greenfield has received numerous awards for her writing for children, including recognition by the Council on Interracial Books for Children for her "outstanding and exemplary contributions in children's literature."

Noteworthy Features

Each stanza tells its own "story" in rhyme. The narrator tells of things she loves: listening to her cousin's way of speaking, racing under a hose on a hot summer day, and laughing with her friend. The repetition of the phrase, "Honey, let me tell you" in each verse accents the rhythm that flows through the words: "Honey, let me tell you that I love to take a ride, I love to take a family ride." The poem can be interpreted on two levels. For the younger reader, it might be a list of things that are fun to do. The more perceptive reader will detect the underlying message of love: each of the verses describes an activity that costs nothing, that includes family members and friends, that defines love of family, of neighbor and of self. The one verse that describes something that the narrator does not love-going to sleep early, an action that separates her from family-also fits that pattern.

Illustrator
Jan Spivey Gilchrist

Publisher
HarperCollins, 1978

ISBN
0064430979

TC Level
8

A Field Guide to the Classroom Library, Lucy Calkins and the Teachers College Reading and Writing Project, Heinemann, ©2002 Teachers College, Columbia University; http://www.heinemann.com/fieldguides

Teaching Ideas

Readers might discuss the underlying ideas each stanza emphasizes. Perhaps they'll come to see that the poet is saying that love, not material things, is important. Teachers might ask students to compare the activities in each verse to see if there is an underlying theme that runs through the poem. "What is the one important thing that Greenfield mentions in each verse?"

Teachers might want to have students explore the craft Greenfield uses in this poem. Her use of rhythm, repetition, and rhyme are worth admiring, and the poem becomes yet another example of the list structure (see also Butterworth's *My Mom Is Excellent*, Rylant's *When I Was Young in the Mountains*, and Howard's *When I Was Five*).

Poetry is best appreciated when it is read aloud. Students might work together to prepare a choral reading of the poem, deciding when to read lines as a chorus, when to use solo readers, etc. One or two members of the group might pantomime the action as the rest of the group repeats the lines.

Book Connections

If students enjoy this poem, they might enjoy reading the original collection by Greenfield, *Honey, I Love and Other Love Poems*.

Genre
Poetry; Picture Book

Teaching Uses
Teaching Writing; Interpretation; Read Aloud

A Field Guide to the Classroom Library, Lucy Calkins and the Teachers College Reading and Writing Project, Heinemann, ©2002 Teachers College, Columbia University; http://www.heinemann.com/fieldguides

How a House Is Built

Gail Gibbons

Book Summary

How a House Is Built provides a chronological narration of the process of constructing a home, from the architect's drafting table to the laying of the foundation to the finishing touches of the landscapers.

Basic Book Information

This nonfiction picture book is 30 pages long. The bottom of each page contains roughly two sentences of text below a large illustration. Most of the illustrations are labeled with the names of the machines, tools or jobs that the workers are carrying out. The font of the labels is a little smaller than the mid-size font of the text itself, but not so small as to intimidate. There is no index, table of contents, or subheading structure. At the end of the book, there is a final page entitled "Simple Shelters of the Past." It depicts eight homes, with a sentence describing each one.

Noteworthy Features

Merely glancing at its rudimentary colors and smiling construction workers makes *How a House Is Built* at first seem slightly less sophisticated than its text actually is. It does not provide a glossary or any direct definitions of the technical terms, so readers must rely on the illustrations and context of the words to clarify most meanings. Having prior knowledge will help readers tremendously as they try to figure out the definitions from context. For instance, *septic tank* and *septic system* are not explained directly.

The final page looks at "Simple Structures of the Past." Some students and teachers may take issue with this page, as many of these structures are still in use around the world. The word "simple" may also be misleading. For example, building an igloo requires many fewer people than building a large, two-story house, but it also requires specialized skills and experience that very few people have.

Students might also notice that none of the dwellings in the book appears to contain multi-family units, the kind in which the majority of children in cities reside. Students who question this text may become interested in finding out how building apartment buildings is different than building one-family homes.

Teaching Ideas

This is an excellent book for readers who are interested in construction or heavy machinery. The text makes it relatively easy to take notes, so this may be a good book for a beginning note-taker.

Because most pages contain few sentences, *How a House Is Built* gives

---

Illustrator
Gail Gibbons

Publisher
Holiday House, 1990

ISBN
0823412326

TC Level
8; 9

A Field Guide to the Classroom Library, Lucy Calkins and the Teachers College Reading and Writing Project, Heinemann, ©2002 Teachers College, Columbia University; http://www.heinemann.com/fieldguides

readers short, isolated bursts of text in which to practice using context clues. During a whole-class strategy lesson or teacher-student conferences, students might be prompted to look at a sentence such as, "The mason is almost finished building the chimney." Many students will not know what a mason is, but they can work on strategies to figure it out. Are all of the people in the illustration masons? Which is labeled "mason"? What is that figure doing? What materials is he using? Many students may not conclude that masonry involves general work with stones, but that it has to do with building chimneys.

Because no other examples of masonry exist in the book, this conclusion is logical. It is important to remember that readers who learn to use context clues effectively sometimes begin with limited definitions. However, because they read carefully and glean information as they go, they revise their definitions with every book that they read, forming increasingly accurate and complete ideas about new words they encounter.

Some students may think that books such as this one are compilations of facts, loose gatherings of information. It helps to confer with readers so they see that lists are arranged according to logic. In this book, the logic is sequential. However, the information *could* have been presented in a different order. It could have first listed the easy things about building a house, and then listed the hard things.

Alternatively, it could have listed the tasks that require many builders, and then the tasks one builder could do on his or her own. During teacher-student conferences, it is interesting to note what readers think a book's structure is. Understanding structure helps many children make meaning of what they read. Students may note that the first four pages of the book provide general information about houses, while the rest of it moves chronologically. Observing how they deal with this structural shift may tell teachers a bit about how children understand nonfiction at this level.

Book Connections

Gail Gibbons has written dozens of careful, nonfiction picture books. Gibbons' *From Seed to Plant* follows a similar chronological structure, and her *Tool Book* relates thematically to *How a House Is Built*. Byron Barton's *Building a House* offers students more reading on this topic.

Genre
Nonfiction; Picture Book

Teaching Uses
Independent Reading; Partnerships; Content Area Study; Reading and Writing Nonfiction; Critique

A Field Guide to the Classroom Library, Lucy Calkins and the Teachers College Reading and Writing Project, Heinemann, ©2002 Teachers College, Columbia University; http://www.heinemann.com/fieldguides

How Is a Crayon Made?

Charles Oz

Book Summary

This book explains how crayons are made, including mixing the pigment in a color mill, mixing the pigment into the clear wax at the crayon factory, then cooling into crayon shapes. The text then describes the labeling and sorting process, and ends with an explanation of boxing the crayons into the packages customers can buy at the stores.

Basic Book Information

This nonfiction picture book has about 25 pages. Each page has one or two photographs of some aspect of the crayon production process. Each page also has from one to ten lines of text describing that process. After a brief introduction, the text is a step-by-step narration of the production process. There is no table of contents, glossary, or index.

Noteworthy Features

The most remarkable parts of this book are the photographs of the machines and the factory in which crayon production happens. The gritty and powerful mechanization process, highlighted by the bright, friendly colors of the familiar crayons makes the book's illustrations captivating to many readers.

Some pages have very few lines of text, making browsing the book possible. Some pages, however, have many lines of text, and readers probably can't browse them effectively. On these pages, readers can only guess at what the pictures show when they don't read the entire text.

In the descriptions of the process, the author uses many technical terms, especially for the kinds of machines that are needed in the process. Usually, these technical terms are defined soon after they appear, or their functions are described. Readers should be encouraged to keep reading even when they get to words they aren't familiar with since they will soon find out what the words mean.

Readers often find that whole worlds can open to them after reading this book. Suddenly they wonder where all sorts of things come from and how all sorts of things are made. The book opens a new realm of inquiry for many readers.

Teaching Ideas

There are many questions that readers can routinely ask themselves when they read a book, even an apparently unbiased, nonfiction book. Whose story is this, and who benefits from it being told this way? How else could the story be told? Whose perspectives aren't given in this account? In this

Publisher
Scholastic, 1988

ISBN
0671694375

TC Level
8; 9; 10

A Field Guide to the Classroom Library, Lucy Calkins and the Teachers College Reading and Writing Project, Heinemann, ©2002 Teachers College, Columbia University; http://www.heinemann.com/fieldguides

text, the machines involved in the process are in the foreground of the story, and the people involved in the process are in the background of the story. Another way to tell the story would be to put the story of the factory workers into the account. In which country are the crayons made? What are the effects on health and the environment? All of these aspects of crayon production are not included in this story, and perhaps they shouldn't be. In any case, those aspects of crayon production are there to think about.

Readers can also talk about the assumptions in the first paragraph of the text. Is it so hard to imagine a world without crayons, really? In many countries, people live without them, and in the past people did as well. Certainly crayons are familiar to many Americans. Is that the author's point? Readers sometimes discuss reasons why the author wrote the opening line the way he did.

Some teachers use this book to teach budding writers about one way to organize descriptive nonfiction-dividing it into steps. This text is an excellent model for writers trying to relate a step-by-step process to their readers.

Genre
Nonfiction; Picture Book

Teaching Uses
Content Area Study; Interpretation; Critique

A Field Guide to the Classroom Library, Lucy Calkins and the Teachers College Reading and Writing Project, Heinemann, ©2002 Teachers College, Columbia University; http://www.heinemann.com/fieldguides

I See, You Saw

Nurit Karlin

Book Summary

I See, You Saw is about two mischievous cats and what they see as they take a walk one sunny day. This tongue-twister of a book is made up of the dialogue between these two slightly competitive cats as they banter playfully back and forth. For example, "I see, you saw./ No. I see, you saw./ I saw the seesaw first!/ I see a bee./ I saw the bee./" The humor is based on word play, and can be confusing to a reader.

Basic Book Information

I See, You Saw is a *My First I Can Read Book*. The book has 24 pages and contains five double-page spreads. The watercolor illustrations are subtle and yet support the text. The actual text and numbering begins on page 5. The format of the text "seesaws" back and forth and up and down across the pages, with one or two sentences on each page. Homonyms such as *can/can, fly/fly, duck/duck,* and *fish/fish* are used throughout the book. There is one homophone (see/sea) and one case of onomatopoeia (quack, quack). Punctuation is varied and includes periods, question marks, exclamation points, and quotation marks. In some editions there are three places where the closed quotes are missing (pages 6, 7, and 10) and should be corrected by the teacher before using or placing this book in a class library.

Noteworthy Features

Although this book uses many simple, high frequency words that young children will quickly recognize, words are often used in odd ways that may confuse to beginning readers. They may read the words, and not comprehend their meaning within these sentences and will have to reread to get it. The syntax is awkward at times and doesn't always sound like natural language: "I saw the duck fish the fish" (page 22) and "I saw you duck the duck" (page 23). The layout does not have any set or predictable pattern.

Teaching Ideas

Prior to using this book, teachers should do a thorough book introduction to elicit children's prior knowledge. One teacher said this to a child before he read the book, "Today we are going to read a story about two cats and their adventure. The title of the book is *I See, You Saw*. Here are the two cats we are going to read about [pointing to them]. Let's take a look. First the cats see a can, and then a fly, a seesaw and then a bee and then they see a saw. They use the saw on the seesaw. How funny-that sounds so similar. Then the cats see a duck and a fish and then they meet a frog who knows they did something bad by sawing the seesaw."

Series
My First I Can Read Book

Illustrator
Nurit Karlin

Publisher
Harper Collins Juvenile Books, 1998

ISBN
0064442497

TC Level
4

One reason to have this book in a classroom library is because some readers like books that puzzle, intrigue, and challenge. As far as cleverness goes, this book is in the category of the *Amelia Bedelia* books, although it's a considerably easier text. The point could be made to any reader of this book that being able to read the words alone is not enough. Readers must try to develop an understanding of words based on context, as well as the visual.

While *My First I Can Read Books* are usually geared to very early grades, the sophistication of the word play in this book makes it more appropriate for more fluent readers.

Book Connections

Other books by this author include *The Fat Cat Sat on the Mat* and *Little Big Mouse*. For more on homonyms and homophones read *See the Yak Yak* by Charles Ghigna and Fred Gwynne's books, *The King Who Rained* and *A Little Pigeon Toad*.

Genre
Picture Book

Teaching Uses
Independent Reading; Small Group Strategy Instruction

I'm in Charge of Celebrations

Byrd Baylor

Book Summary

The narrator tells us about some of the 108 celebrations she has created for herself in the desert of the southwestern United States. After she takes part in an extraordinary natural event, such as observing a green cloud shaped like a parrot or walking along a trail close to a coyote, she records the occasion in her notebook and decides on a fitting way to celebrate the anniversary in the future. She laughs when people ask her if she is lonely in the desert, because she has become so familiar with the desert and the creatures that inhabit it.

Basic Book Information

Two-page spreads of text and illustrations comprise this 26-page picture book. Each double-page spread contains two or three columns of text, with columns holding from one to five words. Streaks of color from the sparse illustrations angle around the text. Byrd Baylor is the author of four Caldecott Honor books, including three illustrated by Peter Parnall.

Noteworthy Features

Short lines and stanzas give *I'm in Charge of Celebrations* the feel of a poem. With words such as "you" and "Friend," the narrator addresses readers directly. Though her voice is simple and colloquial, her language occasionally becomes lyrical. For example, when describing the gyrations of whirlwinds she has seen, the narrator uses a series of line breaks and the repeated word *and* to convey a sense of a twisting that picks up speed like a whirlwind itself: ". . . moving / up from the flats, / swirling / and swaying / and falling / and turning, / picking up sticks / and sand / and feathers / and dry tumbleweeds."

The book is arranged so that each celebration begins on a different page, much like the books that contain a compilation of poems about the holidays in a calendar year.

Many readers will not be familiar with the desert landscape in this book. Some will imagine that a desert is nothing but sand, and be surprised that the text names so many plants and animals that thrive in this habitat. Many will not know what a yucca is, and some might not know what a cactus is. In general, the least familiar words in the book are not likely to interfere with basic comprehension, though teachers can remind children of strategies to get the gist of unknown words.

Teaching Ideas

I'm in Charge of Celebrations serves the writing workshop not only as a

Illustrator
Peter Parnall

Publisher
Simon and Schuster, 1986

ISBN
0689806205

TC Level
7

A Field Guide to the Classroom Library, Lucy Calkins and the Teachers College Reading and Writing Project, Heinemann, ©2002 Teachers College, Columbia University; http://www.heinemann.com/fieldguides

model of good writing, but also as a model of writers' habits. In the story, the narrator keeps a notebook. She tells what she writes down and why. Students can look at how the narrator uses her notebook and get ideas for working with their own writers' notebook. Teachers might encourage children to notice the natural world-even the ants crawling through cracks in the playground blacktop-to see if they can find something to write about and celebrate.

Before reading *I'm in Charge of Celebrations*, teachers may begin by reading a different book about the everyday events that children experience (e.g., Sandra Cisneros' *Hairs /Pelitos*). Teachers might ask, "How do you suppose this author got the idea to write a whole book about this? I bet that because she's a writer, she really notices the littlest things. I could write a book about my hands. I've got this green magic marker on my thumb from this morning when we were working on our science studies, and I've got a scar on my finger from when I fell off my bike when I was six. I'm noticing that there are a lot of stories, right in my hand." Soon the class might imagine stories from daily life they could put down on paper.

The illustrations of the book, with their broad swaths of unusual colors, often do not immediately attract children's attention, though they do invite questions. Why is the rabbit portrayed in the middle of a circle? Why is the tail of the falling star touching the narrator and going all around her?

Book Connections

Byrd Baylor and Peter Parnall's Caldecott Honor books are *The Desert Is Theirs*; *Hawk, I'm Your Brother*; and *The Way to Start a Day*. Eve Merriam's *The Wise Woman and Her Secret* and Norma Farber's books of poems are good companion texts.

Genre
Picture Book

Teaching Uses
Teaching Writing; Read Aloud; Independent Reading

Jamaica's Find

Juanita Havill

Book Summary

Jamaica, while playing alone in the park, comes across a red sock hat and a cuddly, stuffed gray dog. Instead of placing both items in the lost and found at the park house, Jamaica returns only the hat and takes the stuffed animal home. At home, Jamaica shows off her dog to her family, which is not thrilled about having a dirty stuffed dog sitting at the dinner table. Once Jamaica is asked to take it out of the kitchen area, she begins to think about whether she did the right thing by keeping the dog. She overhears her mother mention, "It probably belongs to a girl just like Jamaica." While sitting in her room and talking to her mother, Jamaica feels empathy for the owner and decides that she wants to return the dog to the park house. After bringing back the stuffed dog, Jamaica meets a girl named Kristin, the original owner of the stuffed animal. As Jamaica happily reunites Kristin with her missing dog, the girls exchange smiles and become friends.

Basic Book Information

This picture book is a winner of the 1987 Ezra Jack Keats New Writer Award and a Reading Rainbow Selection. This 32-page picture book has at least one illustration for each pair of facing pages. The text in the book can be found on both sides of the page and superimposed over some pictures. The watercolor illustrations in the book closely represent the written text.

Noteworthy Features

The text itself has been placed to fit around the illustrations. As such, words are not in any consistent place on the page. The illustrations, however, support the text carefully. The characters' expressive faces and postures can help children understand the emotions the text on each page describes.

Teaching Ideas

This book is about honesty, compassion, and making good decisions. Jamaica's moral dilemma of dealing with right and wrong is a thread woven from the beginning to the end of the book. In and outside the classroom, there are many ways in which children can learn from this book.

The book can be a mentor text for children who are trying to write their own personal narratives. Many children retell incidents in their own lives without consciously shaping them as stories. They would benefit from a reminder of the features of narrative, and from examples of successful, cohesive stories.

This book also lends itself to teaching the strategy of prediction. Readers could use prior knowledge and looking at the cover to predict what the story

Series
Jamaica series

Publisher
Houghton Mifflin Company, 1986

ISBN
0590425048

TC Level
5

will be about. Throughout the text, they can predict what will happen next
and explain the textual basis for their predictions.

Book Connections

Juanita Havill has written two other books with the same main character,
Jamaica and Brianna and *Jamaica Tag-Along*. In this text, as well as Rod
Clement's *Grandpa's Teeth*, the main characters deal with issues of honesty,
making choices and attending to their consciences. *Believing Sophie*, by
Hazel Hutchins, and *Fanny's Dream*, by Caralyn Buehner, both address the
major themes presented in *Jamaica's Find* and show how characters resolve
similar problems.

Genre
Picture Book

Teaching Uses
Independent Reading; Teaching Writing; Character Study; Critique

A Field Guide to the Classroom Library, Lucy Calkins and the Teachers College Reading and Writing Project, Heinemann, ©2002 Teachers
College, Columbia University; http://www.heinemann.com/fieldguides

Jessica

Kevin Henkes

Book Summary

Ruthie Simmons is an only child who has an imaginary friend named Jessica. This friend goes everywhere and does everything with Ruthie. Anything that Ruthie does wrong gets blamed on Jessica. When Ruthie goes to Kindergarten, Jessica follows her. Ruthie displays her feelings of apprehension through Jessica. The turning point in the book comes when Ruthie lines up to march to the lavatory and needs a partner. Ruthie feels that Jessica, her imaginary friend, suffices, but she soon finds that another little girl is inviting her into a partnership. Ruthie says she will be the little girl's partner, only to find this new friend of hers is named Jessica. The book closes as the two walk hand-in-hand down the hallway. This story is about growing up and making new friendships.

Basic Book Information

The illustrations in this picture book are beautiful and match the text perfectly. The text is varied throughout the book and can be found in different sizes and places on the page. The book begins and ends with the same words: "Ruthie Simmons didn't have a dog. She didn't have a cat, or a brother, or a sister."

Noteworthy Features

This story articulates a lot of feelings many young children feel on the first day of school. Children will relate to Ruthie's worries about finding a partner in line, about the first day of school, and about not wanting to take responsibility for a mistake such as spilling juice.

Although the text and illustrations roughly go together, the text can be found in different sizes and different locations on the page, which will be tricky for readers. Otherwise, the text is relatively straightforward.

The most confusing part of the book may be the ending. Some students may not understand that Jessica, the imaginary friend and Jessica, the real friend, are two different entities. This may create some misunderstanding, and it will be important for children to reread for clarification if the ending does not make sense to them.

Teaching Ideas

This would be a perfect book to read aloud to children in primary grades on one of the first days of school. This text could spark conversations about how the class members feel about the start of a new year and this could help children understand that many others, too, are anxious.

Because *Jessica* follows a classic story structure, the text could also help

Illustrator
Kevin Henkes

Publisher
Mulberry Paperback
Books, 1989

ISBN
0688158471

TC Level
5

A Field Guide to the Classroom Library, Lucy Calkins and the Teachers College Reading and Writing Project, Heinemann, ©2002 Teachers College, Columbia University; http://www.heinemann.com/fieldguides

children develop a sense for the elements that reoccur in all stories. Readers could read or listen to the text with an eye toward noticing the characters, setting, and plot. Readers could talk about a change that happens in the book, one that is central to the characters and the plot. Readers could also notice the passage of time in this book. The book especially dramatizes the changes that occur in Ruthie, who begins the novel with an imaginary friend and moves on to meeting a true friend.

Readers will probably be confused by the first pages of the book. The text tells us that Jessica went wherever Ruthie went, but the picture shows just one girl, alone. "Huh?" the engaged reader will ask. It is important for children to learn that the first pages in a book are often a bit confusing, and that's okay. By reading forward, one begins to see things more clearly. The dawning realization that Jessica is an imaginary friend is important to the story, and the wise teacher won't ruin the surprise by previewing this for the reader.

The font in this book invites readers to take great pleasure in reading the book with expression. Ruthie's parents are not unlike the parents in *The Carrot Seed* who say over and over, "It won't come up." Her parents are also reminiscent of the sister in Bernard Waber's *Ira Sleeps Over* who firmly suggests that Ira not bring his blanket to the sleep over.

Book Connections

Kevin Henkes also wrote *Chrysanthemum*, *Chester's Way*, and *A Weekend with Wendell*. If students enjoy this story, they will enjoy his other works.

Genre
Picture Book

Teaching Uses
Author Study; Read Aloud

Julius

Angela Johnson

Book Summary

Maya gets a pig as a present from her granddaddy. She loves the rowdy, fun-loving beast, Julius, and they do everything together, from making messes to making cookies, from making noise to watching old movies. They disturb the orderly household and have the time of their lives doing it. They both learn from each other, too. Julius teaches Maya to swing at the park, dance to old jazz records, and eat peanut butter right from the jar without getting any on the ceiling. Maya teaches Julius some manners and personal hygiene. They live happily ever after.

Basic Book Information

Illustrator Dav Pilkey has won the Caldecott award for his book *Paper Boy*.

Noteworthy Features

Kids tend to love the exuberant and colorful illustrations in this book, and choose it right away when they see it on the shelves.

The plot of the book is a bit unusual, and while it almost certainly won't leave anyone confused, it may leave some readers a bit surprised when the book is over. There is no real conflict, or problem to resolve, or characters that change; many experienced readers who have come to expect such elements in a book and may be surprised not to find them. These readers may turn the last page and close the book with a "Is that all?" feeling. This is an elusive moment to catch in readers, but one that if caught, can lead to fertile discussion of reading expectations and necessary story elements. Probably the only way for young readers to catch this thought-if they have it at all-is for them to be keyed in ahead of time to be listening for their final thoughts and expectations and emotions when they get to the end of the book. This would probably be done by the teacher before a read aloud of the book, or before a group sets out to read the book together.

Teaching Ideas

Sometimes, readers get off on the wrong track when they read the line in the middle of the story that goes, "But Maya knew the other Julius too. . . ." Readers who are thrown by this line tend to be the ones who saw Julius' antics so far as fun and funny. The turn in the story is supposed to revolve around the fact that until this point in the story, the writer intended to describe Julius' *annoying* habits and after this line, she intends to describe the *fun* things he and Maya do together. Readers who thought the first set of antics sounded fun, however, will see no change in the kinds of activities described, and so the pivotal sentence is an oddity in the story. These readers might be waiting still for what the "other Julius" is going to turn out to be. This mistake can also contribute to a reader feeling at the story's end that something is missing or that nothing has happened.

The anxiety-free, fun-loving, caring tone in this book of friendship captures the fancy of many readers. The heart of this book seems to be a celebration of friendship, and most readers feel this right away. In fact, this may be a good book to help young readers understand what it means to talk about the theme of a book. The book certainly isn't about real pigs or about getting in trouble when you behave badly, or learning to take turns. Although all these things occur in the book, the story as a whole is about how much fun it can be to have a good friend. Most kids can see this easily and thus begin to develop a sense for theme.

Once in a while, a group of readers becomes irritated with Maya and Julius. They consider them an undue burden on their parents and too irresponsible, especially in their tendency to mess up the house. These readers want to see some repercussions fall on the kids or a resulting change in their behavior as they become more responsible. Other readers see the depiction of the perfect friendship between the two characters as unrealistic and misleading to real friends who will certainly have disagreements from time to time. These readers tend not to like the book, but their wary attitude toward the book leads them to do some good reading work to learn plenty as they gather evidence to show the delinquency of both Maya and Julius.

Genre
Picture Book

Teaching Uses
Author Study; Independent Reading

A Field Guide to the Classroom Library, Lucy Calkins and the Teachers College Reading and Writing Project, Heinemann, ©2002 Teachers College, Columbia University; http://www.heinemann.com/fieldguides

Little Bear's Visit

Else Holmelund Minarik

Book Summary

Four separate stories tell of Little Bear's visit to his grandparents. In the first story, "Grandmother and Grandfather Bear," Little Bear arrives at his grandparents' with a warning not to "tire them out." After some much-loved snacks, and a little exploring, Little Bear's grandfather settles in to tell Little Bear a story, and promptly falls asleep. Little Bear asks Grandmother to tell him a story instead. Grandmother tells the second story, "Mother Bear's Robin," to Little Bear. This story takes place when Little Bear's mother is a girl and finds a robin that is too young to fly. She nurtures and loves the robin in every way. When she discovers the robin is sad because he misses his home in the wild, she sets him free. In "The Goblin's Story," Little Bear's grandfather, who has awakened from his nap, tells Little Bear a scary story. A goblin, walking in the woods, becomes frightened by a sound of "Pit-pat-pit-pat-pit-pat" behind him. The sound follows him all the way to his hiding place in a tree. When he gets up the nerve to look out, he discovers his own shoes have been following him all along. In "Not Tired," Little Bear rests on the couch waiting for his parents to pick him up. When they arrive, he "tricks" them into believing he is asleep, so all four sit around and talk about how sweet he is and how much they love him, and how they want to take him fishing. He "wakes up," asks if they will *really* fish together, and they all talk about how Little Bear has fooled them. In the midst of this talk, Little Bear truly falls fast asleep!

Basic Book Information

Little Bear's Visit is part of the *I Can Read Book* series.

Noteworthy Features

The number of sentences per page, as well as the length and difficulty of each sentence, vary considerably throughout the book. There are many short, repetitive, simple sentences (e.g., "The robin ate. It grew. It sang. Soon it could fly"). There are also somewhat more complicated and lengthy sentences (e.g., "He liked to look at all the nice things, the pictures, Grandmother's flowers, Grandfather's toy goblin that jumped up and down in a jar").

There are numerous high frequency words throughout the text. The more difficult words (e.g., *oriole, coffee, hurrah*) can usually be figured out contextually. These things, in combination with the manageable length of each story, make this a good book for children beginning to read their very first chapter books.

Series
Little Bear

Illustrator
Maurice Sendak

Publisher
Harper Trophy, 1979

ISBN
0064440230

TC Level
6

A Field Guide to the Classroom Library, Lucy Calkins and the Teachers College Reading and Writing Project, Heinemann, ©2002 Teachers College, Columbia University; http://www.heinemann.com/fieldguides

Teaching Ideas

It is important to show young readers how to plan for reading longer books. For example, a teacher may say, "I notice that this book is divided into four separate stories. Each one has a different title, so it is probably about something different each time. Today, I am going to stop at the end of one story so I can talk about what I noticed with you. When I read, I am going to put a Post-It note on the parts I want to talk about the most so that when I'm finished, I can come *back* to those parts. This way I will not have to stop right in the middle of a story."

While reading texts such as this one, readers can try out some more sophisticated reading strategies: rereading difficult, enjoyable or funny parts; using a Post-It note to mark places they may want to reread and discuss with a reading partner; rereading to feel "strong" or rereading what they've read so far.

Little Bear's Visit can also be used to study character. Although Little Bear's character is not deeply developed, he does retain some simple, noticeable characteristics from book to book. There are also recurring characters in each *Little Bear* book. Readers can make character lists, compare the characters to themselves and each other, or simply discuss what they like and dislike about the characters.

Teachers may also use this book as a starting off point to study books in a series. The level of vocabulary and content remains consistent throughout. Readers can read, write, and discuss ways in which the books are similar and different, how the author's voice is the same, and whether the characters, settings, and themes remain the same or change.

Book Connections

There are three other books in the *Little Bear* series. The other titles are *Little Bear, A Kiss for Little Bear*, and *Father Bear Comes Home*. Other books at a similar level include the *Henry and Mudge* series by Cynthia Rylant and some of the more difficult books by Syd Hoff. Series that are slightly harder, and would be a good next step, include the *Frog and Toad* books by Arnold Lobel and the *Oliver Pig* books by Jean Van Leeuwen.

Genre
Picture Book

Teaching Uses
Independent Reading; Partnerships; Character Study

A Field Guide to the Classroom Library, Lucy Calkins and the Teachers College Reading and Writing Project, Heinemann, ©2002 Teachers College, Columbia University; http://www.heinemann.com/fieldguides

Little Penguin's Tale

Audrey Wood

Book Summary

Grand Nanny Penguin gathers the young penguins around her to tell the story of a mischievous Little Penguin. The young penguins role-play whatever she describes the Little Penguin doing. First he runs away to dance with the gooney birds. Then he boats to the Walrus Polar Club and acts wild with animals from all over the world. Though all these are known to be dangerous things to do, he doesn't get hurt. Then tired, he lies down by the deep sea and a big whale eats him up. The penguins listening to the tale at this point begin to cry and Nanny quickly changes the ending. The Little Penguin manages to hop on a boat and get away back home to his friends and Nanny. But he loses his tail feathers to the whale. This new ending to the story seems to satisfy the penguins, and they all go home with Nanny.

Basic Book Information

This full color picture book has fun illustrations that tend to catch a reader's interest. The penguin characters are more like cartoons than like real penguins, and they are drawn with a comic edge to them.

Noteworthy Features

At the end of the story, the Little Penguin loses his tail feathers to the whale and the line of text tells us that is the end of Little Penguin's "tale." Some kids enjoy the play on words while others don't even realize it exists.

Teaching Ideas

There are many aspects of this book to study and wonder about. One of the most obvious is the question of whether the Little Penguin that the Nanny is talking about is one of the "real" little penguins she is taking care of. Or is he copying the story of the penguin from long ago as the Nanny tells it? In the pictures, this would appear to be so, as the penguin is shown wandering off from the group and going on all the adventures Nanny describes. Is Nanny getting the story from watching the little penguin? Maybe this character is just the product of the active imagination of the little penguins. There is plenty of textual evidence and visual evidence to have a lively debate over these questions, and many kids consider them the heart of the book.

Some teachers like to use this book as an example of how composing a story might go. The Nanny is telling her story as she goes along, and changing it according to the needs of her audience. She can try different endings, and settle on one she likes. She gets her ideas from things around her and events she has heard about in the past. She can change what happens according to the effect she wants to create. Teachers often use this

Publisher
Harcourt, Brace & Company, 1989

ISBN
0152474765

TC Level
7

book in the writing workshop.

Book Connections

Other books that have the awareness of themselves as a story or as text written on the page are *The Stinky Cheese Man and Other Fairly Stupid Tales* and other books by Jon Scieszka. These books go even further than this one in referring to themselves as stories and words. There are many other books that have a storyteller telling a story within them, such as Gerald McDermott's *Anansi the Spider*. Of course, Audrey Wood has also written many different kinds of picture books for children, including *The Napping House* and *Moonflute*.

Genre
Picture Book

Teaching Uses
Independent Reading; Interpretation; Critique

A Field Guide to the Classroom Library, Lucy Calkins and the Teachers College Reading and Writing Project, Heinemann, ©2002 Teachers College, Columbia University; http://www.heinemann.com/fieldguides

Machines at Work

Byron Barton

Book Summary

Machines at Work is a survey of machines used in construction. It begins with a picture of construction workers on their way to work and the words, "Hey, you guys! Let's get to work." Various machines are shown at work: bulldozers, cranes, and steamrollers.

Basic Book Information

This book is illustrated in the style that has made Barton famous-bold, uniform colors and dark outlines around the basic shapes and parts in the pictures.

Noteworthy Features

Many young readers love machines, particularly ones they know from their environment. Many of the machines in this book are seen on construction sites all over cities.

There is not a lot of difficult text, but the text that is machine-related (*build, lift, cement, rubble, load,* and *dump*) could be challenging. Sight words included in the text are *up, now, let's, eat, the, go,* and *stop.* Although the illustrations are supportive of the text, they do not usually match one-to-one with the text.

Teaching Ideas

Because there are many machine-related words combined with the sight words of the text, teachers will want to help readers get started with this book. The book can be introduced by showing the cover and explaining, "This book is all about big machines that work to build buildings and roads. What is the machine on the cover? What job it is doing? Have you ever seen this machine in use anywhere?" As children respond, the teacher can take a picture-walk through the book and ask questions or elicit responses from the readers that use the challenging words from the page. For example, on the page that shows a wrecking ball knocking down a building, the teacher can say, "What is happening in this picture? What is this machine doing? Why does the machine swing that big heavy ball? Are the workers trying to build a building or are they trying to knock it down?"

In some cases, it is appropriate for the teacher to "give" the word to a reader who is struggling. In this book, there are some words that will be difficult to figure out for some readers, even after using all the appropriate strategies. It is important for the reader to feel some fluency as she reads, and if trying to figure out a word is becoming frustrating and/or discouraging the reader from moving ahead, it is important for the teacher

Illustrator
Byron Barton

Publisher
Thomas Y. Crowell, 1987

ISBN
069401107X

 A Field Guide to the Classroom Library, Lucy Calkins and the Teachers College Reading and Writing Project, Heinemann, ©2002 Teachers College, Columbia University; http://www.heinemann.com/fieldguides

to step in. *Tomorrow, rubble, beam,* and *bulldoze* are examples of words with which readers might need some help.

This book can be used as part of a Byron Barton author study or reading center. Readers may want to compare and contrast the similarities and differences of Byron Barton books. Teachers may ask, "What can we learn about Byron Barton from the books we have studied? Where do you think he lives? What kinds of things does he like? What do you think he does when he wants to write a new book?"

This book can also be used as part of a reading center of books (at a similar level) about machines, or books about building things. Readers can notice what seems to be included in all their books in the center, and what is specific to one or another book. Readers can categorize books into smaller groups, such as machines that are driven, machines that you hold in your hand, machines that build, machines that knock things down, machines used in cities, and machines used on farms.

Book Connections

Byron Barton has written and illustrated many books for children that are similar to this one. Some of these titles include *Airplanes, Trucks, Boats, Building A House, Trains, Airports, Wheels,* and *Zoo Animals.*

Genre
Nonfiction; Picture Book

Teaching Uses
Content Area Study; Author Study

Madeline
Ludwig Bemelmans

Book Summary

In simple, irresistible rhyme, *Madeline* is the story of a little girl at a French boarding school who wakes up one night in terrible pain. She is rushed to the hospital to have her appendix out. Her classmates and her caretaker, Miss Clavel, visit her to see if she is getting well and to examine the scar on her abdomen. That night, after the visit to the hospital, all the other girls want to have their appendixes out, too. Miss Clavel tells them to be thankful they are well, and to have a good night.

Basic Book Information

This Caldecott Honor book is the first in a world-famous series. Even sixty years after their first publication, these books continue to be favorites of children everywhere. The pictures alternate between full color plates and simple black and white and yellow sketches.

Noteworthy Features

The simple, short-line rhymes give extra support to those children trying to read *Madeline* for the first time. The patterns also make the stories very easy to memorize, especially the shorter ones. Sometimes the rhymes are a bit of a stretch, like "arm" and "warm."

The *Madeline* books all contain historic buildings and landmarks in their illustrations. Several have lists at the back naming the famous architecture in the pictures.

Children sometimes get confused by some of the details that represent either the French part of the story or the fact that it was written so long ago. The doctor calls the hospital by dialing "DANton-ten-six," a style of telephone number that no longer exists. They also don't know why Madeline would be standing on a chair to be measured in her underwear by a man with some small "sticks" in his mouth. Some children aren't familiar with the formal attire of nuns and wonder why Miss Clavel and the nurse at the hospital dress so oddly. The muffs the girls all wear while they are ice-skating also tend to be unfamiliar.

Teaching Ideas

Partners may want to place Post-It notes on all the interesting places that are illustrated throughout the book. In this particular edition, the illustrations are listed in the back for clarification. This historical information could extend over into a social studies unit about Paris. Teachers may want to use the *Madeline* series to compare cultures of two major cities, such as Paris and New York.

Series
Madeline

Illustrator
Ludwig Bemelmans

Publisher
Puffin Books, 1939

ISBN
0140501983

TC Level
7

A Field Guide to the Classroom Library, Lucy Calkins and the Teachers College Reading and Writing Project, Heinemann, ©2002 Teachers College, Columbia University; http://www.heinemann.com/fieldguides

For students who may have had a similar experience to Madeline's (being hospitalized, having an appendix burst), this could lead to a text-to-self connection, where the student may be able to say, "This reminds me of. . . ."

Teachers may also want to encourage a character study as students become more familiar with Madeline through different books in the series. Students may be able to make more and more connections about Madeline, other characters in the story, or places they visit. Students may discuss similarities and differences with book partners.

Book Connections

The books in this series do not have to be read in a particular order. However, it makes sense to read *Madeline* first, followed by *Madeline's Rescue*. Other books in this series include *Madeline and the Bad Hat*, *Madeline and the Gypsies*, *Madeline's Christmas*, and *Madeline in America and Other Holiday Tales.*

Genre
Picture Book

Teaching Uses
Independent Reading; Character Study

Madeline in America and Other Holiday Tales

Ludwig Bemelmans

Book Summary

Madeline's grandfather leaves her a fortune upon his death, and the whole Paris boarding school travels to Texas to hear the reading of the will. The girls enjoy adventures and sights in Texas, from visiting oil wells and eating chili to seeing a huge department store and riding horses through a cattle stampede. Madeline gets lost and the Texas rangers come out in full force to find her, in the depths of the department store. Everyone celebrates her return with lavish gifts on Christmas day. When Madeline says she will quit school because of her newfound wealth, the lawyer reveals grandfather's wisdom-the money is not hers until she turns twenty-one. The girls all return to boarding school, excited from their recent Texas adventure.

Basic Book Information

This large-scale book contains several stories about Christmas, some about Madeline, some about author's memories of Christmas, others about general good will and peace at Christmas time.

Noteworthy Features

This story is illustrated in the style of Ludwig Bemelmans by his grandson, so the pictures are slightly different then in other *Madeline* books, and all in full color. In this story, the pictures are less crucial to the understanding of the plot than they are in others, but they are still necessary to understanding the tale.

Understanding a bit about Texas (or at least its stereotypes) may help readers appreciate this story, although it isn't necessary, as the story introduces these elements gradually.

Teaching Ideas

There are a couple of possible conversations a teacher could support after reading this book aloud. Some teachers don't like the portrayal of Christmas in this story as simply a time to get lots and lots of presents from the wealthy. In this tale, there are no talks of feelings, or of generosity or of the joy of giving, there is only a depiction of the girls getting clothes and shoes and new hats and all kinds of toys for Christmas, all being rolled into the room by the delivery boys. This might be the basis for a conversation, even a teacher-started conversation. What do you think the delivery boys are feeling about all this? What do you think the girls are missing when

Series
Madeline

Illustrator
John Bemelmans Marciano

Publisher
Scholastic, 1991

ISBN
0590043064

TC Level
7

A Field Guide to the Classroom Library, Lucy Calkins and the Teachers College Reading and Writing Project, Heinemann, ©2002 Teachers College, Columbia University; http://www.heinemann.com/fieldguides

Christmas, or any holiday celebration, becomes only about getting as many gifts as possible?

There are also possibilities for discussion in Madeline's comment that "there'll be no more school, that is the best part, for who is rich is already smart." Children often take this comment at face value without thinking through if they agree or disagree with Madeline. Some usually wonder what she means by this. Children also often have a lot to say about the reasons Miss Clavel could have for asking Crockett, the Lawyer, to stop spoiling the girls. What could possibly be wrong with giving them so many toys?

Book Connections

Other books in this series include *Madeline and the Bad Hat, Madeline and the Gypsies, Madeline's Rescue, Madeline's Christmas* and *Madeline*.

Genre
Anthology of Short Stories; Memoir; Picture Book

Teaching Uses
Independent Reading; Interpretation; Critique

A Field Guide to the Classroom Library, Lucy Calkins and the Teachers College Reading and Writing Project, Heinemann, ©2002 Teachers College, Columbia University; http://www.heinemann.com/fieldguides

Madeline's Rescue

Ludwig Bemelmans

Book Summary

Madeline falls into the river and a stray dog saves her life by pulling her out. All the girls fall in love with the dog, but the board of trustees decides the dog, Genevieve, cannot stay at their boarding school. Lord Cucuface kicks the dog out onto the street. Miss Clavel and the girls are determined to get her back. Finally the dog returns on her own, to everyone's great happiness. At first the girls fight over whom the dog should sleep with, but finally, when Genevieve has puppies, everyone is content.

Basic Book Information

This book is one of a series about Madeline, and has the alternating pattern of four-color illustrations and black, white and yellow illustrations, all in the spare line drawing style of the illustrator.

Noteworthy Features

As always with the *Madeline* books, the dialogue isn't referenced with such tags as, "said Madeline" or "said Lord Cucuface." The pictures help to clarify who is speaking.

Like the other books, there are a few odd rhymes that can cause children a bit of confusion: "thorough" and "sorrow," "back" and "scat," and "safe" and "grave." This usually presents rhythm problems, since children expect a rhyme, and then think they have missed something when it doesn't come.

As in the other *Madeleine* books, the text includes French terms, but children can figure out the meaning of words such as *gendarmes* by using context clues.

Teaching Ideas

The pictures in this book are crucial in helping the reader understand the story. On one page for example, there is a tapping sequence that is hard to understand unless the reader looks at the page and sees it is Genevieve's tail tapping on the ground. At the end of the book, when the words read ". . . there was enough hound/ to go all around" only the picture makes it clear that the dog had puppies. Because of this, it is important for teachers to model for children how the pictures can help a reader understand the story.

Children may want to critique the values that brought Lord Cucuface to kick the dog out of the school. Was that fair? Was the students' response appropriate?

Series
Madeline

Illustrator
Ludwig Bemelmans

Publisher
Puffin Books, 1951

ISBN
0140502076

TC Level
7

A Field Guide to the Classroom Library, Lucy Calkins and the Teachers College Reading and Writing Project, Heinemann, ©2002 Teachers College, Columbia University; http://www.heinemann.com/fieldguides

Book Connections

The books in this series do not have to be read in a particular order. However, it makes sense to read *Madeline* first, followed by *Madeline's Rescue*. Other books in this series include *Madeline and the Bad Hat*, *Madeline and the Gypsies*, *Madeline's Christmas*, and *Madeline in America and Other Holiday Tales*.

Genre
Picture Book

Teaching Uses
Independent Reading; Character Study; Critique

A Field Guide to the Classroom Library, Lucy Calkins and the Teachers College Reading and Writing Project, Heinemann, ©2002 Teachers College, Columbia University; http://www.heinemann.com/fieldguides

Martha the Movie Mouse
Arnold Lobel

Book Summary

In this rhyming book, Martha the mouse is cold and hungry and lives in alleys eating garbage. One day she happens upon a movie house and inside finds a mouse paradise. There is popcorn, candy, movies, and best of all, a man, Dan, who befriends her. Martha is in heaven until one night a moviegoer hears her singing along with the movie and screams in fright. Martha feels unwanted and leaves. Eventually, however, the harsh conditions outside drive her back. Later, when Dan the projectionist is in trouble with a broken projector, Martha saves the day by entertaining the waiting audience with her singing and dancing. She is a great success and becomes very famous in addition to making Dan very thankful.

Basic Book Information

In this large, old-looking book, the text is separated into two columns. The pictures are not full color, but do have a certain drama in the line drawings.

Noteworthy Features

Teachers tend to appreciate the spunk of Martha, who bounces back with enthusiasm after stewing at first over her rejection. The mouse is a great example to us all. She leaves in a self-pitying sulk, and then comes back with energy and enough self-confidence to stand up in front the people who screamed at her and perform to help her friend. Some students don't read the book exactly this way, but instead see a mouse who comes back to show those people who thought she was just a dirty rat, and then becomes rich and famous.

Teaching Ideas

The layout of text in this book can cause confusion. The two-column format may need to be discussed with readers before they start the book.

Learning to read the rhythm in this book is perhaps its greatest challenge to most readers. Those who can't see the rhythm immediately should try reading it aloud for a few pages until they can feel it, and can hear where the stresses and rhymes should be. If reading aloud isn't working, a reading partner might help by reading to the reader so more than one ear is listening for the rhythm, and the listener isn't distracted by the decoding. If this doesn't help children get the rhythm of the book, the teacher could read a few pages aloud so children can hear the rhyme better.

It can be interesting to watch a reader try to read it and not notice the rhyme at first. How long does the reader go and what finally cues her into the pattern? Does the reader guess the pattern right away because of the

Illustrator
Arnold Lobel

Publisher
Harper Collins, 1966

ISBN
0064433188

TC Level
6

short lines of text? Does the reader go back and reread the first lines before becoming aware of the pattern?

Book Connections

If they are doing an Arnold Lobel author study, children may want to know that some of his other books to include are *Frog and Toad Are Friends*, *Frog and Toad Together*, *Frog and Toad All Year*, and *Days with Frog and Toad.* This book is substantially more difficult to read than those.

Genre
Picture Book

Teaching Uses
Independent Reading; Interpretation; Critique

A Field Guide to the Classroom Library, Lucy Calkins and the Teachers College Reading and Writing Project, Heinemann, ©2002 Teachers College, Columbia University; http://www.heinemann.com/fieldguides

Messy Bessy

Patricia McKissack; Fredrick McKissack

Book Summary

The story is told by a narrator who talks to the main character, an enterprising and spirited girl named Bessy. The book begins with an illustration of Bessy gleefully painting an elephant and the words, "Look at your room, Messy Bessy." Bessy sees paint on the walls, books on the chair, toys in the dresser drawer, and games everywhere. Then she sees gum on the ceiling and jam on the window! The narrator tells Messy Bessy to get the soap and water and soon she's mopped and scrubbed and shoved stuff in her closet so the room is clean.

Basic Book Information

This book is a *Rookie Reader*, part of a series published by Children's Press, a division of Grolier. It is one of many *Messy Bessy* books written on a range of levels. These books have all been written by Patricia and Fredrick McKissack, whose awards include the Coretta Scott King Award, the Jane Addams Peace Award, the Newbery Honor Award, and the Catholic Library Association's Regina Medal.

Noteworthy Features

In this day and age when many children play only video and computer games, it's refreshing to see that Bessy's bedroom and life spill over with projects of all sorts. She's painting an elephant that she later pins onto her wall. Her chair is filled with a towering pile of books, and her bureau seems to hold more stuffed animals than clothes. She's got toys everywhere: a robot, a model of the planets, a drum and a horn, a dinosaur puzzle, a few games, and a doll house.

There is just one line of print on most pages, but the book is more challenging than it might seem at first glance. Although there is a bit of repetition here, readers can in no way assume that being able to read one page will help them read the next. Even the repeated refrains vary often in ways that require readers to stay on their toes.

The sentences are long, often encompassing three pages. This text pushes readers toward fluency and phrasing in a way that is helpful. There is some rhyme that acts to support readers taking in bigger chunks of the text as they read.

The story can be thought of as having two parts. Pages 3 through 19 show the narrator urging Bessy to look closely at the mess in her room. On page 21, the narrator's voice changes: "So Bessy rubbed and scrubbed . . ." which tells of Bessy's actions in the past tense.

Series
Messy Bessy

Illustrator
Richard Hackney

Publisher
Children's Press, 1987

ISBN
0516270036

TC Level
4

Teaching Ideas

Children will read this book many times, doing different kinds of work each time. The first challenge will be to look over the text and the pictures in preparation for reading comprehension. The book opens with familiar sight words. Here, the text isn't supported by the pictures, but most children who can read a book at this level will recognize *look, at,* and *you* so the reader will be able to get started with the text.

One can anticipate that a reader might be stymied by the text saying, "See *colors* on the wall." A reader may expect the sentence to say, "See *paint* on the wall" or "See *hand prints* on the wall" but the reader should see from the print that neither alternative works. The phrase, "See gum on the *ceiling,*" may also pose difficulties. If a teacher wants to offer some help before the child reads, one option is to do a book-walk together and to mention the colors on the wall and the gum on the ceiling in a conversational way as we look at the pictures. *Busy* is another word that could use similar support. All of these sources of difficulty could simply be left for the child to tackle, and if the child is reading with 90 to 95 percent accuracy and with understanding, the child should have resources for tackling difficulty (and ultimately should be able to bypass it for a bit, if need be).

When a child reads this text, a teacher who observes can gain great insight. If for example, the student reads on page 18 "get the mope," the teacher will see the child using phonics and not meaning. To highlight meaning, the teacher will respond, "You said, 'Get the *mope.*' Does that make sense?" The teacher might also say, "Check the picture, what could it be?"

Another example would be if the child read on page 9, ". . . hat on the floor," the teacher might prompt the child. "You said, '. . . *hat* on the floor.' I'm glad that you made sense and that you looked at the picture, but do the letters look right?" The child will probably be able to correct the word *hat* to *coat.* In cases such as this, children are probably relying on the picture, not the print.

If a reader is encouraged to reread, thinking deeply about the text and expecting to grow ideas, the reader may: notice paint on the girl's overalls and on the closet walls; comment that the set-up of stuff in the room changes from one picture to the next ("On page 9, it almost looks like the turtle is playing checkers."); and wonder who is talking to Bessy.

Book Connections

It would be interesting to put this book alongside others that are similar. *Tidy Titch* would be a great comparison text, as would *Poppleton in Spring.*

Bessy can be contrasted with other characters as well. A contrast with Jamie Lee Curtis' character in her book, *When I Was Little,* would yield an interesting discussion about gender stereotyping.

Genre
Picture Book

A Field Guide to the Classroom Library, Lucy Calkins and the Teachers College Reading and Writing Project, Heinemann, ©2002 Teachers College, Columbia University; http://www.heinemann.com/fieldguides

Teaching Uses
Independent Reading; Language Conventions

A Field Guide to the Classroom Library, Lucy Calkins and the Teachers College Reading and Writing Project, Heinemann, ©2002 Teachers
College, Columbia University; http://www.heinemann.com/fieldguides

Miss Nelson is Missing!
Harry Allard

Book Summary

The sweet teacher, Miss Nelson, has a class that is misbehaving terribly. The next day Miss Swamp, an ugly teacher in an ugly black dress, shows up instead of Miss Nelson, orders the children around and gives them loads of homework. They don't even get a story read to them. The children miss Miss Nelson and go looking for her, but near her house they only see Miss Swamp. When Miss Nelson finally comes back the children don't misbehave at all. Back at home, Miss Nelson closes her ugly black dress into the closet and swears never to tell.

Basic Book Information

This 32-page book has at least one illustration on almost every page. Pages that contains text hold roughly three sentences each. Other titles in the Miss Nelson series include *Miss Nelson is Back* and *Miss Nelson has a Field Day*. James Marshall and Harry Allard have collaborated on many titles besides these, *The Stupids Step Out*, *I Will Not Go to Market Today*, and *The Tutti-Frutti Case*.

Noteworthy Features

Miss Nelson Is Missing! offers many supports for readers. Vocabulary is fairly simple. The pictures, too, provide support, in that they correspond very closely to the words they illustrate.

They provide a better match to the words than is usual in picture books, to the point that even without the words, a reader browsing the pictures could build a relatively accurate outline of the plot for him or herself

Many children catch on to the fact that Miss Nelson is Miss Swamp before the characters in the story catch on, which can be very empowering. It makes readers feel smart to have caught on to the joke or the trick in the story.

Teaching Ideas

Because this is a book which tends to catch on in a classroom, so that lots of children in the room read it within the space of a few weeks, many children come to the book already knowing a summary of the plot, or at least knowing that Miss Nelson and Miss Swamp are the same person. Clearly, this makes it a lot easier to read. In fact, it can make reading it almost like rereading it. This feature of the book makes it an excellent choice for teachers ready to emphasize and build on the social aspect of reading.

In teacher-student conferences, one good way to tell how well students understand this book is to listen for where they think Miss Nelson has gone.

Series
Miss Nelson books

Illustrator
James Marshall

Publisher
Houghton Mifflin Company, 1977

ISBN
0590118773

TC Level
7

A Field Guide to the Classroom Library, Lucy Calkins and the Teachers College Reading and Writing Project, Heinemann, ©2002 Teachers College, Columbia University; http://www.heinemann.com/fieldguides

Children who actually believe that Miss Nelson has left for Mars or been eaten by sharks - two of the scenarios that the kids in the story imagine as a fate for Miss Nelson -are confused, and either need to read easier books for a while or discuss *Miss Nelson is Missing!* with a partner in order to make more sense of it. Helping readers who are struggling with this book work through it is valuable because of its social power in the classroom.

Miss Nelson is Missing! raises many questions children can discuss. Some partnerships will talk about why the kids in the class behave badly and why, in general, nice people are often exploited. Some readers may talk about the ethics of Miss Nelson lying to her class.

Some teachers use this book as a read aloud to start discussions they feel the class needs to have before having a substitute teacher in the classroom.

Book Connections

Students who like *Miss Nelson is Missing!* may wish to read the other books in this series, *Miss Nelson is Back* and *Miss Nelson has a Field Day*. Those who enjoy guessing what has happened to Miss Nelson may wish to take on some of the chapter book mysteries at this level, such as the *Nate the Great* series.

Genre
Picture Book

Teaching Uses
Independent Reading; Partnerships; Critique

Miss Rumphius

Barbara Cooney

Book Summary

The narrator tells the story of her Aunt Alice. Alice once lived by the sea and worked with her grandfather, an artist. Alice hoped, like her grandfather, to go faraway places and then grow old by the sea. He told her that she must also do something to make the world more beautiful. Eventually, Alice did travel the world, and she did find a house by the sea, and she did something to make the world more beautiful: she planted bushels and bushels of lupines. Now the narrator, little Alice, says that she, too, will travel the world and grow old by the sea. Her Aunt Alice tells her that she must also do something to make the world more beautiful. And she will.

Basic Book Information

Miss Rumphius was written and illustrated by Barbara Cooney, who was the recipient of the American Book Award for this story.

Noteworthy Features

Although the book is generally straightforward for readers at this level, at the very beginning of the book, the text doesn't match the picture. The first paragraph of the book describes The Lupine Lady as an old, small lady who lives among the flowers in a house overlooking the sea. The picture, on the other hand, matches the next paragraph, in which Alice is a little girl living in the city overlooking the sea. This can be confusing or distracting to some children as they try to get oriented to the book; they see the place overlooking the sea, but at first none of the rest matches up.

Teaching Ideas

Teachers may want to study movement through time with their students. In the first paragraph, Miss Rumphius is introduced to the reader by her young great-niece. Then we are taken back to when Alice was a young girl. Students may want to discuss this for clarification before they begin independent reading.

There are "clues" mentioned throughout the book as to where Miss Rumphius travels abroad. Teachers may encourage students to use outside sources to decode where Miss Rumphius is located. For example, a tropical isle "where people kept cockatoos and monkeys as pets" or " Land of the Lotus Eaters" may be worth investigating.

This books falls into more than one genre. "Once upon a time" gives it a fairy tale feel, while the telling of the story could fall under memoir. Teachers may want to encourage students to think about stories that have been told and retold to them by family members, to share with their

Illustrator
Barbara Cooney

Publisher
Puffin, 1982

ISBN
0140505393

TC Level
8

partners or with the class, or to explore further during writing workshop.

This story also reads like a folk tale, with the message, "You must do something to make the world beautiful" at its beginning and end. This clear message will make it an easy book for students to use to find a theme, or to practice interpreting a text.

Students who take the message of this book to heart may end up starting a project to do their part to make the world a more beautiful place. Teachers can be on hand to support and encourage this important reading behavior. Good readers often let reading change lives and change behavior.

Book Connections

Barbara Cooney has written and/or illustrated many books including the Caldecott Award-winning *Ox-Cart Man*. Oftentimes, the books she has written or has illustrated have messages that embrace the cycle of life and encompass a long time period.

Genre
Picture Book

Teaching Uses
Independent Reading; Interpretation

Monkey See, Monkey Do
Marc Gave

Book Summary

Monkey See, Monkey Do is about a group of monkeys who "see" and then try to "do" things that the humans around them can do. For example, the monkeys "walk" and "run" to a picnic alongside their human friends, and they "bend" and "reach" with people doing exercises until they tire themselves out.

Basic Book Information

This is a thin, emergent literacy-type picture book. The illustrations are full color and the layout and book size are like the familiar I Can Read books.

Noteworthy Features

The text has large, generously spaced print. The word *monkey* or *monkeys* begins each sentence. Every other line rhymes (second and fourth line). The rhyme pattern helps children use known words to decode unknown words. Familiar sight words include *a, and, in, on,* and *the*. Humorous content and language may support readers in making sense of this text.

Some of the challenges in this book are inconsistent text placement, frequency of rhyming words and illustrations that do not always match the text.

Teaching Ideas

Teachers may want to explain the phrase "Monkey See, Monkey Do." Since this is a rhyming book, readers can use words they know to figure out unfamiliar words by changing the beginning letter or letters. Teachers may also want to model reading in a singsong or chant-like way to support fluency.

This text has several teaching uses. Some examples are the study of direction words and opposites, reading with fluency and expression and using rhymes and spelling patterns to decode words.

Genre
Picture Book

A Field Guide to the Classroom Library, Lucy Calkins and the Teachers College Reading and Writing Project, Heinemann, ©2002 Teachers College, Columbia University; http://www.heinemann.com/fieldguides

Publisher
Scholastic, 1993

ISBN
0590458019

TC Level
4

Teaching Uses
Independent Reading

Mouse Soup
Arnold Lobel

Book Summary

A weasel captures a mouse with the intention of making him into soup. In order to distract the weasel the mouse convinces him he must put stories in his soup, which the mouse proceeds to tell him. When the weasel goes out to collect ingredients from the mouse's stories, the mouse escapes.

Basic Book Information

This short book for early readers has the look of the Frog and Toad books.

Noteworthy Features

The story of the mouse's capture acts as a frame for the four stories he tells. The stories are set apart as separate chapters with headings.

The text is of varied length, the majority of which is dialogue. The color pictures illustrate the main action of each scene, which makes comprehension easier.

Teaching Ideas

This book is appropriate for readers familiar with dialogue, readers ready for books that include a table of contents and chapters, and readers learning to predict text from pictures.

One possible way to introduce the book is to say, "This is the story of a mouse who uses his imagination to get out of a dangerous situation." Children will be interested in the clever way the mouse tricks the weasel into letting him escape, a theme that is repeated in the first of the four stories the mouse tells.

In a conference, a teacher might ask a reader to identify the "moral" of the remaining three tales the mouse tells. The child will probably talk about the fact that all the stories tell different ways of turning something sad or frustrating into something positive. A child could also be asked to discuss the "moral" of the book as a whole. The child might say the moral is that the reason the mouse is able to save himself is because he reads books, and therefore had stories to tell the weasel.

Book Connections

If students are engaged in an Arnold Lobel author study, they might be glad to know some of his other books include *Frog and Toad Are Friends*, *Frog and Toad Together*, *Frog and Toad All Year* , and *Days with Frog and Toad*.

Illustrator
Arnold Lobel

Publisher
Harper Trophy, 1977

ISBN
0064440419

TC Level
6

Genre
Picture Book

Teaching Uses
Independent Reading; Partnerships

Mr. Popper's Penguins

Richard Atwater; Florence Atwater

Book Summary

Mr. Popper's Penguins is the comic story of a semi-employed house painter whose passion for Admiral Byrd's polar adventures leads him (and his surprised family) to become caretaker of, at first one, and thentwelve, mischievous penguins.

With the help of practical Mrs. Popper and their children, Janie and Bill, Mr. Popper ingeniously creates a proper polar home in the basement of their house. It isn't long before the financial strain of a large, fresh-fish-eating family leads the Poppers to a brief career on the stage, and to a solution that pleases everyone.

Basic Book Information

This Newbery Honor book has 132 pages and 20 numbered, titled chapters of between four and nine pages each.

Noteworthy Features

Mr. Popper's Penguins is a rare combination of humor, science, history and fantasy. Although the slapstick antics of the Poppers and their penguins are in the foreground of the story, a reader also gets a taste of the 1930s atmosphere, learns something about the explorer Admiral Byrd, and gets information on penguin diet and behavior.

Set in a small town during the 1930s when Admiral Richard Drake was exploring Antarctica, *Mr. Popper's Penguins* contains what might be unfamiliar vocabulary and settings (e.g., "Pullman" train and "vaudeville" stage shows), but its delightful wackiness should keep readers involved. Engagingly comic illustrations, chronological narration, and short chapters will be assets to less patient readers. In general, there are fewer reading challenges (in terms of vocabulary, structure and dialogue) than in other books in this grouping.

Teaching Ideas

Mr. Popper's Penguins makes a good read aloud, but is also appropriate for independent reading.

Mr. Popper's Penguins can accompany other nonfiction research on the 1930s, penguins and the Antarctic. This research may help with comprehension of the book. For example, if readers collect information on penguins, they can then discuss how Mr. Popper accommodated the penguins' needs.

Kids can work on interpreting the message of the story. Commonly, students decide one message is that with enough enthusiasm, one can

A Field Guide to the Classroom Library, Lucy Calkins and the Teachers College Reading and Writing Project, Heinemann, ©2002 Teachers College, Columbia University; http://www.heinemann.com/fieldguides

Publisher
Little Brown, 1938

ISBN
0590477331

TC Level
12

accomplish nearly anything. Mr. Popper's eccentricity and passion, while bringing strange looks from the plumber, are assets to himself, his family and the penguins. Other readers decide on different messages, for instance, that odd people learn more. As long as kids are supporting their interpretations with textual evidence all of the messages they point to are fair game, and should generate lively discussion.

The characters of Mr. and Mrs. Popper are well drawn. Mr. Popper remains an irrepressible dreamer while Mrs. Popper is an utterly down-to-earth woman who ends up sharing Mr. Popper's love of the penguins. Students may want to study these characters and come to these conclusions about Mr. and Mrs. Popper's natures. Some students even do little character studies about the individual penguins!

Genre
Chapter Book; Fantasy; Historical Fiction

Teaching Uses
Read Aloud; Independent Reading; Character Study; Content Area Study

Mrs. Wishy-Washy

Joy Cowley

Book Summary

This book is an extended version of the simpler text, *Mrs. Wishy-Washy's Tub*, also by Joy Cowley. The cow, the pig, and the duck all play in the mud. Mrs. Wishy-Washy finds them, puts each in the tub and scrubs them down. Satisfied that they are now clean, she leads them into the yard and heads inside. No sooner is she gone then the three animals head back for the puddle and the lovely mud.

Basic Book Information

This is one of the Story Box books, and is written by Joy Cowley, the beloved author of countless books for early readers. As a Story Box book, this book looks like it belongs in a kit of identical little books but in this library it is interspersed with a lovely variety of shapes and sizes of books. The Wright Company provides professional development as well as books for teachers, and has been a major force in supporting the move toward literature-based classrooms. The company uses its knowledge of reading development to publish texts that are supportive of early readers.

There are fifteen pages of text in this story. The sentences are short-most contain only four or five words. The repeating patterns of some of the sentences make reading easier. The syntax is varied, with a number of the sentences in reverse order, that is, predicate/subject. Elizabeth Fuller's cartoon-like illustrations portray the action well, making word recognition easier for the young reader.

The layout has features that put this text at a higher difficulty level than the introductory books from Wright Group. The text is located inside the lines that frame the picture, and placement varies. Sometimes it appears at the top of the page, other times at the bottom. On one page, the sentence begins at the top and continues underneath the illustration. On a couple of other pages, the sentence begins on the left-hand page and continues onto the right-hand one. In these cases, the sentence is a compound one, the division coming before the conjunction "and."

There are thirty-six different words in this story, a fact that also increases the difficulty level of the book. The plot sequence is a simple problem/resolution with a circular structure-at the end, the animals wind up where they began, making a humorous ending that is enjoyable for beginning readers.

Noteworthy Features

The third person narration, with sentence patterns that provide practice in less common sentence structure, introduces students to more varied text. Clues in the pictures encourage inferring-the expressions on the faces of the

A Field Guide to the Classroom Library, Lucy Calkins and the Teachers College Reading and Writing Project, Heinemann, ©2002 Teachers College, Columbia University; http://www.heinemann.com/fieldguides

Illustrator
Elizabeth Fuller

Publisher
Wright Group, 1998

ISBN
0399233911

TC Level
5

characters, as well as their movements, add to the humor of the story. There is some dialogue in the form of comments made by Mrs. Wishy-Washy, rather than conversation. The vocabulary Cowley uses is made up of common words that will be familiar to some young readers.

Teaching Ideas

If students have read the simpler version of this story, *Mrs. Wishy-Washy's Tub*, teachers might introduce this book by comparing the two, and asking for someone to recall the simpler version. If this book is their first encounter with Mrs. Wishy-Washy, teachers might introduce the book by giving the title and asking them why they think she might have a name like that, and to predict from the cover and title page what Mrs. Wishy-Washy may be getting ready to do.

Teachers might do a very brief walk-through of the book, discussing a few of the illustrations with students. Because the story has a humorous, unexpected ending, teachers may want to save the last page for children to discover in their independent reading. Students can discuss the illustrations, particularly the expressions on the characters' faces and their gestures, to infer how they are feeling. A teacher might even follow this discussion with a variation of a shared reading. The teacher might first read each page aloud alone, while pointing to the words, and then students might chime in together as the teacher and the class reread the page together.

Teachers might discuss the repeated pattern of some of the sentences with a single word change. They might remind students that they could use the illustrations and the letter sounds in a new word to unlock the word. The cow, for example, is jumping in the picture; the pig is rolling. The letters "j" and "r," together with the pictures, help in the decoding. Teachers may want to coach the reader to reread when encountering difficulty in decoding, to cross-check the pictures for help, and to self-correct when necessary. The teacher can also encourage readers to get into the habit of monitoring for meaning.

Teachers might want to discuss features of punctuation and what the various marks signal. Commas, for example, signal a pause in reading. Quotation marks signal words said aloud. The larger print used for the word "LOOK" signals this word was said louder. A hyphen joining two words signals that these two words are read as one word.

Teachers might use this story to discuss the past-tense verb ending *-ed* in the words *jumped*, *rolled*, and *screamed*. *Paddled* might also be used as an example, although the teacher can explain that since the "e" is already there, we don't need to add another one. The words *said* and *went*, while past tense as well, are irregular and should not be included in that discussion.

There are a number of activities teachers may use to review this book. They may ask students to retell the story and discuss why they enjoyed it. Teachers might then want to contrast the book with an informational book on farm animals, discussing actions in this book that ordinarily do not happen in real life. For example, in real life, animals do not get washed in a tub. Students should realize that nonsense stories like this one are written to amuse and entertain, rather than to inform.

A Field Guide to the Classroom Library, Lucy Calkins and the Teachers College Reading and Writing Project, Heinemann, ©2002 Teachers College, Columbia University; http://www.heinemann.com/fieldguides

Book Connections

If students enjoy this book, they will find Joy Cowley's *Splishy-Sploshy* equally amusing. They may also enjoy another wonderful washing story, *Tiny's Bath* by Cari Meisler (Puffin, 1988).

Genre

Emergent Literacy Book

Teaching Uses

Partnerships; Small Group Strategy Instruction; Language Conventions; Independent Reading; Interpretation; Read Aloud

Nicky Upstairs and Down

Harriet Zeifert

FIELD GUIDE

Ⓑ Ⓒ

Book Summary

Nicky is a cat who plays in the basement and upstairs of his house. Every time his mother calls for him, he runs up or down the stairs. When his mother calls for him, he hides underneath the sink. Finally, he comes out of hiding and runs halfway up the stairs. Nicky triumphantly tells his mother, "I'm not upstairs! I'm not downstairs! I'm right in the middle."

Basic Book Information

This is a picture book with cute illustrations that are particularly loved by cat-owners.

Noteworthy Features

It is noteworthy that *Nicky Upstairs and Down* contains many wrap-around sentences. In addition, there are some sentences that continue across two different pages (you must turn the page for the continuation). The punctuation in *Nicky Upstairs and Down* is quite sophisticated and includes quotation marks, commas, exclamation points, and ellipses.

The illustrations in the book do not fully support the text. For instance, on one page it says, "Nicky's house has a downstairs." The corresponding illustration shows Nicky lounging on a chair in his living room.

Teaching Ideas

Nicky Upstairs and Down contains wrap-around sentences. Teachers may need to work with readers on following one idea across two lines. Even more challenging, are the sentences that are continued over the course of two pages. It is essential that students retain the initial idea of the sentence as they turn the page.

One of the ways that this book indicates a continuation on the following page is through the use of ellipses. If appropriate, ellipses may be something that a teacher decides to focus on during their teaching points (in a guided reading session) or reading mini-lesson.

Nicky Upstairs and Down contains a number of compound words, such as *upstairs, downstairs,* and *everywhere.* For readers who are still working on one-to-one matching, it is important for teachers to ensure that children are pointing only once under these compound words. For children for whom these words are somewhat unfamiliar, chunking may be a powerful strategy. Children feel like empowered readers when they discover that if they know the words *up* and *stairs,* then they also know they word *upstairs.*

This book elicits much discussion around different themes in whole class readings, partnerships, or independent work. Children may relate to the fact

Illustrator
Richard Brown

Publisher
Penguin Group, 1987

ISBN
0140368523

TC Level
4

A Field Guide to the Classroom Library, Lucy Calkins and the Teachers College Reading and Writing Project, Heinemann, ©2002 Teachers College, Columbia University; http://www.heinemann.com/fieldguides

that Nicky's mother always needs to know where he is. Young readers might want to speculate about why Nicky's mother is always asking, "Nicky, where are you?" Another point of discussion might be centered around Nicky's response. Children might also envision alternative solutions to Nicky's.

Another teaching option might be to compare animal characters in various books that talk and act like people against those that don't.

Genre
Picture Book

Teaching Uses
Independent Reading; Language Conventions

A Field Guide to the Classroom Library, Lucy Calkins and the Teachers College Reading and Writing Project, Heinemann, ©2002 Teachers College, Columbia University; http://www.heinemann.com/fieldguides

Oliver
Syd Hoff

Book Summary

Oliver, an elephant, travels with ten other elephants across the sea to work in a circus. When they arrive, the circus man claims he ordered only ten elephants, so Oliver continues looking for work. He tries a zoo, but it already has enough elephants. He tries - and fails -to be a family pet. He tries to ride people like a horse but that doesn't work out either. Then he plays with children in a playground, showing he can be a dancing elephant. The circus parade comes down the street but no one notices. They are all watching Oliver dance. The circus man realizes he can use Oliver in the circus after all. Oliver goes off to the circus but promises never to forget the children.

Basic Book Information

This is a short chapter book, though it doesn't technically have chapters. It is somewhat longer than many others on this level.

Noteworthy Features

This narrative is told in the third person with simply structured sentences. The passage of time is implied, rather than indicated through transitional phrases that would make it more explicit. Some simple inferences are required - the taxi driver tells Oliver "you need a moving van," implying that he is too big for the taxi. When the children say, "Don't forget us," Oliver says, "Of course not, elephants never forget. And even a rhinoceros would remember the fun we had." This is meant to be a joke but some readers may not understand. Vocabulary is simple with a few words, such as *type* or *weigh*, which may be unfamiliar to some readers. The story contains a good deal of dialogue, which is referenced, though the speaker is sometimes identified at the end, and sometimes in the middle of the dialogue, rather than at the beginning.

Teaching Ideas

A teacher will want to look over the books in his or her classroom, anticipating the challenges they may pose for readers and planning ways to translate these challenges into learning opportunities. As children begin to read longer books like *Oliver*, one of the challenges for them is to avoid "tunnel vision." Sometimes at this transitional stage, readers crawl through books with their noses close to the print, saying each word in its turn but not accumulating the words into sentences, let alone into a coherent story. Children will have learned about the importance of chunking letters into rhymes in shared reading and word work. They're likely to know that it's easier to read r-i-n-g if one sees *ing* as a unit. The ability to do so "on the run" while reading will improve children's fluency, allowing them to focus their attention on making meaning.

It's helpful for children to know that when they read a book like this, they can also chunk bigger portions of the text, noticing how some of the pages go together as a unit. A teacher could set it up for children to do this sort of chunking by introducing the book by saying, "This is *almost* a chapter book. If it *did* have chapters, I think pages 7-14 would be Chapter One and it would be named 'Oliver's Problem.' You could read to learn about his problem. A lot of stories tell you the problem right up front, and this is one of them. Then, the next chapter might be pages 15-40, and it would be named 'Oliver Keeps Trying.' The next big chunk would be Chapter 3, pages 41-64, and it might be called, 'Things Get Better.'" Instead of *telling* these divisions to a reader, a teacher might ask children to read with a Post-It and that idea in mind saying, "If *you* were to divide this story into chunks like chapters, how would they go? Mark what seems like the beginning of a new chapter with your Post-it and be ready to explain your thinking."

To help young readers stay in this, or any other book, longer for the purpose of deepening their comprehension, teachers could support children in asking questions about the text. After modeling with read alouds, he or she might invite readers to jot their own questions on Post-Its as they read and come together with a partner before or after reading to talk over their questions. In *Oliver*, for example, students may question why most people in the book don't appear surprised to see Oliver walking around on the street. Or, they might notice that Oliver is the only *named* character in the book - everyone else is "the lady" or "the man." What could be the reason the author did this? Or that the girls and women in this book all wear skirts or dresses. Is this true in Hoff's other books?

Book Connections

Other Syd Hoff books include *Sammy the Seal*.

Genre
Short Chapter Book

Teaching Uses
Independent Reading; Interpretation; Small Group Strategy Instruction

A Field Guide to the Classroom Library, Lucy Calkins and the Teachers College Reading and Writing Project, Heinemann, ©2002 Teachers College, Columbia University; http://www.heinemann.com/fieldguides

"Pardon?" said the Giraffe

Colin West

Book Summary

The little frog in this story is trying hard to ask the giraffe, "What's it like up there?" The giraffe is so tall he cannot hear the frog. Therefore the giraffe keeps asking "Pardon?" as the frog hops up on bigger and bigger animals to reach the giraffe. The frog finally hops onto the giraffe's nose. This tickles the giraffe and he sneezes, sending the frog down to the ground. The giraffe ends the story by asking the frog, "What's it like down there?"

Basic Book Information

This is a trade book by a well-known children's author. It is not part of a series as many other early readers are. The book contains 123 words over 17 pages. There is a repetitive pattern in the conversation between the frog and the giraffe that will provide some support to the reader.

Noteworthy Features

The title does not help a reader know what will happen in the book. The repetitive pattern will help the reader once the reader recognizes it. The pattern also lends itself to the teaching of fluency and phrasing.

Teaching Ideas

If a teacher chooses to provide an introduction to this book for a reader or partnership, she might say, "In this book the frog is trying to ask the giraffe 'What's it like up there?' but the giraffe cannot hear him so he says, 'Pardon?' Do you know what pardon means?" Once the readers know it's another way to say excuse me, the teacher can suggest they read to find out what happens as the frog hops higher and higher.

When the frog finally reaches the giraffe's nose the pattern changes and this page may be a challenge for the reader. In a conference, the teacher might prompt the child to search the picture for the meaning while also searching the print to see if there are words, or word-chunks, the child knows. This orchestration of meaning and visual cues will need to be modeled, prompted and/or practiced many times before it becomes automatic for the early reader.

Genre
Picture Book

Publisher
Harper and Row, 1986

ISBN
0397321732

TC Level
4

Teaching Uses
Independent Reading

A Field Guide to the Classroom Library, Lucy Calkins and the Teachers College Reading and Writing Project, Heinemann, ©2002 Teachers
College, Columbia University; http://www.heinemann.com/fieldguides

Peter's Chair

Ezra Jack Keats

Book Summary

Peter has a new baby sister, and things have changed. He has to play more quietly, and his parents are using all of his old things for her. His high chair is getting painted pink, like the crib and the cradle. He finds his old chair and decides to run away with it. When he tries to sit in it, though, he realizes it is too small. By the time mother calls him inside for a special lunch and a hiding game, Peter feels differently. As he sits in the adult chair around the table, he asks his father if they can paint the little chair pink for his sister Suzie.

Basic Book Information

Caldecott award-winning author and illustrator Ezra Jack Keats offers this picture book, illustrated in his usual collage format, set in a city with the character of young Peter and his small dog Willie, both of whom are featured in many of his other stories. This picture book has about thirty pages. On each double-page spread, there are from one to five lines of print, always on only one of the pages. There is some dialogue, all of which is referenced with a "speaker tag." The book is not based on patterns or repetition, but is instead a story told in chronological order of one afternoon in Peter's life.

Noteworthy Features

As in many of Keats' books, in order to understand the full story, the reader will need to examine the pictures closely. Sometimes the text refers to events described in the illustrations, as when Peter's mother thinks she has found Peter, but it is only his shoes he has placed at the foot of the curtains.

This story begins in the middle of the action. While some readers find this type of opening to be a great hook because it draws them into the book, others find it disconcerting because they begin reading without knowing who, what, where, why, and when.

Teaching Ideas

The primary instructional purpose of *Peter's Chair* in Library A, is as a read aloud. This instruction is based on the research of Elizabeth Sulzby, whose work with kindergarten children informed her of the importance of recreating parent-child interactions around books in the kindergarten classroom. At home, children often ask parents to "read it again" when they hear a favorite story. In school, the teacher's multiple readings of emergent literacy books helps children become familiar with rich narrative, hear the inflection and pacing of storybook language and learn to use detailed

Illustrator
Ezra Jack Keats

Publisher
Penguin, Puffin, 1967

ISBN
0140564411

TC Level
6

illustrations to assist them in remembering storyline.

After the story has been read to children at least four times, multiple copies of the book should be added to a basket of "Stories We Love." Children will have opportunities to return to these books at independent reading time. They will refer to the pictures and use their memory of the teacher's reading to recreate the story on their own. Given the opportunity to do this, children pass through a series of predictable reading stages from simply "labeling" pictures on the page, to telling the story off the pictures, to using progressively more dialogue and storybook language, and then moving toward a more "conventional" reading where they use the print. To go on this journey, it is important for children to hear the story read aloud many times, have a lot of opportunities to reread it to a partner and have a supportive teacher nearby who thoughtfully coaches into their reading.

To support this process, teachers can select books that contain more text than emergent readers could decode on their own, that can not be easily memorized, that have elements of drama and suspense, and that have characters that many young children can relate to.

After children have heard *Peter's Chair* and *The Snowy Day*, teachers might want to create an Ezra Jack Keats reading basket. This would be a good time to also introduce *Whistle for Willie*, another book with Peter as the main character. A few of the books together would make excellent material for a character study of Peter. In each of the books, including this one, Peter has some unvoiced, and unexplained, emotions and conflicts that he works through by the end of each book. Readers sometimes like to put these events together to show how Peter has grown. Readers also sometimes like to put the books in chronological order as best they can, based on the kinds of things Peter is doing in his life in each book. In which books does he have his dog Willie? In which books doesn't he? Clues of this sort add to the puzzle of the correct order for the stories.

In classrooms with older children, this book can serve other purposes. Because there are so many similarities between Keats' books-recurring characters and settings, style of illustration and their interdependence with the text and the story structure-he makes a great author to study and this book makes a good addition to such a study. Through read aloud, partner and independent reading, or even in a reading center, readers can build collective knowledge about Keats and his style. What tends to be similar about his books? How is each unique? What can we say about his writing style? His choice of language and setting?

A few of his books together would also make an excellent character study of Peter. In each of the books, including this one, Peter has unvoiced, unexplained emotions and conflicts he works through by the end of the book. Readers sometimes like to put these events together to show how Peter has grown. Readers sometimes put the books in a chronological order as best they can, based on the kinds of things Peter is doing in each book. In which books does he have his dog Willy? In which books doesn't he? Clues of this sort add to the puzzle of the correct order for the stories.

Since the books never explicitly state how Peter is feeling or why, readers need to infer these emotions based on Peter's behavior and their own personal experience. This book is good to read aloud, even in the upper grades. It helps students build their ability to infer and to understand books based on their own experience. Since nearly everyone has experienced a

A Field Guide to the Classroom Library, Lucy Calkins and the Teachers College Reading and Writing Project, Heinemann, ©2002 Teachers College, Columbia University; http://www.heinemann.com/fieldguides

reluctance to share or a discomfort with change, many readers in a class should be able to bring their personal experiences to this story.

It's helpful for readers to look for places in a story when a character really changes. Why does the character change? In this case, why does Peter suddenly feel okay about letting his baby sister have the chair? At first, many readers say it is because the chair no longer fits him, but with further discussion, they come to a deeper understanding of Peter's changing feelings about himself and his role in his family. This type of discussion, both with the whole class and between partners, can teach children to ask these questions when they read on their own.

Book Connections

Ezra Jack Keats has written many great books for children, including *The Snowy Day*, *A Letter to Amy*, and *Whistle for Willie*.

Genre
Picture Book

Teaching Uses
Author Study; Interpretation; Small Group Strategy Instruction; Language Conventions; Character Study; Read Aloud; Independent Reading; Partnerships

Pippi Longstocking
Astrid Lindgren

Book Summary

Fearless and pigtailed, Pippi Longstocking moves next door to Annika and Tommy, and proceeds to demonstrate how charming life can be when you have the right attitude. Only nine years old and an orphan, she is strong as an ox and a whiz at making pancakes. *Pippi Longstocking* is an outrageous tall tale with a daring, oddball heroine. Pippi is many of the things younger readers, particularly girls, wish to be but aren't allowed to be. She gets to be entirely free of grown-ups and other adults (such as schoolteachers), free of bedtimes and set mealtimes, free of homework, heedless of manners, free even of having to be truthful. In addition, she never suffers from loneliness or fear, or from other problems that come to normal children when their parents are absent. Unlike more conventional young heroines, Pippi fights and subdues bad guys, entertains by being disruptive, is not cowed by criticism, always says what she means, and constantly draws attention to herself.

Basic Book Information

Lindgren has written over 80 books and has received many awards for her work, including the Lewis Carroll Shelf Award for *Pippi Longstocking* in 1973; the Hans Christian Andersen Award in 1958; and the International Book Award from UNESCO in 1993. There are many other *Pippi* books that follow this one, including *Pippi Goes on Board* and *Pippi in the South Seas.*

Noteworthy Features

The funny, eventful plot of *Pippi Longstocking* consists of episodic adventures. Dialogue is clear and interesting. The small Swedish village where the book takes place does not get much emphasis, as Pippi's activities take center stage.

Teaching Ideas

A comparison study of Pippi and different sorts of female heroines might yield interesting insights. How does Pippi differ from Amber Brown or Ramona Quimby, and how is she the same? Clearly, Pippi Longstocking has quasi-magical powers that these realistic characters lack, but readers can look for more subtle aspects, such as the difference between how Pippi's and the others' outrageous behavior is received. A comparison between Pippi and another fantastic heroine, such as Roald Dahl's Matilda, would reveal more similarities, but the heroines still have sizeable differences. Readers can examine how they deal with their foes (Pippi is direct, while Matilda is secretive) and think about why that is. Who approves of these heroines, and

Publisher
Viking Press, 1950

ISBN
0140309578

TC Level
11

who disapproves of them? What do these heroines want in the end? Older readers might want to consider what the various books say about how girls (or children in general) should act.

Another area to look into is Pippi's love of storytelling. As shown in the coffee party chapter, Pippi can't *stop* telling stories. Part of what makes Pippi's stories so compelling and funny is the uncertainty of whether she is lying or not. What do the students think? Teachers may direct students to consider-is she lying or telling the truth about her amazing life? Why would she lie?

Book Connections

Ramona and Her Mother is part of a series about Ramona Quimby, written by Beverly Cleary. The *Amber Brown* books by Paula Danziger and Judy Blume's *Fudge* series both feature girl heroines.

Genre
Chapter Book

Teaching Uses
Read Aloud

Poppleton

Cynthia Rylant

Book Summary

Poppleton is the first book in a series about a pig and his friends. There are three separate, yet connected, stories in the book. In the first story, "Neighbors," Poppleton the pig moves from the city to the country. He thoroughly enjoys his new life, which includes napping in the sunroom, planting in the garden and sharing meals with his new neighbor, Cherry Sue (a goat). When Poppleton begins to tire of eating every meal with Cherry Sue, they discover that they both want to be alone sometimes, but have been afraid to hurt one another's feelings by saying so. After their talk, they become even better friends. In the second story, "Library Day," the reader learns about Poppleton's passion for spending Mondays at the library reading his favorite books. Poppleton follows the same routine, brings the same reading "tools" (such as a tissue, in case there is a sad part in the book he's reading), and buries his head in a good adventure for the day. In the third story, "The Pill," Poppleton cares for his sick friend Fillmore (another goat), who refuses to take his medicine until Poppleton hides it in a piece of Cherry Sue's heavenly cake. Fillmore proceeds to eat the whole cake to "find the pill." When Fillmore says he still needs a whole *other* cake to get his pill down, Poppleton decides to become sick too! The two friends spend the next few days in bed together and "polish off" 27 cakes.

Basic Book Information

Poppleton is the first in a series of books about Poppleton and his friends. The book is 48 pages long and separated into three stories listed in a table of contents. The stories stand alone and can be read separately or as part of a larger story. Every page is illustrated.

This wonderful series does not have to be read in any particular order, but students should read several *Poppleton* books because the characters reveal themselves across the series. Readers will come to know Poppleton so well that they'll find themselves smiling when he returns to old antics we've seen in earlier books.

The *Poppleton* series has a great deal in common with *Frog and Toad* because both series tell of friendships that endure ups and downs, which result from the differences between the friends. The *Poppleton* series should be read after readers have experienced *Henry and Mudge* and *Mr. Putter and Tabby* (also written by Cynthia Rylant), as *Poppleton* is more complex. Over the course of the series we get to know not only Poppleton but also his friends Hudson, Cherry Sue, Marsha, Gus and Fillmore.

Noteworthy Features

The text of *Poppleton* is simply written but hilarious and heart-warming.

Series
Poppleton books

Illustrator
Mark Teague

Publisher
Scholastic, 1997

ISBN
059084783X

TC Level
7

A Field Guide to the Classroom Library, Lucy Calkins and the Teachers College Reading and Writing Project, Heinemann, ©2002 Teachers College, Columbia University; http://www.heinemann.com/fieldguides

Most of the humor is readily accessible to the early reader, but some of the more subtle humor (e.g., when Poppleton reads, he holds "lip balm for a dry part") may go unnoticed.

Most of the story lines are simple and easily understood. There are some sections, however, in which the young reader will have to infer the motivation behind a character's actions, for motivations are not explicitly written into the text. Young readers may have trouble understanding that Poppleton soaks Cherry Sue with a hose because he is frustrated that she once again wants to eat with him, or that Fillmore refuses to hear in *which* piece of cake his pill is hidden in so that he will have an excuse to eat as much cake as possible.

This book, like the others in the series, is episodic, meaning each chapter stands on its own; young readers need not remember a continuous plot for the entire book. Each chapter has a supportive title. The illustrations support some part of the text on each page. Pages have anywhere from two to five sentences of text. There is dialogue throughout the book, all of which is referenced at the beginning or end of the sentence.

Teaching Ideas

Because this is the first book in a wonderful series, teachers will probably want to do some small group work to support children as they read it, setting the stage for them to read the remaining books more independently. In a book introduction, a teacher might say, "This is a book about Poppleton. Poppleton is a pig who loves naps, gardening, reading books at the library and chocolate cake. He has just moved from the city to the country and is becoming friends with his new neighbors, Cherry Sue and Fillmore. Just like when we make new friends, Poppleton doesn't always know what to say or how to act."

The straightforward humor is a great topic for discussion in read aloud and partnerships. For example, when Poppleton soaks *himself* with the hose to apologize for soaking Cherry Sue, the teacher and students can all have a good laugh and talk about why that's funny. The more subtly humorous parts can be discussed at greater length. For example, a teacher may say, "It's funny, but a little surprising, when Poppleton soaks Cherry Sue with the hose after she invites him over for lunch. Cherry Sue is being nice. Why is Poppleton acting like that? How do we know?" This discussion may inform children trying to write humor, and it may also give them new ways to think and talk about humor in their own, independent reading.

Poppleton presents several opportunities for readers to make some personal connection to the characters. Their experiences are not especially deep, but they do mirror the lives of children enough for some discussion. For example, in the story called "Library Day," Poppleton is totally committed to and invested in his love of books. A teacher may say to young readers, "I know exactly how Poppleton feels when he packs the same things each time he goes to the library. Every time I sit down to read my favorite book, I have my favorite bookmark in my hand and I always drink a cup of tea."

A Field Guide to the Classroom Library, Lucy Calkins and the Teachers College Reading and Writing Project, Heinemann, ©2002 Teachers College, Columbia University; http://www.heinemann.com/fieldguides

Book Connections

Other titles in the Poppleton series include *Poppleton and Friends* and *Poppleton Forever*. Cynthia Rylant's *Henry and Mudge* and *Mr. Putter and Tabby* series are comparably difficult. Arnold Lobel's *Frog and Toad* books touch on similar themes of friendship.

Genre
Short Chapter Book

Teaching Uses
Independent Reading; Character Study; Partnerships; Small Group Strategy Instruction; Critique

Poppleton in Spring
Cynthia Rylant

Book Summary

Poppleton in Spring is a collection of stories about Poppleton the pig and his animal friends doing springtime activities. Poppleton decides to have a spring-cleaning. He can't bring himself to throw out things like unmatched socks, old buttons and rocks, so he brings them to his neighbor and friend, Cherry Sue, who also happens to be cleaning. In the end, Cherry Sue ends up with a clean attic and Poppleton ends up with a house overflowing with things. Then Poppleton goes to buy a new red bike from his friend, Marsha. He gets overwhelmed by too many choices and can't make a decision. In the final story, Poppleton buys a new tent in order to sleep outside. All his friends, except Cherry Sue, think he is silly, and Gus thinks that Poppleton will catch pneumonia. But Poppleton doesn't care what they think because he read some good books by flashlight and he paid attention. . . and saw a new flower open up that night.

Basic Book Information

Poppleton in Spring is the fifth book in the *Poppleton* series. It is 48 pages long. There are lively pictures on every page, most matching the text. Occasionally the text and illustrations do not match. On page 46, the text says, "Then Poppleton went back inside, and closed his blinds and slept in his bed all day," but nowhere in the picture are blinds shown. Also, on page 27, the text reads, " 'Red,' croaked Poppleton." The picture shows Poppleton looking very sad. Children may not be able to figure out what croaked means and it is repeated three times.

This wonderful series doesn't have to be read in any particular order, but it is good for students to read many of the books in the series because Poppleton's character reveals itself across the series. Readers will come to know Poppleton so well that they'll find themselves smiling when he returns to old antics they've seen in earlier books. "There he goes again," they might say.

The *Poppleton* series has a great deal in common with Lobel's *Frog and Toad*-both series tell of a friendship that endures ups and downs that occur because of the differences between the friends. As Poppleton is more complex, the *Poppleton* series should be read after readers have experienced *Henry and Mudge* and *Mr. Putter and Tabby* (also written by Cynthia Rylant). Over the course of the series readers get to know not only Poppleton but also his friends Hudson, Cherry Sue, Marsha, Gus and Fillmore.

The books in this series are episodic chapter books that make it easier for young readers to hold on to the plot because each chapter stands on its own.

Series
Poppleton

Illustrator
Mark Teague

Publisher
Scholastic, 1999

ISBN
0590848224

TC Level
7

A Field Guide to the Classroom Library, Lucy Calkins and the Teachers College Reading and Writing Project, Heinemann, ©2002 Teachers College, Columbia University; http://www.heinemann.com/fieldguides

Readers don't have to hold onto one plot line that unfolds slowly over the course of the book. Each chapter has a supportive title.

Noteworthy Features

This book is in many ways characteristic of Rylant's writing. She uses lots of lists and her books often have echoes, with early events reoccurring in later parts. The first list in this book comes when Poppleton looks at all his things. "Things and things" Rylant writes. Then she says, "There was a box of unmatched socks. There were jars of old buttons. One whole shelf was full of rocks." One of the first patterns in the book begins on page 13, when Poppleton, after spring-cleaning his junk, eyes Cherry Sue's yarn. "May I have it?" Poppleton asks, and Cherry Sue-who is also spring-cleaning-says, "Of course." Next Poppleton sees her thumbtacks, then her shoelaces, and each time he asks, "May I have it?" and each time Cherry Sue says, "Of course."

In this book, new friends of Poppleton are introduced: Marsha, who works at the bicycle store, and Gus, the mail carrier. The reader can't help but notice that everywhere Poppleton goes, he deals with friends-his friend the librarian, his friend the bike store sales clerk, his friend the mail carrier.

Each episode is set in Poppleton's familiar neighborhood and the cover of the book shows a map of this small town. Neither the bike store nor Poppleton's house are shown on the map, although the library is there, as are both Poppleton and Cherry Sue.

A third-person, omniscient narrator describes each character's actions and feelings. For example, on page 10, the narrator says that Cherry Sue "couldn't hurt Poppleton's feelings," and on page 15, Cherry Sue "was so nice."

Teaching Ideas

In *Poppleton in Spring*, Poppleton the pig has three different experiences: he and Cherry Sue decide to do some spring cleaning, he goes to buy a new red bike; and he sleeps out in his back yard in a tent to "pay attention" to spring.

There is much more dialogue in this series than in *Henry and Mudge* and *Mr. Putter and Tabby*. Occasionally the dialogue reference is embedded in the text and not at the ends of lines. This will probably be new for readers at this level. The dialogue is also more difficult because pronouns, rather than proper names, are used to identify who is speaking. There is some vocabulary that might challenge readers. *Attic* might be difficult for urban students, while many readers will have difficulty with *croaked*, *blinds*, and *pneumonia*.

The humor is also a source of some challenge for readers. Many students may not "get" the section that starts on page 13, when Poppleton covets Cherry Sue's yarn, her thumbtacks and her shoelaces, all of which she never uses. It helps to clue readers into the humor as they read by telling them that Poppleton is funny, and suggesting they be on the lookout for humor as they read. Still other readers will need more scaffolding. Some teachers have found it helps to simply have them put a Post-it note on pages 13 to 16

A Field Guide to the Classroom Library, Lucy Calkins and the Teachers College Reading and Writing Project, Heinemann, ©2002 Teachers College, Columbia University; http://www.heinemann.com/fieldguides

labeled "funny." When conferring with individual readers, teachers will often ask students what was so funny about these pages. Students can then find and put Post-its on other parts that are funny in this book or books in the series.

Poppleton is a rich character who doesn't change greatly in any one book, but is revealed in the way he handles everyday situations. Some students jot down what they learn about Poppleton and notice when Poppleton acts in characteristic ways across several stories. In *Poppleton*, he gets more and more frustrated over Cherry Sue's invitations to eat every meal together, and finally explodes, dousing her with water. In *Poppleton in Spring*, his frustrations grow when he is in the bike shop, and he finally explodes, running out of the shop in a fit. In *Poppleton*, Poppleton's love of books is evident, and this again is the theme in one of the chapters in *Poppleton in Spring*.

Poppleton in Spring is a great book for working with students on phrasing and fluency, as well as reading dialogue. A teacher might gather students together for a small strategy lesson. One teacher pointed out that the narrator sounds like he or she is talking to the reader. "We're going to read pages 5, 6 and 7 aloud to ourselves. Listen to yourself and make it sound like a story is being told," she said. "First, let's look on pages 6 and 7. There are words that repeat themselves here. Our eyes can pick up on that quickly." Each student then read aloud side-by-side (but not in unison; their starting times were staggered a bit to keep them out of sync with each other). The teacher listened in for students who needed coaching. One teacher said to a reader, "Put your words closer together, read faster, faster." Another asked a child to remove her finger, as it was slowing her down.

After a bit, the teacher told readers that reading fluently and smoothly is easier if you think about what the character is probably feeling. To read page 11 accurately, for instance, it is important to know that Cherry Sue doesn't want to hurt Poppleton's feelings. "Of course," said Cherry Sue. "We'll put them in my attic."The same work can be done with pages 12-15. Children can then disperse to read the next chapters on their own, trying to maintain fluency and phrasing. The group would probably need to reconvene several times for more of the same work.

Book Connections

Poppleton in Spring is similar in difficulty to *Henry and Mudge* and *Mr. Putter and Tabby*, also by Cynthia Rylant. The first story in this book is very similar to Pat Hutchins' book *Tidy Titch*. Readers might have a great time noticing ways the two stories are similar and different. After children have read the *Poppleton* series, teachers might recommend that they move to any book in the *Nate the Great* series by Marjorie Weinman Sharmat.

Genre
Short Chapter Book

A Field Guide to the Classroom Library, Lucy Calkins and the Teachers College Reading and Writing Project, Heinemann, ©2002 Teachers College, Columbia University; http://www.heinemann.com/fieldguides

Teaching Uses
Independent Reading; Character Study; Language Conventions

Ramona and Her Mother

Beverly Cleary

Book Summary

Ramona Quimby is a second-grader who wants to know that she is appreciated by her mother, and also by the world. Ramona weathers, with poignant humor, many storms: her mother's entry into full-time work, an unaffectionate babysitter, a "perfect" older sister, and family financial problems. Ramona's common concerns are treated with warmth, humor, and appropriate seriousness, and the solutions are both comforting and realistic. At the end of the story, Ramona feels secure about her mother's love and the family's future.

Basic Book Information

Ramona and Her Mother is the third of seven books predominantly about Ramona. Read in order, the books give a year-by-year accounting of Ramona's life from kindergarten to fourth grade. However, they need not necessarily be read in this order as each book can also stand alone.

Noteworthy Features

The text is clear, lively and well written, and the characters are multi-dimensional. The incidents described in the story will be familiar to many readers and exemplify how vivid writing and a sense of humor can make even mundane events-a new haircut, a parental argument-a pleasure to read about. The vocabulary is varied but mostly simple. More complicated words can usually be understood in context. The author uses Ramona to define more complicated words; in one paragraph she describes Ramona's thoughts, using the word "satisfying" twice and "satisfactory" once. Ramona tries out expressions on her family, such as "the devil made me do it" and repeats unfamiliar words, such as *scrimp* and *pinch*.

Teaching Ideas

A teacher may introduce the main character in the book by saying, "Ramona Quimby is a second-grader who just wants to be loved. Everyone calls her big sister Beezus 'her mother's girl,' and treats Ramona without the respect she deserves. Ramona tries her hardest with the cranky babysitter, parents who sometimes squabble, and other wrinkles of family life, but still, sometimes 'everything goes wrong, one thing after another, like a row of dominoes falling over.' It doesn't seem fair. But you'll see in this book that after a bunch of funny adventures, Ramona finds out she really is appreciated."

A teacher might draw her students' attention to the subtle ways in which Ramona matures within this book and more dramatically, across the series

Illustrator
Alan Tiegreen

Publisher
Avon Books, 1979

ISBN
038070952X

TC Level
10

of books. Students may draw parallels between Ramona and their lives by talking or reading with a partner.

This book is a fine example of how writing about ordinary life can be made interesting by attention to detail, language, dialogue, and characterization. A teacher might use vignettes from this book in the writing workshop to demonstrate to children that life's details can be written in ways that captivate readers and reveal personalities. Students might place Post-Its on their favorite incidents from the book, and then use those sections as models for their own writing.

Book Connections

Ramona and Her Mother is part of a series about Ramona Quimby, written by Beverly Cleary. The *Amber Brown* books by Paula Danziger and Judy Blume's *Fudge* series are both rather similar to this series.

Genre
Chapter Book

Teaching Uses
Read Aloud

A Field Guide to the Classroom Library, Lucy Calkins and the Teachers College Reading and Writing Project, Heinemann, ©2002 Teachers College, Columbia University; http://www.heinemann.com/fieldguides

Rosie and Tortoise

Margaret Wild

Book Summary

Rosie the hare is very excited about the birth of her new baby brother. But when he is born early, he is so tiny that she is shocked. Her parents ask if she would like to hold him, or push the carriage and she always says no. Little by little Bobby grows, but still Rosie keeps her distance. One day, her father asks Rosie why she doesn't like her brother. She explains that she is afraid of him because he is so small. Her father tells her a fable about a slow, steady tortoise that finds his way home with the help of his good friend, the hare. Rosie understands and accepts the message in her father's story. That night, she holds her brother for the first time and affectionately calls him "Little Tortoise."

Basic Book Information

This picture book has gentle illustrations in pastel colors.

Noteworthy Features

The "story within a story" structure is rather complicated. Some children are confused by the abrupt change of characters and story when Rosie's dad tells her a fable. Although the typeface changes to italic when the fable begins, some readers have to flip back and forth a few times to realize a new story has started.

Teaching Ideas

Students may need some guidance in personal response to read this book well. In partner or group talk, some students may be able to make connections between how Rosie was feeling and how they've felt before, in response to a new brother or sister. This connection may be beneficial for reading comprehension or in writing workshop. Teachers may prompt students by asking, "Have you ever been responsible for something very small and delicate and alive? How did you feel-brave or scared?" Readers can question each other until they think they are beginning to gain insight into Rosie's feelings.

Partners may want to practice character voice by reading to each other. When the father starts to tell the story of the hare and the tortoise, students may find it beneficial to emphasize a change in tone.

When a story has a theme or teaches a lesson, it is helpful for students to discuss what they are thinking and feeling about that message. Partners or a group may want to compare the message(s) they receive from the reading of this text and discuss the validity and the fairness of these messages.

Illustrator
Ron Brooks

Publisher
DK Inc., 1999

ISBN
0789426307

TC Level
5

Genre
Picture Book

Teaching Uses
Independent Reading; Interpretation; Critique

Rosie's Walk

Pat Hutchins

Book Summary

As Rosie the hen goes for a walk, a fox follows behind her. Seemingly by accident, the hen manages to get the fox caught up in obstacle after obstacle as he pursues her. She arrives home for dinner without incident, with the traumatized fox nowhere in sight.

Basic Book Information

This book has detailed pictures and a short prepositional phrase in the midst of some white space on each page. The font is larger than most books at this level and has no serifs.

Noteworthy Features

The story in this book is played out not only in the words but also in the pictures. The pattern of the story is the hen that walks obliviously around the farmyard with the fox trailing behind her, encountering hazard after hazard. First the text explains where Rosie walked, using a prepositional phrase that is fully illustrated in the picture. Then, the illustrations on the wordless pages that follow, show the trouble the fox gets into as he tries to follow her.

Teaching Ideas

Many teachers like to have this book on hand when they are working with children on making predictions based on clues in the text and pictures. The kinds of things that happen to the fox are based on a predictable pattern; one page shows clues of what could happen to the fox and the next page shows what actually does happen. To figure out what will happen to him, students have to think about the physical evidence presented in the picture, and put that together with what they know has happened to the fox in the past.

Just as this book is good for helping students work on prediction, it is also good for helping students make meaning out of a text in ways that go beyond the words. If a student merely reads the text and does not pay attention to the pictures, the story is boring and pointless-in fact it doesn't make much sense at all. As teachers confer with students about their reading of this book, they may want to be sure that they are monitoring their own comprehension closely enough that they'll pick up on the connection. In most cases, if two students are reading the book together, at least one will notice something is happening in the pictures and soon they will both be involved in the fuller story.

This book can also help those students who are just learning English with

Illustrator
Pat Hutchins

Publisher
Simon & Schuster, 1968

ISBN
0020437501

TC Level
4

A Field Guide to the Classroom Library, Lucy Calkins and the Teachers College Reading and Writing Project, Heinemann, ©2002 Teachers College, Columbia University; http://www.heinemann.com/fieldguides

prepositions. In the pictures, it is very clear what Rosie is doing, and once students can read the words, the graphic illustration of where Rosie is may stick in their minds better than abstract concepts of "through" and "over."

Book Connections

Other books by Pat Hutchins include *Goodnight Owl, Titch, You'll Soon Grow Into Them, Titch,* and *The Doorbell Rang.*

Genre
Picture Book

Teaching Uses
Author Study; Teaching Writing; Partnerships

Roxaboxen

Alice McLerran

Book Summary

A group of children with powerful imaginations create the imaginary town of Roxaboxen with the things they find in the desert. White rocks outline roads, bits of colored glass and abandoned crates form houses for the children, and a prickly cactus patch serves as the jail when the youngsters speed in their imaginary cars. There are market days and wars and gallops on horses and much more. The place they make and the adventures they had there as children have stay vivid in their adult memories.

Basic Book Information

Alice McLerran is the author of many well-loved books including, *The Mountain That Loved a Bird, Secrets, I Want to Go Home, Dreamsong, Hugs, Kisses, The Ghost Dunce*, and *The Year of the Ranch*. Her book *The Legacy of Roxaboxen* won the ALA Best Books Award for Young Adults in 1999. In the spring of 2000, the City of Yuma dedicated a restored Roxaboxen, which this book is based upon, as a natural desert park.

Noteworthy Features

The way this story moves through time may be difficult for students to understand. The descriptions and the life of Roxaboxen all take place more than fifty years ago. At the end of the book the narrator refers to the children who invented the place as grown-ups. Some children may not understand that so much time has passed since the events described in the book actually happened.

Teaching Ideas

Keeping track of the characters in this story may be challenging. They aren't introduced at the beginning of the story, but instead are mentioned in passing if what they have done is relevant to the description of the village of Roxaboxen. This makes some children think the characters have been introduced before and they missed it. Others try hard to hold onto all the different characters' names, when many characters are only mentioned once. For a character like Marian, who appears more than once, it may be worthwhile for readers to take note.

The Author's Note explains that Roxaboxen is a real place and the characters are real people. When reading the book aloud, most teachers choose to read this note too, as children tend to be interested in it. Some children even ask which child is the mother of the author.

Some readers believe the book is really about the power of imagination and community-that given enough freedom and enough raw materials,

Illustrator
Barbara Cooney

Publisher
Scholastic, 1991

ISBN
0140544755

TC Level
8

instead of toys that beep and buzz and come with scripts, children can create wonderful and enriching experiences for themselves. In this interpretation, the book is a celebration of creativity and ingenuity, a celebration of making something special out of something others might see as insignificant. Given this interpretation, teachers may want to use Roxaboxen in writing workshop, to show how through writing one can make something significant out of something others might think is small and unworthy.

Other readers see the book as a metaphor for people all over the world building societies, deciding what each community needs and will tolerate. Given this interpretation, teachers sometimes use this book to launch discussions about the communities the children in the classroom can envision, strive for, and help create. A particular group of readers might come up with yet another interpretation. Of course, all these interpretations are possible and both teachers and students can believe, find support for, and make use of more than one.

Genre
Memoir; Picture Book

Teaching Uses
Read Aloud; Teaching Writing; Independent Reading

Running

G. Porter; P. Teft Cousin; C. Mitchell

Book Summary

Running tells the story of Kisha, and her first relay race with her team, the "Tigers." As the race begins, Kisha, the fastest one on the team, is confident that her team will win. They have been practicing every day. Kisha wins the race, inches ahead of the other team, to the sound of a cheering crowd.

Basic Book Information

This small-format book has easy-to-understand pictures and short, inspirational text.

Noteworthy Features

The text is written as fiction, but does a nice job of relating a couple of technical elements of a relay runner's experience. For example, as Kisha's team gets ready for the race, they are shown stretching and preparing.

There are some elements of racing that are not fully explained, but the reader can figure out the meaning from context. (For example, on page 5, the text states: *POP went the starter signal, and the first runners on the relay teams began to run.*) In the cases where the meaning is not further explained or explained with contextual information, the elements are usually not critical to the understanding of the whole story.

The text is relatively simple but there are some sentences with dependent clauses, something early readers often find challenging.

Although the book is quite short, the vocabulary is rather difficult and may be challenging for some readers. Some difficult vocabulary includes *stretched, prepared, practicing, announcer, signal, baton,* and *thought.*

Teaching Ideas

This is a good book for readers who are comfortable reading independently, and can do it with some fluency, focus and stamina. Independent readers may find themselves making personal connections to this story. Readers can discuss with a partner or write in a notebook about a time when they ran in a race or competed in a sport. Readers can relate their experiences of what they needed to do to prepare for their individual sport and how they felt before, during or after the competition.

This book can be used as part of a reading center. A teacher might work with readers to figure out to which kind of reading center this particular book may belong. Readers can generate a list of ideas, and then develop a center where this book is included. For example, this book could be a part of a center about sports, running or competition, or a center that includes only stories where the main character has set a goal and achieved it (!), or a

Illustrator
Michael McBride

Publisher
Wright Group, 1997

ISBN
0780291883

TC Level
4

center that has books that tell a story, and yet seem like nonfiction. Teachers may guide students to ask questions about the book and to "defend" their answers as to why this book fits into the center they've described.

Teachers may also want to use this book as part of a larger study of nonfiction. As mentioned above, the book is written as a story, and yet it has the look and feel of nonfiction. Teachers may use this book to begin talking with readers about the elements of fiction and nonfiction. Readers may want to talk about another "category" of books that does not seem to fit either group. Or perhaps, expand their definition as to what a nonfiction book is, and to decide how this book might fit within a larger, more flexible definition.

As a read aloud, teachers may use this book to model skimming and browsing before reading to find unfamiliar words or words related to a particular subject. Teachers may model such pre-reading activities in a strategy lesson with the whole class, a partnership, or a guided reading group. Teachers might say, "The book we are going to read today is about a little girl who is running in a relay race. A relay race is a special kind of race because four people run it, one right after the other. The first runner has to pass a baton, which is like a stick, to the second runner. The second runner runs to the third runner and passes the baton to her, and so on. I've noticed a lot of new words in this book that are about running and races. Let's make a list of words we know and words we've noticed while browsing through other books, that might be in a book about running in races."

Genre
Picture Book

Teaching Uses
Independent Reading; Content Area Study

Sail Away
Donald Crews

Book Summary

The book takes you through the trials and tribulations of a day of sailing. As the book begins, it looks like a great day for sailing. It is bright and beautiful, and there is just enough wind to enjoy the day. Halfway through the day, however, the sky turns cloudy and gray, and the sea turns rough. Finally, the sails come down and the boat returns home.

Basic Book Information

Donald Crews captures the sights and sounds of a day of sailing by creating illustrations that are large and captivating and by placing a few carefully chosen words next to these beautiful pictures. The size and shape of print is particularly engaging in this book and add to the overall meaning of the text. Some of his words are gigantic, almost filling up a whole page, while others slant as if they are being pulled by the wind of the story.

Noteworthy Features

It may be necessary to discuss some of the vocabulary words that are specific to sailing, such as *dinghy, motor, mooring*, and *lighthouse*.

Teaching Ideas

This book is also particularly appropriate to use as a model in writing workshop once children have heard or read it, perhaps as a read aloud. One possible way of introducing it in the writing workshop is to say, "Let's notice the kinds of things Donald Crews did as a writer so we can try some of those things in our own writing." Children will notice things such as: how the story begins and ends in the same place; the use of sound words (*Whoosh!*); the use of ellipses; different kinds of punctuation ("!"); repetition ("Sailing, sailing")' ;arger print (SEAS SWELL); dialogue ("Shorten sails").

As a mini-lesson in a writer's workshop, one teacher discussed Donald Crews' writing technique saying to her students, "For the last couple of days, I've been sharing stories by Donald Crews. We've been listening to him as readers. Today I want us to think about him as a writer and what he does as a writer. One of the reasons why I love his writing is because he only uses a few words, but he is able to say so much. He uses strong, detailed, powerful words and repeats them. For example in this book he writes, 'Putt...Putt...Putt...Past the lighthouse.' He brings you right in, so you feel like you're there on the boat. He slows down the moment, stretching it out with the sound of the engine, 'Putt...Putt...Putt.' Now let's imagine you're looking at a child on a swing in the playground. Close your eyes. Take a moment to picture it and think about a few words or details you would use

Illustrator
Donald Crews

Publisher
Greenwillow Books, 1995

ISBN
0688110533

TC Level
5

to stretch out that moment. How would you describe what you see, the sounds you'd hear? What words would you use? Turn to your partner. The partner on the left should keep their eyes closed, the partner on the right, share those few words they imagined to describe the scene. Partner on the left, can you see a picture in your mind from the words? If not, think about what word might have made it more powerful. Today everyone is going to try to write like Donald Crews. Take one moment, like the girl on the swing, but chose your own moment, and stretch it out. Think of a few powerful words and details that'll bring your reader into the moment and make them feel like they're right there, too."

The next day, as a follow up to this mini-lesson, the teacher discussed how she noticed that students often write about a lot of different things without focusing on detail. She pointed out again that Donald Crews focused on one thing, a boat, in this case, and wrote around it.

Book Connections

Donald Crews is the author of numerous children's books including *Shortcut* and *Big Mama's*.

Genre
Nonfiction; Picture Book

Teaching Uses
Teaching Writing; Content Area Study

Sammy the Seal
Syd Hoff

Book Summary

Sammy the Seal wants to leave his home at the zoo so he can discover what life is like in the outside world. He walks around the city like a tourist looking at skyscrapers, restaurants, pet stores, and people working. Finally, he ends up in an elementary school classroom where he makes friends, sings songs, plays at recess, and ultimately learns to read. Although Sammy has a fulfilling day, he decides in the end to go back to his home at the zoo, with a promise from the schoolchildren that they will visit him.

Basic Book Information

The majority of the text is composed of high frequency words, such as *their, was, were, said, little, come, know, like, one, look, where, what, jumped, wished, made,* and so on. There are several proper names that may be more difficult for the early reader as well as some more challenging common words such as *ground, caught,* and *whistle.*

Noteworthy Features

Children love this simple, yet hilarious tale of Sammy's adventures in "their" world. Although the text is simple, the author, Syd Hoff, is a master at creating humor with few words, by matching them with direct illustrations or writing with simple puns, double entendres, and little twists. The majority of the text is written in short simple sentences. Quotation marks, exclamation points, and question marks are used throughout. Each page is brightly illustrated and always matches at least one sentence of text on the page.

The story is written with a combination of sentences that are straightforward fun (e.g., "Hooray for fish!" said the seals.) and somewhat more sophisticated fun (e.g., "That is a lovely fur coat," said a lady. "Where did you get it?" "I was born with it," said Sammy.). Although the story is simple, it plays on the fantasy that many children have of having a pet in school, and makes it seem believable that Sammy can easily make friends with children, learn to read and play volleyball! The story is continuous and the text covers 57 pages making it rather difficult for early readers to make their way all the way through it in one sitting. It would probably make sense to plan to read this story in more than one sitting, although there is no natural "halfway" point at which to stop.

Teaching Ideas

The most obvious and strongest characteristic of this book is its humor. When introducing *Sammy the Seal* a teacher might say, "This is the story of

Illustrator
Syd Hoff

Publisher
Harper Trophy, 1959

ISBN
0064442705

TC Level
5

a seal who leaves his home in the zoo to learn about the world outside the zoo. He has never seen the world and he is surprised by what he sees. Some funny things happen too, like when he jumps into someone's bathtub for a drink or when he spends a day in school! Can you imagine some of the things that may surprise or confuse Sammy?"

In a conference, teachers may also discuss with readers the ways in which they relate to Sammy. They may identify with his restlessness and desire to learn about new things. They may also discuss the "lesson" Sammy learns that although the outside world is interesting and fun, he is still happier at home.

Because of its length, this book may also be a good choice for early readers who are anxious to read "harder" books or books they perceive to be more like chapter books. In this case, the teacher will need to instruct the readers in the use of strategies that will support them through a longer text. For example, teachers might model how to set goals by using a bookmark or a Post-It note to mark a stopping place. Teachers might also demonstrate how to pick up the thread of a story on another day by backtracking a bit to review the story in their minds before starting up again.

Some more sophisticated reading strategies for students to try would be: rereading difficult, funny or confusing parts; putting a Post-It note on parts they want to discuss with a reading partner; rereading what they've read so far to "feel strong" in their reading; rereading what they've read so far before reading on at a second or third sitting.

This book also provides opportunities to teach about words with *-ed* endings as there are many simple *-ed* words in the book, such as *jumped, wished, walked, looked* and *learned*.

Book Connections

This book is similar to others written by Syd Hoff. Some titles include: *Danny and the Dinosaur, Oliver, Mrs. Brice's Mice, Stanley, Oliver, Danny and the Dinosaur Go to Camp,* and *The Horse in Harry's Room.* It is also similar in text difficulty and length to other books in the *I Can Read Books* series.

Genre
Picture Book

Teaching Uses
Independent Reading; Partnerships

A Field Guide to the Classroom Library, Lucy Calkins and the Teachers College Reading and Writing Project, Heinemann, ©2002 Teachers College, Columbia University; http://www.heinemann.com/fieldguides

Snowflake Bentley

Jacqueline Briggs Martin

Book Summary

Wilson Bentley loved snow. He even examined snowflakes as a child in the deep cold blizzards of winter. By the time he was a young man, he had decided he would find a way to photograph them so that everyone could see their uniqueness and beauty. Some people have never understood his passion, and some, even today admire and learn from his life, his work, and his photographs.

Basic Book Information

The Caldecott Medal graces the cover of this beautiful, down-to-earth, Nonfiction book. The woodcuts inside it give the feel of rustic 1920s Vermont, and warmth and appeal of the pictures may be what makes it makes it generally a popular choice even when the children know nothing of its story.

Noteworthy Features

The text is constructed in an unusual way. The story is told along the bottoms or tops of the pages, and then black-bordered columns on the sides of certain pages offer more information about the part of the story on those pages. The information on the sidebars does tend to make some readers lose the thread of the "main" story if they stop to read them while on the first read. Since the information is related to the main story and usually a bit more complicated, it might be most appropriate for readers to ignore them the first time through and instead, read them the second time they read the book. Perhaps it is easier to follow if the reader imagines, or really hears, two voices, one for the "main" text, and one for the marginal text. It might also be appropriate for readers to decide for themselves how to handle the two kinds of reading, and for readers to discuss and compare their conclusions.

Teaching Ideas

The messages of this story often make it a perfect choice for us to read aloud to children at the beginning of the year when they are learning or relearning how to use writers notebooks. Wilson's appreciation for an ordinary thing like snow-his passion for studying it and learning even more about it than anyone had ever known, his finding the patterns and beauty in its deepest structure-can inspire and serve as examples for children trying to learn how to observe, feel passionate about, study, and see patterns in the things in their own lives that may at first seem ordinary.

Illustrator
Mary Azarian

Publisher
Houghton Mifflin, 1998

ISBN
0395861624

TC Level
10

Genre
Nonfiction; Picture Book

Teaching Uses
Reading and Writing Nonfiction; Content Area Study; Independent Reading; Read Aloud; Teaching Writing

Swimmy
Leo Lionni

Book Summary

In this Caldecott Honor book, a small black fish named Swimmy loses all his little red brothers and sisters to a hungry tuna. He encounters many wondrous things as he swims alone scared and very sad. When he comes across another school of little red fish, he encourages them to stop hiding, and "SEE things!" and he thinks of a way to keep them all safe. The school swims in the shape of "the biggest fish in the sea," and Swimmy makes the eye. While swimming together in this formation, they chase the big fish away.

Basic Book Information

This is a very popular, classic work by well respected children's author Leo Lionni.

Noteworthy Features

Text averages from one to five lines per page, though one sentence continues across six double-page spreads. The lines of print seem to "swim" in the ocean-like page spreads and the small typeface may be somewhat obscured in the lush artwork, presenting a possible challenge for beginning readers.

Teaching Ideas

Before reading this book teachers may want to preview a few of the challenging vocabulary words related to the sea: *mussel, medusa, lobster, sea anemone,* and *school* (as it refers to a large group of fish). Students may also have difficulty with some other words like: *swift, fierce,* and *hungry.*

There are many similes and metaphors in the story, but if children miss them, they probably will not miss the main storyline, though they may get sidetracked in their thinking.

A few children have been known to focus in on the similes and metaphors in the text to the extent that it confuses them. Swimmy describes a lobster, "Who walked about like a water-moving machine." They wondered how could Swimmy be saying that the lobster reminds him of a machine? He doesn't know any machines, does he? And a child might ask why do the sea anemones look like "pink palm trees swaying in the wind"?

In a class discussion about the big idea or meaning of *Swimmy,* a teacher may want to start with questions that nudge children toward interpretation, such as: What is really important about this story? What does this story say about the world? What does this story say about my life? What is the point of this story for me?

Illustrator
Leo Lionni

Publisher
Scholastic, 1992

ISBN
0590430491

TC Level
7

Most readers decide that there is a message here: that people who are powerless can work together to vanquish the common enemy-if they have a good leader. Readers find other messages too. Some children think the book's message is that if you lose your family, you have to think of a better way to protect your next family. Some children decide the message is that if you are bullied yourself, you will end up trying to bully other people, too. As in any text, the learning comes not in just taking in another person's interpretation, but instead in deciding if that interpretation fits, or in building a different one, always with supporting evidence from the text. If the class has been studying this theme of community, a teacher might want to challenge the class by asking, "If the little fish, Swimmy, helped *people*, what problems would he see, and how would he help them? How would you?"

Book Connections

Many of Leo Lionni's books including *Frederick*, *The Alphabet Tree*, *Tillie and the Wall* and *Mathew's Dream,* are also parable-like animal fables with powerful messages for study either through the read aloud, in a reading center or as part of an author study.

Genre
Picture Book; Emergent Literacy Book

Teaching Uses
Read Aloud; Interpretation; Content Area Study; Critique; Author Study; Language Conventions

A Field Guide to the Classroom Library, Lucy Calkins and the Teachers College Reading and Writing Project, Heinemann, ©2002 Teachers College, Columbia University; http://www.heinemann.com/fieldguides

The Amazing Bone
William Steig

FIELD GUIDE

Book Summary

Pearl the Pig is enjoying a lovely spring day as she walks home from school. She lingers in town watching the folks at work and play; she lingers in the forest appreciating the flowers and the warm air. As she says aloud "I love everything," she hears an answer, "So do I" and finds a magic, talking bone. She rejoices in her find, and she and the bone, dropped by a grumpy witch a long time ago, chat as they start home. Suddenly, robbers jump from behind a rock and try to steal Pearl's purse. The bone imitates wild animals and scares them away. Pearl and the bone laugh and continue on. Then Pearl is grabbed by a fox who wants to eat her for dinner. The bone imitates a crocodile, but the fox is too smart to fall for the trick. He takes Pearl and the bone home and lights a fire on which to cook them. Just in the nick of time, the bone remembers a spell used by the witch. Using the spell, he makes the fox the size of a mouse so he can't hurt them. Pearl is delighted and takes the bone home to live as a member of her family.

Basic Book Information

This is a picture book with William Steig's classic style of both wiggly-line illustration and fun-with-words, fantastic writing.

Noteworthy Features

Many teachers like to read Steig books aloud to their students because they are so whimsical and unusual, and because teachers themselves love the books. This one in particular has a high level of drama-robbers attack, and Pearl trembling as the fox stokes the fire and makes a salad to eat her with. There is usually enough dialogue to make voices in the reading of the story, too. In this one there is the voice of Pearl, the bone (even casting a spell), and the fox. It can be valuable for a class to see an adult revel in the language, humor ,and fun of a book, especially a book they too can enjoy.

One of the most common ways that teachers use William Steig's books is for teaching children to read books that contain hard vocabulary words in them. Since children tend to love the stories in his books, there is motivation for them to work out ways to read with the tough vocabulary he always uses. Sometimes teachers give each book club a Steig book to read and then the readers come together to discuss the ways they found to manage the tough words.

Illustrator
William Steig

Publisher
Sunburst, Farrar, Straus and Giroux, 1976

ISBN
0374403589

A Field Guide to the Classroom Library, Lucy Calkins and the Teachers College Reading and Writing Project, Heinemann, ©2002 Teachers College, Columbia University; http://www.heinemann.com/fieldguides

Teaching Ideas

Learning to understand a new word from context is not automatic. Many readers come to a dead stop in their reading when they get to a word they don't know. They don't realize that to understand the word it is usually necessary to keep reading for a little while, until the rest of what the line or sentence or paragraph or page is trying to say becomes more clear. Sometimes, reading beyond the words makes the word's meaning exactly clear, and sometimes it only makes it clear within a wide range of meanings. Readers need to learn that, usually, arriving at that wide range of meanings is quite enough, and that further thinking about the word will interrupt the story too much. If children are studying the book in depth this isn't true, of course, but for a general, for-the-story read, this is quite enough for the majority of real-world readers.

Of course, for an in-depth study of any book, children also will need to learn other ways of finding out the meanings of unknown words, from asking a friend to using the dictionary or computer. Steig books can be good subjects for this kind of work.

Some kids like to wonder about the messages of the book. Is the author telling us not to dawdle in the woods or it will be courting trouble? Is he telling us to have hope because friends and help can come from even the most unlikely places? Is he saying that youth and a lust for life will always survive in the end? Is he just presenting a fanciful tale so we don't let our imaginations wither away? Some readers find it very difficult to find messages in Steig's work, and perhaps this makes them all the more fun and interesting and unpredictable.

Steig has written numerous other wonderful children's books, the most highly acclaimed being *Sylvester and the Magic Pebble*. None of his books shy away from unusual and specific vocabulary words that tend to delight (and sometimes confound) both young and old readers. The books often contain an element of magic to enjoy, and the characters are often animals. All the books have his characteristic wavy-line drawings. All his characters, even the humans, are quirky and have interesting emotions. Almost all of the books are witty and humorous for all ages of readers. All of them have happy endings. Readers who are launching themselves on an author study may well find all these things out, and more, on their own. They may want to include some of his cartoons from the *New Yorker* magazine in the body of his work that they study-some have humor accessible to young readers.

Book Connections

If the magic or the big, bad fox were the appealing elements of the story to the reader, those elements can be found in many fairy and folk tales, from *Little Red Riding Hood* and *The Three Little Pigs*, to any of the three-wishes-type stories.

Genre

Picture Book

A Field Guide to the Classroom Library, Lucy Calkins and the Teachers College Reading and Writing Project, Heinemann, ©2002 Teachers College, Columbia University; http://www.heinemann.com/fieldguides

Teaching Uses

Author Study; Independent Reading; Read Aloud; Interpretation

The Artist

Lois Podoshen

Book Summary

The narrator, a young girl, follows her uncle the artist around for a day. Uncle Josh paints everyone in the family, one by one, as the girl watches and paints some herself. At the end of the day, Uncle Josh doesn't have any more yellow paint to use or to mix, but he paints a wonderful picture of her with purples instead.

Basic Book Information

This book has twelve numbered pages. Each page has a watercolor illustration and about two lines of text. Although the book is not entirely patterned, there is a mini-pattern within it, for three pages, "He paints a picture of my [mom/dad/brother] with her/his yellow [tie/dress/cat]." The other sentences before and after this small pattern are short, declarative and without clauses.

The packaging and illustrating of this book make it stand apart from many other books at this level. It has a look and feel of a picture book rather than a book that is a part of a packaged kit.

Noteworthy Features

The last page is a color wheel that names the primary and secondary colors for children, perhaps to help them understand the mixing of paints that occurs in the story.

Teaching Ideas

This book may well inspire children to paint and experiment with mixing colors themselves, just as the narrator and Uncle Josh do.

Beyond the word work children can undoubtedly do with the illustrations in this book, there is a lot of mind work to be done as they read this book.

The illustrations offer details of the painting that Uncle Josh does, and his art can be compared, in most cases, to the real person or object he is using for a model. Readers will find that the artist takes liberties, and makes decisions about what to include or exclude from his paintings. This tends to be of great interest to readers who are artists themselves, and calls for much discussion. Even readers who haven't experienced painting can find interesting ideas in this situation, and the artist's decisions can be likened to the decisions writers must make.

The narrator of the story is also an artist, and in many of the situations where Uncle Josh is painting, she is copying his subject. At the end of the story, Uncle Josh paints a portrait of her with an artist's beret and brushes in

Illustrator
Linda Finch

Publisher
Richard C. Owen, 1999

ISBN
1572741376

TC Level
3

her hand, although isn't she wearing a beret or holding brushes. The readers can figure out things about the girl's character from her behavior throughout the book, and from her uncle's rendition of her. She can be an interesting subject for a character study.

Uncle Josh's liberties with his last painting-his rendition of her in unusual colors and with new props around her-can be taken, along with the rest of the book, to illustrate a theme of artistic creativity and choice. Children may notice that the artist could have painted the girl in colors that more closely matched those she is sporting, but he chooses not to. Often, readers discuss the reasons for this, which often leads to talks that can be about the theme or message of the story.

Book Connections

The content of this book is rather parallel to the content in several other books in this library. Children can discuss this book alongside Tomie dePaola's *The Art Lesson*, Shirley Hughes' *Able's Moon,* and Cynthia Rylant's *All I See.*

Genre
Picture Book

Teaching Uses
Interpretation; Independent Reading; Character Study

A Field Guide to the Classroom Library, Lucy Calkins and the Teachers College Reading and Writing Project, Heinemann, ©2002 Teachers College, Columbia University; http://www.heinemann.com/fieldguides

The Bumper Cars

Beverley Randell

Book Summary

On the first page of the book, Dad and three children approach the bumper car ride, presumably at a carnival or a fair. The text says, "'Come here, Dad,' said James. 'Look at the bumper cars.'" Soon two of the children are in one bumper car and Dad and James (the youngest child) are in a second car. The cars zoom toward each other, "'Here we come. Here we come!'" The cars bump.

Basic Book Information

This is another text in the PM Rigby series, recognizable by the predictable size and shape of all PM readers, as well as the well-known author of these books, Beverley Randell.

The book succeeds quite well at being a very supportive book that isn't a patterned, predictable book but is instead a story. Although the story doesn't contain very supportive illustrations, it is still within grasp for many readers. The secret is the repetition of sight words, usually inside quotes with the pictures conveying what's happening and where.

Noteworthy Features

There are a few noteworthy but subtle details. The girl, not the boy, drives the bumper car. The father at least feigns alarm when the bumper cars seem ready to crash, but James, the youngest child is enthralled by this.

The emergent reader will find continued support from the pictures, but clearly will see that the text is not illustrated precisely. Much of the book is written in dialogue. On pages that contain more than four lines of text, there is substantial space to support the reader in moving through the text.

The last page has only one word, *bump*, in a substantially bolder, larger font than the words in the rest of the book, highlighted on the page with an exclamation point.

Teaching Ideas

Children who read many PM readers will recognize the characters in this book, but for other readers it can be overwhelming to meet four characters within the first two pages of a book. James, the youngest child, will probably be most noteworthy to readers who may notice that for a while, his facial expressions (page 7) suggest that he thinks he is going to be left behind on this ride. Some children may think he's unlucky to need to ride with his Dad but if the teacher urges them to study the text closely, they'll probably conclude that James didn't mind riding with his father.

Series
Rigby PM

Illustrator
Elspeth Lacey

Publisher
Rigby, 1997

ISBN
0763515086

TC Level
2

If a child looks over the book quickly from the opening cover on, the child should be able to put together the separate pictures, developing a hunch for the story from the pictures alone. This is good work for a reader to do because the pictures (at this level of text) soon become less helpful in word-solving and more helpful as a way to give oneself an introduction to the text. If two children skim through the pictures, talking about them, they'll probably know this is a story about Dad and three kids going on the bumper cars (although the name of the ride might require some help), and they'll know that the youngest child rides in the bumper car with Dad.

Readers will need to point under the words as they read them. They'll probably find it challenging to read the story-they won't be able to rely on pictures or patterns-and it'll be important once they've worked through the text to reread in order to put the words together and make it sound like people are talking. The goal isn't for children to read with dramatic expression as if they were in a play, but it is important for them to read with fluency and phrasing (not like robots). The best way to achieve this is to reread the text often, making it sound more like talk. Readers will want, in their rereads, to pay attention to the punctuation marks because these road signs will help readers read the text well.

This is an excellent text to use with a group of students who are ready to be notched up a level from Level 1 books to Level 2 books. The large number of high frequency words will serve as anchor words. Since the characters and story plot of the book are straightforward and probably be familiar to many readers, it will be easier for the reader to predict the next event. A book introduction would serve these students well. A teacher might say, "Kate and James are old enough to drive their own bumper car. Nick is too young and must ride with his dad. Read and find out what happens as the bumping begins." As the teacher observes a child reading, she will want to be sure the reader is cross-checking the meaning with the visual clues, and recognizing that the words and illustrations together carry the message. This may be a newly developing concept for the early reader who was able to remember most previous texts.

This is an excellent book for children to read in a partnership. They love to take on the roles of the characters. One child could take the role of Nick and the other child the role of Kate, practicing reading with fluency and expression. This would also provide an opportunity to teach the value of rereading for the purpose of not only developing fluency but also planning and thinking what kind of voice would best convey the meaning.

Children who have been encouraged to have conversations and talk back to texts often will linger on their own personal experiences of riding in bumper cars. They will also talk about Nick and how he must feel to still have to go with his dad and sit on his lap. They may wonder how old Nick is, "When can he ride by himself?"

This book could be a welcome addition to a reading center of books that contain sound words. Often, sound words are associated with animals making noises, and this would be an example of a sound that is not inherent to the object, but rather is a sound made by cause and effect.

Genre
Picture Book

A Field Guide to the Classroom Library, Lucy Calkins and the Teachers College Reading and Writing Project, Heinemann, ©2002 Teachers College, Columbia University; http://www.heinemann.com/fieldguides

Teaching Uses
Language Conventions; Partnerships; Independent Reading

A Field Guide to the Classroom Library, Lucy Calkins and the Teachers College Reading and Writing Project, Heinemann, ©2002 Teachers College, Columbia University; http://www.heinemann.com/fieldguides

The Carrot Seed
Ruth Krauss

Book Summary

This beloved classic has been around for years because it is simply written and holds the important theme of keeping hope alive. It is the story of a little boy who plants a carrot seed. Everyone in his family tells him that it won't grow. The little boy continues to believe that the seed will grow, despite the discouraging behavior of his family and the seed's lack of progress. He tends to the plant, and eventually the carrot seed sprouts and grows, "just as the little boy had known it would."

Basic Book Information

Many people credit Ruth Krauss, the author of this book, and Margaret Wise Brown with being the two people to break open the field of picture book writing. Ruth Krauss has also written *The Happy Day*, which is a Caldecott Honor Award winner, and *A Hole is to Dig*. *The Carrot Seed*, like these other books, is considered a classic.

Noteworthy Features

The book is illustrated in single lined drawings with shades of brown and white. When the carrot comes up, green is introduced. Then on the final page, there is an orange carrot. The old fashioned feeling of the book doesn't take away from the brilliance of Crockett Johnson's art. The expressions on characters' faces are especially worth noticing.

Some teachers think this book is easier than it is. There aren't a lot of words on the page but the illustrations won't do a lot to help the readers figure out words. Readers also need to be alert to changing patterns. The book is filled with literary language, which can pose some challenges for readers who are more used to the syntax of oral language. For example, the phrase, "Everyone kept saying it wouldn't come up," isn't the sort of phrase people would normally say.

Teaching Ideas

In the A library, the primary instructional purpose of this book is as an emergent literacy read aloud. Through the teacher's multiple readings of this text, children become familiar with the story. After the teacher has read the story at least four times, copies of the book could join a basket of "favorite story books." When they are given the book to read during independent reading time, readers can then use the pictures and their memory of the teacher's readings to recreate the story. When they have had the opportunity to do this, their reading progresses from simply "labeling" pictures on the page, to telling the story off the pictures using progressively

Illustrator
Crockett Johnson

Publisher
HarperCollins, 1945

ISBN
0064432106

TC Level
4

more dialogue and storybook language, to more "conventional" reading using the print. It is important for children to hear the stories read aloud many times, and to have a lot of opportunities to reread it with a partner while a teacher is near by to thoughtfully coach the reading.

The Carrot Seed is a classic story written around the familiar motif of the youngest child who prevails in the end. This is not unlike the story of Cinderella, the youngest of the daughters who in the end marries the prince or of Titch who has only the littlest things, but whose seed grows into the mighty plant.

The characters' facial expressions provide an opportunity to demonstrate the importance of reading the pictures and how they can be used to help in making inferences. When the mother and father say, "I'm afraid it won't come up," there is a picture of the mother and father leaning into the picture with wide eyes and concern on their faces. When the big brother leans into the picture, he has a smile on his face and he pronounces, "It won't come up." Teachers can point out the facial expressions of the characters and demonstrate, using their own voice inflection, how they imagine the characters might sound when they speak.

One teacher, during a guided reading book introduction, discussed how the illustrated facial expressions help us to understand the story. She said, "The mother looks worried here in the picture. How do you think she would say the words, 'I'm afraid it won't come up.'" One young reader replied, "Oh, she doesn't want to disappoint the boy, so she says it softly, carefully. She doesn't want him to be hurt."

When young readers are working in partnerships, they may alternate the pages, taking on the parts of different characters while reading this book to each other. Readers can practice the different ways the lines could be said. This can develop a reader's sense of fluency and phrasing.

Although this is a Level 4 book, it can be used with more advanced readers in upper grades who are ready to understand that stories often have themes. Some teachers talk about the theme as the "under story," or as the story beneath the surface. In *The Carrot Seed*, the boy's undying belief in his seed illustrates the value of keeping faith in each other and in ourselves.

This is one theme in *The Carrot Seed*, but of course each reader needs to construct her own sense of a book's theme. One first grader noticed that this book is about the way some people and things grow-slowly at first, and then in bursts. This child pointed out that the carrot was rather like Leo from *Leo, the Late Bloomer*. Other readers will think that this book carries the message that if someone believes enough, their belief will come true. This interpretation doesn't always match our life experiences, and readers who know that things don't always turn out well may question *The Carrot Seed*.

All this can make for some great book talk. Teachers may remind children that if they suggest a theme is present in a book, they must demonstrate accountability by returning to the text for supporting evidence.

Book Connections

This book might be added to a reading basket of "Books about people who believe in themselves or others," along with *Leo the Late Bloomer* (Windmill, 1971) and other more recent books by Robert Krauss.

A Field Guide to the Classroom Library, Lucy Calkins and the Teachers College Reading and Writing Project, Heinemann, ©2002 Teachers College, Columbia University; http://www.heinemann.com/fieldguides

Genre
Picture Book

Teaching Uses
Independent Reading; Partnerships; Critique; Interpretation; Read Aloud; Language Conventions

The Chick and the Duckling

Mirra Ginsburg

FIELD GUIDE

A C

Book Summary

The Chick and the Duckling is a story of a duckling exploring his world as a chick follows close behind and mimics each of the duckling's actions. Every time the duckling tries something new he says what he is doing, "I am taking a walk." "Me too," said the chick. Finally, when the chick almost drowns while trying to swim like the duckling, he is saved by the duckling and decides to stop mimicking him.

Basic Book Information

This book has been translated from the Russian story of V. Suteyev. It has 110 words over 29 pages with an average of five to eight words per page. The placement of text changes from top to middle to bottom and some pages have no text. There is one sentence on each page.

Noteworthy Features

The text is highly supported by colorful illustration and will support early reading behaviors such as one-to-one matching and directionality. The same two sentences are alternatively repeated on each page with the only difference being the verb. A small change occurs at the end of the book when the verb changes from *said* to *cried*. The last sentence breaks the pattern that runs through the book. Quotation marks are used in each sentence.

Teaching Ideas

If a teacher wants to support a reader by giving a book introduction, she might tell a student, "This book shows a newborn chick learning from a newborn duckling by copying everything the duckling does. On the first page, it says 'A duckling came out of his shell.' Then a pattern begins when he says, 'I am out!" At the end of the story, there is a surprise for the chick."

This book includes many high frequency words including *I*, *am*, *said*, *the*, *me*, and *too*. For readers who haven't yet mastered one-to-one correspondence, who don't always check the picture against the first letter or who are ready to expand their sight word vocabulary, this book offers many learning and teaching opportunities. The book offers the opportunity for teaching about quotation marks. Although the text is a simple one, there are topics and issues to be discussed within the text. Children can talk in partnerships about "things that birds do." They can also discuss why they believe the chick is copying everything the duckling does and relate this to their own lives. Children may find humor (or grief) in the story when the chick falls in the water and is saved by the duckling. Finally, a good topic of

Illustrators
Jose Aruego; Ariane Dewey

Publisher
Simon & Schuster, 1972

ISBN
068971226X

TC Level
3

discussion could be how and what the chick learns at the end of the story.

Genre
Picture Book

Teaching Uses
Independent Reading; Partnerships

A Field Guide to the Classroom Library, Lucy Calkins and the Teachers College Reading and Writing Project, Heinemann, ©2002 Teachers
College, Columbia University; http://www.heinemann.com/fieldguides

The Doorbell Rang
Pat Hutchins

FIELD GUIDE

Illustrator
Pat Hutchins

Publisher
William Morrow, 1986

ISBN
0590411098

TC Level
6

Book Summary

Ma has made a dozen cookies for tea for Victoria and Sam. She makes wonderful cookies, just like Grandma. As Victoria and Sam start to divide the cookies, the doorbell rings and Tom and Hannah from next door come in. Now the four children start to divide the cookies but the doorbell rings again. The story continues until there are twelve children around the table. Each child can now have one cookie, but the doorbell rings again. Luckily, it is Grandma with an enormous tray of cookies.

Basic Book Information

This book has 283 words. The pages are unnumbered. Repetition, sentence structure, and phrasing are written to support early reading behaviors and will help beginning readers find meaning in the book. This book uses many high-frequency words.

Full-page color illustrations are on each page with the text at the top. The illustrations provide moderate support.

Noteworthy Features

The author uses varied, simple sentence patterns. Sentences are short. The pages have one to four lines of text. The print is well-spaced. One sentence continues onto the next page; this may need to be explained to a reader. In this text, children will have the opportunity to implement strategies such as self-correcting, self-monitoring, and searching for visual information.

Teaching Ideas

Because of the complexity of many of the words in this book, independent readers of *The Doorbell Rang* will probably not rely solely on the strategy of sounding it out.

Students should be encouraged to discuss and analyze the book. Young readers of this book will probably be interested in the quandary the characters are faced with every time the doorbell rings. Sharing chocolate chip cookies with an increasingly large amount of people is not always an easy thing to do! Students may want to discuss the plot or characters in book discussions. Young readers might want to put Post-It notes on a favorite page and talk about it, posing alternate solutions to the cookie problem, discussing how the characters might be feeling, and so on.

Children, with keen observation, may notice that the mother is mopping the floor only to have more muddy shoes trample through the kitchen. In addition to the increasing number of muddy footprints, more and more steam comes out of the kettle and pot, more plates go on the table, and the collection of children's toys grows. The illustrations help to create a sense of chaos.

An engaging aspect of the book is that the problem grows in intensity each time the doorbell rings. Young writers in grades 2 and up might want to emulate this "snowball" effect in their writing by setting up a problem in their stories and then adding layers to it. Building suspense could be the topic of a writing mini-lesson.

The Doorbell Rang also provides a strong example of the use of dialogue. The story is primarily told through what the characters say to one another. Teachers may want to coach children on what the quotation marks mean, and then concentrate on how to read dialogue with fluency. At first, children may want to use different voices for each of the characters in order to distinguish them.

Book Connections

There are several other books about these same characters that young readers may want to try.

Genre
Picture Book

Teaching Uses
Author Study; Read Aloud; Language Conventions; Teaching Writing

The Gardener
Sarah Stewart

Book Summary

When the Great Depression keeps her parents from earning a living, young Lydia Grace goes from her family's farm to the city to work in her Uncle Jim's bakery. Lydia Grace embarks on a mission to make her sour-faced uncle smile and to make her new home one that she can call her own. As each month passes, Lydia Grace brings obvious physical changes to her environment and even subtler emotional changes to her uncle.

Basic Book Information

A 1998 Caldecott Honor book, *The Gardener* holds 19 double-page spreads of illustrations. Letters from Lydia Grace to her family are situated on the upper corners of twelve pages, surrounded by the text's expressive illustrations.

Noteworthy Features

The pages of *The Gardener* must be read in order, because each letter builds chronologically on the previous one. The letters share consistent features: a greeting to Lydia Grace's family, a salutation, and often a postscript about the results of Lydia Grace's latest attempt to make Uncle Jim smile.

When hearing the book read aloud, young readers pick up on the book's style almost immediately. Children start to see the text's repeated structure at the appropriate places in each letter.

Readers will want to pay close attention to the illustrations. Those illustrations begin before the title page and continue after the copyright information at the back of the book. Unlike many books, the front and end papers do not merely reproduce drawings from the middle, but are part of the narrative itself. In total, there are seven double-page illustrations without text, none of which should be passed over quickly.

The passage of time is marked not only by Lydia Grace's experiences in the city, but also by the life cycle of her garden. The reader sees the growth of flowers from seeds to full bloom.

The sentences in each letter are fairly long with some terms that are specific to making bread and gardening. One way to help these long sentences make sense is to remind children to practice reading with expression. This might take a little practice.

Teaching Ideas

Used during independent reading or whole-class read alouds, *The Gardener* is a great book for the teaching of inference. The essential plot is easy to follow, but subtleties in the text offer students a wealth of information.

Illustrator
David Small

Publisher
Farrar, Straus, and Giroux, 1997

ISBN
0374325170

TC Level
8

From Lydia Grace's first letter alone, children can infer the following (and possibly more): Lydia lives with both her parents and grandmother, that the family is struggling financially, that Papa is deeply upset at the prospect of his daughter's leaving, that Lydia Grace behaves responsibly, that Grandma pushes her to excel and that Uncle Jim and Lydia Grace have not seen each other for years-if they have ever seen each other at all.

During a read aloud, students can turn and talk to each other periodically to discuss everything they can infer about Lydia Grace and her relationship to her family. In teacher-student conferences, teachers may want to check to see how much students are picking up by reading between the lines.

The illustrations in this book offer just as many inferential possibilities as the text, so even if teachers read it aloud to a whole class, *The Gardener* should be available for students to hold in their hands. Halos of white encircle many of the key parts of illustrations to help focus readers' attention. These luminous splashes often contrast with the other parts of the illustrations, popping boldly forward from the backgrounds of a bleakly gray train station or the drab, brown city Lydia Grace finds when she first steps out of the taxicab in front of Uncle Jim's bakery. Once they know the story well, students can even flip through the book a few times without reading the text, looking for details that are not in Lydia Grace's letters. On the title page, for instance, children might notice Grandma and Lydia Grace proudly returning with lettuce from their garden, while Mama and Papa look down glumly at what may be Uncle Jim's invitation for Lydia Grace to come to the city.

Students without prior knowledge of the Great Depression may struggle to understand why Lydia Grace has to leave home to work at such a young age, or why Uncle Jim almost smiles when his bakery is nearly full of customers. Children might be helped with a quick introduction to this historical period.

Book Connections

Sarah Stewart and David Small have teamed up previously to produce *The Money Tree* and *The Library*. Martina Selway's *Don't Forget to Write* also uses letters to narrate a story of a girl adjusting to life in a new place, in this case her grandfather's farm.

Genre
Picture Book; Historical Fiction

Teaching Uses
Read Aloud; Partnerships

The Horrible Thing with Hairy Feet

Joy Cowley

Book Summary

Lucy goes over the river to the farm. Then she crosses the farm to get to the field of thistles until she comes upon a tin shed. There she finds the horrible thing with hairy feet that screams that he is going to eat her. She runs out of the tin shed, through the field of thistles, across the farm, and over the river until she gets to town. Meanwhile, the horrible thing with hairy feet is back in the tin shed laughing, because everyone knows he only eats chocolate biscuits.

Basic Book Information

This short, emergent literacy book is in Rigby's Literacy 2000 series.

Noteworthy Features

Joy Cowley, also the author of *Mrs. Wishy-Washy*, wrote this book and it is very much a product of the New Zealand countryside. The opening page shows a river with a wonderful rope bridge spanning it, and beyond there is a field of purple thistles and then a tin shed. Many American children will find all of this represents a world unlike their own, and will be intrigued and challenged by words like *thistles*.

The story has three parts. First it sets the scene saying, "Over the river there is the farm. And on that farm there is a field of thistles." Then once the route has been traveled in this fashion, the story travels the same path only now it says that a girl named Lucy "went over the river to the farm. She went across the farm to the field of thistles." Finally, after the big fright, Lucy retraces all her steps through the field of thistles, across the farm and over the river.

Teaching Ideas

If a teacher wanted to confer with children in a partnership before they read this book, the teacher might decide to use this time to preview words that pertain to direction. She might say, "In this book, the author takes you on a journey and we go through one place, across another . . . you'll see. To read this, you'll need to know some words that can be a bit tricky-words like *across*. Can you find *across* on page 12? What do you notice about the word? Another direction word that's tricky is on the very next page, page 13. Can you find the word *through*-'she went *through* a field of thistles.'" The teacher might say, "There is also a made-up word; look on page 6. Joy Cowley makes up a word here to show that the floor squeaks and has holes in it and is a bit rough."

Illustrator
Martin Bailey

Publisher
Rigby, Literacy 2000 Series, 1988

ISBN
0868677035

TC Level
5

Genre
Emergent Literacy Book

Teaching Uses
Independent Reading

The Hundred Dresses
Eleanor Estes

Book Summary

The Hundred Dresses won the Newbery Honor when it was first published in 1944, and has continued to offer insight and humility to children and adults alike. Wanda Petronski is different from all the other kids at school: she wears an old faded dress and muddy shoes; she has a funny name and lives in the poor part of town. Peggy and Maddie tease her daily, but miss her when she doesn't come to school because they must suspend their teasing game. The game is called the Hundred Dresses game, and in it Peggy repeatedly gets Wanda to tell everyone that she has a hundred dresses at home "all lined up in my closet." When Wanda wins the class competition for her drawings (of her hundred dresses), Maddie convinces Peggy that they must apologize. However, they are too late: the Petronskis have moved. As Wanda's absence extends into many days, the class receives a letter from Wanda's father telling them that Wanda will not return to school. They are moving to a big city where their name won't be made fun of and they won't be called "Polack." By the end of the book Maddie has become reflective, vowing never again to stand by and allow someone to be teased or bullied. Peggy, however, remains the same.

Basic Book Information

This 80-page book has 7 chapters, with illustrations on nearly every page. The story is told in the third person from Maddie's point of view. There is frequent dialogue to show Wanda's and Maddie's interactions with others. Eleanor Estes is also known for her beloved *Ginger Pye*, which received the NewberyMedal, and for *The Moffats*.

Noteworthy Features

This book is available in several formats, ranging from a large picture book to a slim chapter book. Older children may feel that the large picture book looks babyish, and so perhaps using the 6" x 8" version, illustrated in full color, can solve this perceived problem.

Since this book was written in 1944, there is some language that will seem foreign to readers. At one point in the book, the narrator points out that Wanda's forehead shined, like she used "Sapolio" on it. Not many young people will know that sapolio was a form of margarine used in the 30s and 40s. The practice of oral reading in school may also need some explaining. Some readers may not know what "Polack" refers to and that it is a derogatory term for people of Polish descent.

The story begins almost immediately with a shift in time as Maddie remembers how the Hundred Dresses game began one day outside of school. This invites readers to do some good work right away, and

Illustrator
Louis Slobodkin

Publisher
Voyager Books, 1944

ISBN
0156423502

TC Level
9

encourages lively conversation. Readers may realize, at this point, that it'd be helpful to keep some record of the time line of the story.

Many readers do not catch on to the fact that Peggy is cruel, particularly those who do not yet realize that words in a book may not be true. Because the narrator states that Peggy would never think of herself as cruel, for she often defended those who were being bullied, readers tend to accept this as gospel. They don't read between the lines enough to see the real truth of the statement. Readers need to understand that even though Peggy may protect "small children from bullies" and cry for hours when she sees an animal mistreated, she doesn't hesitate to tease Wanda about her lie because Wanda isn't an "ordinary person." Peggy thinks it's okay to tease Wanda because she deserves it and because she's different. This goes to the root of cultural, racial and ethnic bias and should be pointed out to students if they don't see this.

Teaching Ideas

The Hundred Dresses is a book commonly used to address classroom community issues such as bullying. Rather than preach that bullying is wrong, this book tells the story of Wanda Petronski and humanizes the issue, letting readers draw their own conclusions. It is a great book for a read aloud, especially in the beginning of the school year or when the issue of bullying arises. It is short and can be read over a couple of days, and it can support a great deal of conversation that will probably center around the characters of Wanda, Maddie and Peggy. In almost any fictional story, readers could benefit from collecting information and growing theories about the main characters. Such a character study would be rich for readers of this book. The readers will benefit from being reminded that one gets to know a character by attending to what he or she says, does and does not say or do. One class, studying *The Hundred Dresses*, decided to use a T-chart, setting up the names of the characters on one side of the T and their personality traits on the other, referencing the pages they used for evidence.

Using a T-chart to list character traits can be very helpful in making the story more organized and concrete for unsophisticated readers. Many readers think that Wanda is lying and that Peggy is doing the right thing by showing her up to everyone. The story does move quickly, so using a T-chart will slow down the story and help clear up many readers' misconceptions. T-charts could be made for Wanda, Maddie and Peggy, listing on the right side their attributes and on the left, textual evidence to support it. When students think that Wanda is lying, they will need to prove it. This will keep the readers on track with what is really going on and cut down on confusion.

Readers could talk about Peggy as a character, or they could read aloud excerpts of the text in ways that show her character. One partnership of readers used photocopied pages of dialogue between Wanda and Peggy, talking about her voice inflection and meaning. One teacher who was trying to show her class that Peggy was not as nice as she appeared, asked, "Why does Peggy call Wanda 'the child'?" She went on to say, "When Peggy says, 'Your hundred dresses sound beautiful,' she says it like this, 'bee-you-tiful.' Look at that on the page. How does that sound when you say it like it is written?" The readers practiced saying "bee-you-tiful," and discovered that it

A Field Guide to the Classroom Library, Lucy Calkins and the Teachers College Reading and Writing Project, Heinemann, ©2002 Teachers College, Columbia University; http://www.heinemann.com/fieldguides

sounded like Wanda was being mocked. From there the readers better understood the character of Peggy.

Book Connections

Other books by Eleanor Estes include *The Moffats* and *The Middle Moffat*. Though these Newbery Honor Books are somewhat longer and more challenging than *The Hundred Dresses*, the series is warm and humorous and a favorite of many third graders. Eleanor Estes also wrote *The Curious Adventures of Jimmy McGee*, *The Witch Family* and the Newbery Medal winner, *Ginger Pye*.

Genre
Short Chapter Book

Teaching Uses
Read Aloud; Character Study; Independent Reading

A Field Guide to the Classroom Library, Lucy Calkins and the Teachers College Reading and Writing Project, Heinemann, ©2002 Teachers College, Columbia University; http://www.heinemann.com/fieldguides

The Iron Giant
Ted Hughes

Book Summary

At the start of the story, the Iron Giant falls from the top of a seaside cliff, breaking into separate parts. Then his hand finds an eye and eventually an arm, and bit by bit the giant reconstructs himself. The next chapter begins with Hogarth, a farmer's boy, seeing the giant's eyes rise up above the cliff top. Hogarth runs home, breathless, and soon his father has gotten a double-barreled gun. The plot tells about the Iron Giant terrorizing the countryside by eating all the machines. The farmers plot to capture him and ultimately do, aided by Hogarth. The Iron Giant escapes and Hogarth saves the day by realizing that the Iron Giant will be happy eating their old metal objects in the junkyard. When Earth is threatened by an alien invader, the Iron Giant is sent to save the planet. The alien is pacified by the heat of the sun and becomes gentle, playing beautiful, calming music. In the fashion of fairy tales, there is a happy ending, with a moral if you want to find it. There are bad guys and good guys.

Publisher
Alfred A. Knopf, 1999

ISBN
0375801537

Basic Book Information

Ted Hughes was the poet laureate of England and this beautiful story (79 pages) reads like poetry. This book was written in 1968 and originally titled, *The Iron Man*.

Noteworthy Features

Though this book is only 79 pages, with five chapters, it is somewhat challenging. One of its difficulties involves its genre. It is science fiction and fantasy. This book leans more to the fantasy side of its genre but is told in fairy tale fashion. Hughes tells the story in self-contained chapters.

There is little characterization. There is much inference work to be done with this book and much interpretation. There are great opportunities for work with symbolism and allegory.

Teaching Ideas

Teachers will want to read this book aloud. Passages from the book can be used as mentor texts for writers wanting to learn to use words to create a mood, to recreate a moment, or to paint pictures.

The book can be used to introduce children to the genre of fantasy. How is fantasy different than realistic fiction? What sorts of things tend to happen in fantasy stories? There aren't many accessible fantasy stories; mostly the genre is for more experienced readers.

Finally this book poses lots of wonderful challenges for readers who are working to become skilled at retelling stories, paying attention to story

A Field Guide to the Classroom Library, Lucy Calkins and the Teachers College Reading and Writing Project, Heinemann, ©2002 Teachers College, Columbia University; http://www.heinemann.com/fieldguides

elements such as the setting, time, and character. In one brief book, time jumps about in ways that will be complex for readers. The character of The Iron Giant is revealed gradually throughout the book.

Genre
Fantasy; Picture Book

Teaching Uses
Read Aloud

A Field Guide to the Classroom Library, Lucy Calkins and the Teachers College Reading and Writing Project, Heinemann, ©2002 Teachers College, Columbia University; http://www.heinemann.com/fieldguides

The Leaving Morning

Angela Johnson

Book Summary

This is a poignant story of a family as they are packing to move. They must say goodbye to all they know, and face the unknown of a new home. The children make lips on the window, reflect on what they will leave behind, and wonder about their new home.

Basic Book Information

The poetic text is set against a backdrop of watercolors showing a family moving. Angela Johnson received the Coretta Scott King Award for her novel, *Toning the Sweep*. This book was recognized as a Child Study Association Book of the Year.

Noteworthy Features

Angela Johnson uses the image of lips on the windowpane to evoke a sense of longing and unknowing. Her sentences are often drawn over pages with the use of ellipses and commas. No one in the text is given a name, "the cousins," are just the cousins. The narrator switches between the singular *I* and the plural *we*, making it sometimes unclear who is telling the story.

Teaching Ideas

Many craft features can be noticed in this stirring narrative. Strong images and scenes of moving help give a feeling of loss and anticipation. Children can start to see what pictures give that feeling. The author uses little moments ("the lips on the window") to tell the story. Internal thinking is used. A thought is carried over several pages with use of ellipses and commas, slowing down the action of the story. There is use of dialogue, and strong adjectives used in doubles (e.g., "soupy, misty morning"). Lists are created, with the most important for last. In addition to examining and using this book as a craft mentor, it is also a good model of writing from one's own life.

Genre
Picture Book

Illustrator
David Soman

Publisher
First Orchard Paperbacks, 1996

ISBN
0531070727

TC Level
7

Teaching Uses

Author Study

The Legend of the Poinsettia

Tomie dePaola

Book Summary

Lucida lives in a village in the mountains of Mexico. One day, as Christmas approaches, Lucida's mother is asked to weave a blanket for the figure of baby Jesus for the Christmas procession. Lucida's mother begins the weaving, but, a few days before Christmas Eve, grows too sick to continue. Lucida tries to finish it, but only tangles it. Ashamed that she has nothing to offer to the statue of the Christ child, Lucida hides as the procession approaches. An old woman finds her and tells her that it is not the gift but the giving that is important, and Lucida grabs up a tangled bunch of green leaves by the side of the road as an offering. People murmur, but as she presents her gift of weeds, they turn into the first, beautiful, red, poinsettia flowers.

Basic Book Information

Award-winning children's author Tomie dePaola began writing at the age of ten. "It's a dream of mine," says dePaola, "that one of my books, any book, any picture, will touch the heart of some individual child and change that child's life for the better" (www.childrenslit.com). DePaola has illustrated over 200 books and has written more than 90 of those 200. He is the author of the Caldecott Honor Book *Strega Nona,* as well as a Newbery Honor Book *26 Fairmont Avenue*, which is the first in a series of memoir including the following titles, *Here We All Are* and *On My Way.*

Noteworthy Features

For readers who haven't had much exposure to other traditions, some talk about the culture or the traditions represented in this story might prove helpful. The text, supported by vivid illustrations, includes simple words and phrases in Spanish with an English translation following for clarity. On the first page there is no definition for *burro*, but the illustration shows a picture of a donkey being fed straw.

Teaching Ideas

Prior to introducing the story, teachers may find it helpful to introduce cultural information about Mexico. Readers will enjoy the story more if they are familiar with or have seen a poinsettia plant before they read the story. The author's note includes more information about the Mexican wildflower that could generate good discussions.

A teacher-led discussion of the book may lead to the theme that when a gift is given with the true spirit of giving, it doesn't matter what the present is, and the gift will be honored by the person who accepts it. That after all, is

Publisher
Scholastic, 1994

ISBN
0590486799

TC Level
8

what the old woman tells Lucida and what she comes to believe in giving the figure of Jesus weeds. Book talks or partner talks may center around this theme, even more so during the holidays. Students may want to discuss further their own interpretation of the story, including background knowledge of their own religious beliefs (or lack thereof). Other myths and legends that students are familiar with could also generate discussion.

Book Connections

Other books by dePaola include *Strega Nona*, *26 Fairmont Avenue*, *Here We All Are,* and *On My Way*. *Hershel and the Hanukkah Goblins* by Eric Kimmel tells the story of Hanukkah in a humorous way for young readers.

Genre
Picture Book

Teaching Uses
Read Aloud

The Lion and the Mouse

Beverley Randell

Book Summary

Adapted from an Aesop fable, *The Lion and the Mouse* is a story about how a mouse teaches a lion a valuable lesson. In the beginning of the story, the lion catches a mouse asleep on his chest. The mouse begs for his freedom. The lion thinks this is quite funny, but lets the little mouse go free. Then the lion is caught in a net. He roars all day, but no one comes to help. That night the mouse hears the lion roaring, and helps to set the lion free.

Basic Book Information

The PM Series was developed by Beverley Randell who continues to be a major author of these books today. The PM Storybooks place a priority on always including the traditional story elements. Even texts that at first appear to be lists are, in fact, stories with characters, a problem, and a resolution. Randell claims, "you will find no traces of mad fantasy, certainly no hint of the supernatural, and the very minimum of surprise twists in plots." She values meaning and wants to teach youngsters to monitor for sense.

Noteworthy Features

Sentence structure varies in this sixteen-page book, with some sentences having as many as fifteen words. The text is full of punctuation marks used for emphasis and characterization. Words are bold for extra emphasis. Some sentences include quotation marks that indicate when one of the two characters is speaking. The illustrations are clear enough for early readers to tell the story in dialogue.

Teaching Ideas

This book could be used to teach characterization and "story voice," since there are only two characters, and they have distinct personalities. Children could learn how and when to speak in character by following the prompts provided by the text.

As children read the text, teachers will want to notice their miscues, realizing that these convey the sources of information a child draws upon in order to read. For example, if on page 9 the child reads, "He didn't see the big *neet* by the tree," and acts as if he is planning to continue on undeterred, the teacher will surmise that the child is attending to phonics but is less attentive to meaning. "You said *neet*, does that make sense?" the teacher might say. On the other hand, other children will be apt to read on page 13, "the mouse came out of her *hose*." The teacher will notice that this could make sense but doesn't match the letters. "You said *hose*. I'm glad that you

Series
PM Storybooks

Illustrator
Pat Reynolds

Publisher
Rigby (New PM Story Books)

ISBN
0435067435

TC Level
4

are making sense, but does that look right?"

To teach a strategy for effective reading, a teacher might say that reading is really thinking about a story, and that one way good readers read is they pay attention to things that surprise them in a story. For example, if you were reading *The Gingerbread Boy* and the Fox said, "Get on my back little gingerbread boy and I'll carry you safely across the river," the smart reader should be thinking, "Huh! I thought foxes ate gingerbread boys. Why is he being so nice?" A teacher could say, "To read this book, first look through the pictures and see if anything surprises you. Let's look at the cover together." The cover will generate lots of "huhs!" because it shows a lion looking down at a mouse that he holds gingerly between his paws.

"Sometimes I get the idea, when I'm just starting a book, that this will be kind of like other books I know," the teacher may want to tell children. "You know what I'm thinking? I'm thinking that this might be one of those, 'The little guy turns out to be tougher' stories.'"

Alternately, a teacher could tell children that sometimes authors write stories hoping they'll convey his messages, "Read this and think about, 'What is the author *really* saying?'" Some will conclude this is a story meant to say, "Good deeds will be rewarded." Others will suggest this is about the little guy winning. Others will conclude that this book suggests the importance of all of us, as individuals, working together in a spirit of generosity.

Genre
Picture Book

Teaching Uses
Independent Reading; Small Group Strategy Instruction

A Field Guide to the Classroom Library, Lucy Calkins and the Teachers College Reading and Writing Project, Heinemann, ©2002 Teachers College, Columbia University; http://www.heinemann.com/fieldguides

The Little Yellow Chicken

Joy Cowley

Book Summary

This story is a delightful twist on the children's classic, *The Little Red Hen*. The little yellow chicken wants to throw a party, but none of his friends will help him. Any time he asks for help, his friend the frog tells him, "Hop it!" His friend the bee says, "Buzz off!" And, the big brown beetle tells the little yellow chicken, "Stop bugging me!" The little yellow chicken manages to throw a great party despite his lack of help. When his friends find out about the event, they come clamoring at his door. In desperation, the little yellow chicken calls his grandmother (the title bird first seen in Cowley's *The Little Red Hen*) for advice. The little red hen tells him not to let them eat all of the food. The kind little chicken, though, can't leave his friends in the cold and welcomes them to the party. Frog, Bee, and Beetle apologize and offer to do all the work next time. On the last page, the little yellow chicken is seen lounging on a chaise and thinking that's a pretty good idea.

Basic Book Information

Written by Joy Cowley, the famous New Zealand author of *Mrs. Wishy-Washy*, this book is part of the Sunshine Collection of books published by the Wright Group.

Noteworthy Features

The Little Yellow Chicken is a challenging book for young readers. Although this is only a 16-page book, it is dense in text. There are approximately four full sentences on each page. The illustrations are colorful and simple, but only moderately supportive of the story. The text is fairly large and well-spaced. *The Little Yellow Chicken* contains many contractions, commas, and dialogue.

The Little Yellow Chicken contains short paragraphs. On the first few pages of the book, text is separated into one paragraph at the top of the page. There are approximately three to four sentences per page. One sentence may wrap around onto multiple lines. Some sentences are quite complex (e.g., "When the shopping was done, the little yellow chicken said to his friends, 'Will you help me do the cooking?'").

Another challenging feature of the text is the use of contractions. On page 2, the author uses the contraction "he'd." Young readers may need to be introduced to the concept that "he'd" stands for "he would."

Lower on the page, one sentence stands by itself (separated from the first paragraph by white space). Sentences do not wrap around onto multiple pages. Since a single idea is presented in full on a page, it makes it somewhat easier for young readers. Children do not have to carry the initial idea of the sentence in their heads as they turn the page for its continuation.

Illustrator
Elizabeth Fuller

Publisher
Wright Group, 1989

ISBN
0780149941

TC Level
5

A Field Guide to the Classroom Library, Lucy Calkins and the Teachers College Reading and Writing Project, Heinemann, ©2002 Teachers College, Columbia University; http://www.heinemann.com/fieldguides

Teaching Ideas

The Little Yellow Chicken is a humorous book for young children. The whimsical illustrations accentuate the comedy. In addition, the little yellow chicken's friends all use funny phrases that reflect their characters. For example, the big brown beetle tells little yellow chicken, "Stop bugging me!" Some children might get the connection automatically. Others may benefit from sharing the book with a partner or the whole class during a read aloud. By sharing in others' reaction to the book, it may add to the enjoyment of the book's humor.

Since this is a somewhat challenging story, it is essential for teachers to assess whether their students are ready for this book. Children can also read this book in partnerships. A combination of partnership and read aloud experiences may provide enough scaffolding for a child to read *The Little Yellow Chicken* independently.

Children who are already familiar with *The Little Red Hen* may recognize that this book is a twist on the classic tale. Teachers may want to suggest reading *The Little Red Hen* for contrast. There are a number of stories that have revisited classic fairy tales and fables. In order to excite children about their classroom library, teachers may decide to promote these types of books. A teacher can put up a temporary display of classic tales and their interpretations. Children may delight in reading two different takes on the same story. Cross-comparisons between books is an important skill that children need to develop.

If developmentally appropriate, a teacher may decide to have a strategy lesson on contractions. On page 2, the contraction "he'd" provides a perfect opportunity for this book to be used as an illustration of an important contraction.

Books should always be springboards for literary discussion at any age. *The Little Yellow Chicken* provides a lot of opportunities for great book talks. Young readers might want to discuss why the little yellow chicken does not heed his grandmother's advice. Another topic for conversation might revolve around the theme of forgiveness: "Do you think that it was a good idea for that little yellow chicken to forgive his friends? Why or why not?"

Genre
Picture Book

Teaching Uses
Independent Reading; Language Conventions

A Field Guide to the Classroom Library, Lucy Calkins and the Teachers College Reading and Writing Project, Heinemann, ©2002 Teachers College, Columbia University; http://www.heinemann.com/fieldguides

The Photo Book

Beverley Randell

Book Summary

The book is about a family photo album that includes pictures of Mom, Dad, James, Nick, and Kate. But Teddy Bear is missing from the album. Mom takes a photo of Teddy Bear so his picture can be in the book too.

Basic Book Information

The book has five to eight words on each of its 16 pages. The print is consistently placed on the left side of the book while the pictures are on the right. There are a number of high frequency words repeated on every page, including *is*, *the*, *here*, *in*, and *I*.

PM Readers is a series published by Rigby. The PM Readers tend to come in kits in which every book looks exactly like every other book. PM Readers feature Ben, Sally, or other characters across a series of books.

Noteworthy Features

There are several patterns that repeat and change in the book: Here is the photo book. / Mom is in the book. / Dad is in the book. / James is in the book. / Here is James. / Kate is in the book. / Here is Kate. / Nick is in the book. Here is Nick. / Here is Teddy Bear. / Teddy Bear is in the book, too.

The photos are clearly labeled with each character's name providing more support for emergent readers.

Teaching Ideas

The Photo Book provides opportunities to practice early strategies such as one-to-one matching and return sweep. A teacher might introduce this book by saying, "This book is about a family-Mom, Dad, Nick, James, and Kate. Their pictures are in the photo book [show family member's picture in the photo album and pointing out the label-Mom, Dad, etc.]. One family member is missing. Can you read and figure out who is missing?" The teacher may wish to point out and possibly have the children frame the word "here." This word frequently provides difficulty for emergent readers and is the initial word in several sentences (Here is James. / Here is Kate. / Here is Nick.). You may also wish to point out the word "photo" with a quick explanation that this might be a tricky word because you might expect to see an *f* at the beginning but in "photo," the letters *ph* make the */f/* sound.

Book Connections

If children have read any of the other books about Mom, Dad, Nick, Kate, and James they may wish to compare the family's adventures. In *The Flower*

Girl, Kate is a flower girl and Nick (really Nicola) decides that she wants to be a flower girl, too, and picks flowers from the garden. Beginning readers love following the adventures of this family and knowing the characters provides a natural introduction to the book.

Genre
Picture Book

Teaching Uses
Partnerships; Independent Reading

The Remembering Box

Eth Clifford

Book Summary

This poignant memoir piece beautifully depicts the relationship between a boy and his grandmother, the past and the present, the old country and a new era. This is a story of family traditions and values being passed from one generation to the next.

Joshua spends every Jewish Sabbath with his Grandma Goldina. It is during this time that Joshua learns of long ago as Grandma Goldina reminisces about growing up in the "old country" and about her life in America before he was born. Sometimes they pull out her remembering box and pore over the treasures inside-a water stick of his great grandfather's, photographs, hair pins, ribbons from different events in grandma's life, a silver bell she used to help her uncle herald in the beginning of Shabbat, and many more. Just before Joshua turns 10, he arrives at his grandma's house to find she has a gift for him: his own remembering box with many of the things that were once in her box. With this passing of treasures, she closes her eyes to rest and does not awaken.

Basic Book Information

The Remembering Box is 59 pages with fourteen chapters ranging from three to six pages in length. There are no illustrations in the text. Dialogue is referenced and occurs only between Joshua and his grandmother. The setting takes place around 1942. Readers will not necessarily need any prior knowledge of this time period in order to understand and appreciate the plot. There are a lot of references to Jewish tradition, language, and culture throughout the text, which add to the rich texture of the memoir.

Noteworthy Features

The text is simple and straightforward. Grandma Goldina has experienced many things throughout her life and she is sharing those things with her grandson. Joshua loves his story telling time with her. He curls up at her feet or next to her in a comfortable spot and listens as her eyes grow distant and her remembering tears fall. He learns about his grandfathers and great grandfathers who lived before him and about traditional Jewish customs that they still practice in his family.

Through Grandma Goldina, Clifford lovingly describes people and things that are dear to her such as traditional Jewish food, the Sabbath blessings, Schmuel the water finder, the knippel grandma and grandpa kept, and Hayim the bell ringer. Grandma's stories captivate us as much as they do Joshua: "My grandfather was a giant of a man. When he walked, the earth shook. When he laughed, the birds fell out of the trees. His hair caught fire from the sun. His eyes were patches of sky."

Publisher
William Morrow, 1985

ISBN
0688117775

TC Level
10

 A Field Guide to the Classroom Library, Lucy Calkins and the Teachers College Reading and Writing Project, Heinemann, ©2002 Teachers College, Columbia University; http://www.heinemann.com/fieldguides

Teaching Ideas

This would be a great text to use as a model of a memoir in the writing workshop. Students could interview a parent or guardian or a grandparent to find out about their own family histories. They could then model their own memoir pieces after this one, as an adult telling a child about times past.

Students could use the text to make a family tree in order to keep track of the characters that are presented through grandma's stories. In partnerships, students could place Joshua and his family on a tree with branches that lead to Grandma Goldina, Grandpa Abba, and the others.

Students might enjoy making their own remembering boxes. They could each find traditional items from their own cultures or religions and/or any items that hold significance for their own families. In small groups they could then share their remembering boxes with their classmates. They could compare to see if they have any items that are similar, or if there are items they've never seen before. They could then individually write about what they learned from another classmate and their family traditions and customs through the remembering box.

Another aspect of the story is Joshua trying to explain things he's learning in school to his grandma. He tells her about thunderstorms, metamorphosis, and the solar system. He brings her magnets and wants her to do an experiment. He shares with her as she shares with him. Students may want to discuss this aspect of their relationship. Both of them have different knowledge in different things. Neither has ideas more important than the other, but because they can share their ideas it makes their relationship special.

The text is filled with rich description. Students might decide to put Post-Its in places in the text where the description paints a picture in the reader's mind: "Joshua noticed his mother's light brown eyes lost their merry look, that her wide smiling mouth took on a pinched, sad expression, and that she twisted a single curl of her sandy brown hair around and around. . . ." This description draws us in to the text. Instead of simply reading words on a page, readers are seeing the picture in their minds.

The element of drama is also present in the text. Joshua enjoys going to the theater to watch Roy Rogers films. Grandma and Grandpa used to scrape and save to go to the theatre where, "For three hours those people on the stage made us live in another world." And when Grandma Goldina tells her stories she often gets up and acts out the part of the people she is describing. Small groups could discuss how telling a story with actions as well as words helps to make it more authentic. They could also discuss how different people might use different gestures for emphasis.

Book Connections

There are many other powerful memoir, or memoir-like, pieces that would be helpful in the writing workshop, giving students a sense of the possibilities they might explore in their own writing. Some examples include *Wilfrid Gordon McDonald Partridge* by Mem Fox; *Nana Upstairs and Nana Downstairs* by Tomie dePaola; and *My Mama Had a Dancing Heart* by Libba

Moore Gray.

Genre
Chapter Book; Memoir

Teaching Uses
Independent Reading; Teaching Writing

The Snail's Spell
Joanne Ryder

Book Summary

The Snail's Spell asks the reader to, "Imagine you are soft and have no bones inside you. Imagine you are grey, the color of smoke." And so the story continues until the child in the illustrations is as small as a snail, and is shown traveling through a garden (alongside a real snail) and living "a snail's life." As the story develops, factual information about snails is woven throughout, until the end, when the child is shown sitting in the garden with a snail in his hand.

Basic Book Information

This lushly illustrated picture book invites those who might otherwise find snails "gross" to explore the subject in a beautiful way.

Noteworthy Features

Factual information is artfully woven into the text. The writer does not get bogged down in too many details, and yet she covers the basic, most important information that children need to know about snails. The illustrations are colorful and beautifully detailed and well worth lingering over as they support and extend the information in the text.

Teaching Ideas

The Snail's Spell can be used to launch or support a whole class or small group science study of snails. Many early childhood classrooms find a "snail study" to be exciting, accessible, and highly supported by available texts for young children. This book does a good job of introducing important facts about snails, which children will then be able to observe in their study.

Teachers may also use this book as part of a reading center organized around the topic of snails. Readers may compare how it is similar and/or different from other books about snails they may have in their reading center basket. Teachers may ask readers to discuss, "What information do you find the same in *all* books about snails? What is in this book that is *not* in the other books you've read? What is *not* in this book, that is in other books you've read about snails?"

Teachers may also want to work with students on developing questions of their own as they read. Questioning the text is an important comprehension strategy and one that can be particularly useful when reading nonfiction.

The Snail's Spell makes a good addition to a nonfiction study, once children have become familiar with some of the characteristics of nonfiction texts. Because this book is really a nonfiction book that looks and sounds like a "storybook" due primarily to the way the author invites the reader to

Illustrator
Lynne Cherry

Publisher
Frederick Warne, 1982

ISBN
0140508910

TC Level
5

imagine along, teachers may want to lead a discussion with readers about what makes this book a nonfiction book. Teachers can ask, "How do we know this book is nonfiction? What makes it seem like it is not? Could it be included in another category as well? Why or why not?"

Because the book is beautifully illustrated and the illustrations are very detailed, many discussions can arise out of the illustrations that may not be "snail-related." Readers may want to "stop-and-say-something" about the garden vegetables they notice and/or are surprised to find growing in the ground. Readers may "hunt" for other creatures that share the garden with the snail, and speculate about why they are there and where each fits in this particular habitat.

Book Connections

How Snails Live, written by Chris Brough is one of many books about snails available for readers at this level. Others are included in the nonfiction module of the C library. Joanne Ryder has also written a number of other nonfiction (and nonfiction-like) books for children with a similar lyrical quality including *Chipmunk Song, Where Butterflies Grow, Each Living Thing,* and *Earthdance.*

Genre
Nonfiction; Picture Book

Teaching Uses
Content Area Study

The Storm

Joy Cowley

Book Summary

This easy-reader story, *The Storm*, describes the sequence of a storm: first the clouds, then the wind, lightning, thunder, rain and finally, a rainbow and the sun.

Basic Book Information

This is one of the *Story Box* books, and is written by the beloved Joy Cowley, author of *Mrs. Wishy-Washy* and countless other books for early readers. Joy Cowley lives on a remote farm in New Zealand. Knowing this, readers might infer that the rural setting of this book may be close to home for her. The Wright Group provides professional development as well as books for teachers and children, and has been a major force in supporting the move toward literature-based classrooms. The company uses a comprehensive knowledge of the development of reading skills to publish texts that are supportive of early readers.

Noteworthy Features

This book helps to introduce early readers to the book format and to simple sight vocabulary words in context. The text is large and bold, providing support for emergent readers. The text is structured as a description of the coming and then passing of a storm rather than a story with a problem and resolution.

Teaching Ideas

A rainstorm is likely to be a familiar phenomenon to most children. Teachers may want to take advantage of this by talking about the title and inviting students to share their knowledge of what happens in a rainstorm by way of introduction. Teachers can then introduce the structure to a reader by showing the first page and saying, "On this page we read 'Here comes the cloud.'" Teachers might invite the student to read the next page, prompting him to use the beginning letter of *wind* along with the picture to decode that word. Readers can then proceed through the pages, with the teacher prompting students as necessary to continue to do the same, using beginning letters combined with information in the pictures to problem-solve unfamiliar words.

This simple story provides a good example of how to focus writing on one specific topic. In a writing workshop mini-lesson, teachers might want to discuss how Joy Cowley wrote only about one thing-a storm. They can invite students to write a story about an event from their own lives that included several things. For example, a story about a birthday party might

A Field Guide to the Classroom Library, Lucy Calkins and the Teachers College Reading and Writing Project, Heinemann, ©2002 Teachers College, Columbia University; http://www.heinemann.com/fieldguides

Series
Story Box

Illustrator
Rachel Waddy

Publisher
Wright Group, 1998

ISBN
0780234499

include friends, games, presents, and a birthday cake. Students can plan for their pieces by first listing those things they connect with the event. They might then be invited to use the pattern, "Here comes the _____" to write a story similar to the one in *The Storm*. When conferring during independent writing time, or in the share, teachers might ask students to reread their story to see if they kept it focused, writing only about their chosen topic-things that go with "birthday party," for example.

Book Connections

The Storm is one of a collection of books published by the Wright Group. Wright Group categorizes it according to their system of leveling as a "Level 1" book. Many of the books in this level follow a similar format.

Genre
Nonfiction; Picture Book

Teaching Uses
Content Area Study; Reading and Writing Nonfiction

The Three Billy Goats Gruff
Paul Galdone

Book Summary

This version presents the traditional folk tale about the three Billy Goats Gruff who want to cross the bridge and go to greener pastures to graze. In their way is a mean troll who lives under the bridge. When the first little goat crosses the bridge and the troll threatens to eat him, he convinces the troll to let him pass because a bigger goat is on his way. This is repeated with the middle goat who convinces the troll to wait for the biggest billy goat. Finally, the big goat comes along and proves too big for the troll to handle. The biggest billy goat gruff butts the troll into the river and joins his brothers on the hill to feast on grass and grow fat.

Basic Book Information

In this 28-page book, the text always appears on one side of the full-page illustrations. The detailed drawings catch the reader's attention and draw him in for a closer look. Generally the pages contain no more than four or five lines of text, though one has nine lines.

Noteworthy Features

This particular version of this folk tale is straightforward. It is short and traditional, adding no new details of its own. Descriptions are simple, such as "mean as he is ugly" for the troll. However, the detailed illustrations allow children to bring a deeper level of visualization to the text.

Teaching Ideas

In Library A, *The Three Billy Goats Gruff* is included as a read aloud. This instruction is based on the research of Elizabeth Sulzby, whose work with kindergarten children informed her of the importance of recreating parent-child interactions around books in the kindergarten classroom. At home, children often ask parents to "read it again" when they hear a favorite story. In school, the teacher's multiple readings of emergent literacy books helps children become familiar with rich narrative, hear the inflection and pacing of storybook language and learn to use detailed illustrations to assist them in remembering the storyline.

After the story has been read aloud at least four times over the course of two weeks, multiple copies of the book should be added to a basket labeled "Stories We Love" (or something similar). Children will return to these books at independent reading time. They will refer to the pictures and use their memory of the teacher's reading to recreate the story in their own rereading. Children who tell you that they "can't read yet" should be encouraged to read it "the best way that they can." Given the opportunity to

A Field Guide to the Classroom Library, Lucy Calkins and the Teachers College Reading and Writing Project, Heinemann, ©2002 Teachers College, Columbia University; http://www.heinemann.com/fieldguides

Publisher
Houghton Mifflin, 1973

ISBN
0899190359

TC Level
4

do this, children pass through different reading stages from simply "labeling" pictures on the page, to telling the story off the pictures, to using progressively more dialogue and storybook language, and then moving toward a more "conventional" reading where they use the print. To go on this reading journey, it is important for children to hear the story read aloud many times, to have a lot of opportunities to reread it to a partner and to have a supportive teacher nearby who thoughtfully coaches into the reading.

Researchers such as Elizabeth Sulzby and Marie Clay, in their studies of emergent readers, have found that when children are given opportunities to do this type of "pretend reading" (referred to as "reading" or "rereading") they go through these predictable stages of reading development. To support this process, teachers should select books with more text than readers could decode independently, books which can not be easily memorized, which have elements of drama and suspense, and characters that young children can relate to.

Young children enjoy repeating the "Trip trap, trip trap" and "Who's that tramping over my bridge" refrains, joining in with the teacher as the story is read aloud. They also naturally begin to dramatize the plot. Teachers might consider supporting this behavior by adding copies of the book to the block area and dramatic play center.

Although this text may be too sophisticated to become a writing mentor for emergent writers, it does serve to build an awareness of story conventions such as repetition, sound words, dialogue in quotes, and a traditional storybook beginning ("Once upon a time...") and ending ("This tale's told out.").

This is also a great book for older readers. Discussions of exactly what the troll looks like, in this story and in other versions can be fascinating for children, and a good exercise in visualization. This can be an even stronger exercise in envisioning if children are willing to let go of the image of the troll in the pictures and create their own from the words alone.

Within the plot alone there are many opportunities for discussion. Was the bridge the troll's to begin with? Did he have a right to block people from using it? Or was it everyone's bridge, and the troll just terrorized people who tried to use it? Did he have a reason for being protective of it? Why didn't the goats try to protect each other, instead of turning each other in as they crossed? Or was it all a big plan to get the troll to fight the biggest goat? If that was the plan, why didn't the biggest goat just go first so that his smaller brothers wouldn't have to risk anything? Why didn't the goats all work together to fight the troll? And why didn't they try to think of a plan that involved outsmarting the troll instead of violence?

Some of the language in the book may be strange to some readers. In the first lines, the book says the name of all three billy goats was "Gruff." Some readers think it's their first name. They find it odd that all three goats would have the same name. Later in the book, the troll calls out "Who's that tripping over my bridge?" and some readers picture the goats actually tripping and falling. This may throw children off track as they try to make sense of the story unless they are familiar with the story or already know what these expressions mean.

Some children even discuss the morality of the story. Did the big billy goat really need to toss the troll into the river to drown? Couldn't he have just threatened or hurt him enough so he would leave the goats alone? Some

A Field Guide to the Classroom Library, Lucy Calkins and the Teachers College Reading and Writing Project, Heinemann, ©2002 Teachers College, Columbia University; http://www.heinemann.com/fieldguides

kids decide the biggest goat is a bully. And why exactly did the troll let the first two goats go anyway? Was he nicer than he looked? Was he just ugly and everyone assumed he was mean? Were the goats appealing to his sense of fair play when they said wait for my bigger brother, or were they appealing to his appetite? And if it was his appetite, couldn't he have eaten them all since the first two were pretty small?

Reading different versions of a familiar fairy tale like this one lends itself to comparison across texts, something we want our young readers to be able to do. As they read each version, they build a set of expectations and knowledge about the story, the characters and the style of each, as well as repeated experience with a familiar vocabulary providing them with opportunities to increase their fluency and comprehension.

Because most everyone does know this story, it's a good one to encourage children to talk to their parents and at-home relatives about. They can bring the fruits of the classroom discussion home to talk over and bring back to the room.

Book Connections

Paul Galdone has written many versions of these old folk tales. Each is fairly simple and fairly traditionally told. His books include *The Three Little Pigs*, *The Three Bears* and other stories that are well known and well loved.

Genre
Picture Book; Emergent Literacy Book

Teaching Uses
Independent Reading; Read Aloud; Language Conventions; Partnerships

The Tiny Seed

Eric Carle

Book Summary

This book tells the story of the life cycle of a tiny seed. The story is told in narrative form, with the tiny seed as the main character. To emphasize the unending continuity of the theme, the author has used a circular structure for the narrative. Beginning in autumn and ending the following autumn, the story goes full circle and full cycle. The process of natural selection (where seeds survive or not, depending on location, circumstances, etc.) weaves its way through the story. Teachers, however, should be aware that all of the information presented is not necessarily scientifically correct. The tiny seed, the smallest seed of all, grows into a plant that is larger and taller than houses. In reality, small seeds usually grow into small plants. Teachers might want to discuss the concept of "poetic license" to avoid children drawing erroneous conclusions.

Basic Book Information

There are 15 double-page spreads, with text consistently starting at the top of a page. Each page is illustrated by Eric Carle in his trademark tissue paper collage style and printed in full color. The text is in bold print and contrasts strongly with the white background of the page. The print size is medium with medium spacing between words and lines. Pages are not numbered.

Noteworthy Features

As a nonfiction book about the life cycle of a seed, the text does not use any sophisticated or technical terms. It is a botany lesson without any botanical language. Instead, the information is conveyed by way of a fiction story told in accessible, everyday language. Although the scenes change often, these scenery changes are clear and direct. The names of the seasons are highlighted by capitalization of the first letter. For example, "It is Autumn," "Now it is Winter," "Now it is Spring," "It is Summer," "Now it is Autumn again." It would be difficult to overlook these markers that indicate the passage of time and a change of scene.

The sentence structure is short and simple, with no clauses and very few complex or compound sentences. Most sentences contain the subject, verb, and object, elaborated with adjectives and adverbs.

Although Eric Carle creates impressionistic illustrations, these pictures are well supported by the text. Each spread contains an illustration of the main idea from the accompanying text.

Teaching Ideas

In Library A, the primary instructional purpose of this text is to support an

Illustrator
Eric Carle

Publisher
Scholastic, 1987

ISBN
0590425668

TC Level
5

A Field Guide to the Classroom Library, Lucy Calkins and the Teachers College Reading and Writing Project, Heinemann, ©2002 Teachers College, Columbia University; http://www.heinemann.com/fieldguides

Eric Carle author study. After listening to many of his books read aloud and having opportunities to reread them on their own, children are likely to notice that many of them are about scientific concepts, and each teaches us something new. These include *The Very Hungry Caterpillar*, *Today is Monday*, *The Very Busy Spider*, and *Have You Seen My Cat?* Children might observe that, although they appear to be nonfiction, they all contain exaggerated truths and even some misinformation.

Eric Carle is a very accessible author for young children to study. Children easily recognize his strong, consistent style of illustrations. The books often contain biographical information, sometimes accompanied by a photograph of the author. Many of his texts contain repetitive patterns and children enjoy joining in on the refrain as the teacher reads aloud to the class.

Eric Carle's books lend themselves to partner reading. After the children have heard the book read to them many times, they will have internalized the story. Using the illustrations to support their retelling, they can then recreate the story as they read to each other in their partnerships.

If the class is doing an inquiry study of plants, this book could be added to a basket of books on the topic. If there were two baskets of books on the topic, fiction and nonfiction, an interesting discussion might ensue around deciding where this book belongs. Children could be encouraged to support their opinions by returning to the text for evidence.

Book Connections

The A Library also contains the book, *The Carrot Seed*. These two books would make an interesting pairing for partner reading or reading centers.

Genre
Picture Book; Nonfiction

Teaching Uses
Author Study; Content Area Study; Partnerships; Read Aloud; Interpretation; Reading and Writing Nonfiction

A Field Guide to the Classroom Library, Lucy Calkins and the Teachers College Reading and Writing Project, Heinemann, ©2002 Teachers College, Columbia University; http://www.heinemann.com/fieldguides

The Tortilla Factory

Gary Paulsen

Book Summary

Children learn about the process of making a tortilla in poetic form. The information communicated by this book provides a general idea of the cycle of life, with the harvest, the work, the cooking, the eating, the harvest again, and so on.

Basic Book Information

This nonfiction picture book is about thirty pages long. On each double-page spread, the text ranges from one to several phrases or clauses. The pages are composed of the oil painting illustrations, which are beautiful and atmospheric more than technical. This book has few of the features usually found in more technical nonfiction-subheads, index, table of contents-instead, there is a simple narrative illustrated with paintings.

Noteworthy Features

The entire text is one unfinished sentence, but it reads more like an unpunctuated poem than a breathless sentence. This is a very simple nonfiction text, with plenty to notice and discuss in the story. This book also presents nonfiction in a nontechnical, simply true sort of way. This can be inviting and nonthreatening to many children who are intimidated or turned off by more traditional nonfiction texts.

Because this story is told with poetic and figurative language, readers who are extremely literal may have some extra work to do in reading it. When, for example, the text says the black earth sleeps, children may at first be puzzled.

The story follows no particular character, following instead the path of the tortilla. Some readers wonder whose hands work the earth, and who is kneading and eating the tortillas. Children who are used to following a character may find this kind of book structure confusing and need some support getting started.

Teaching Ideas

Children who aren't familiar with tortillas will certainly read this book in a different way than children who know them well. For children who don't know them, the reading of the book will hold a certain kind of suspense-finding out what a tortilla is.

As a read aloud, *The Tortilla Factory* can support children's questioning of texts. Some students have asked if the same people who are laboring are enjoying the fruits of their labor-or, are they hungry while someone else eats the tortillas they made? Children could follow such questions to some very

Illustrator
Ruth Wright Paulsen

Publisher
Harcourt, Brace and Company, 1995

ISBN
0152016988

TC Level
7

A Field Guide to the Classroom Library, Lucy Calkins and the Teachers College Reading and Writing Project, Heinemann, ©2002 Teachers College, Columbia University; http://www.heinemann.com/fieldguides

important issues involving labor and equity. If they decide these issues are less relevant here, they will have to determine what the story is mainly about and find evidence to support their determination. In either case, the thinking involved will certainly further their reading.

The Tortilla Factory makes a good addition to a collection of nonfiction texts as it has a different look and sound than lots of other nonfiction. By exposing readers to a wide variety of nonfiction texts, teachers help them develop a working understanding of what distinguishes fiction from nonfiction. Narrower exposure can have a different, unintended result. For example, some groups of young children after studying nonfiction conclude that photographs are the only permissible form of illustration-a logical conclusion given that so much of the wonderful nonfiction now available includes great photographs!

Genre
Nonfiction; Picture Book

Teaching Uses
Independent Reading; Content Area Study; Critique

A Field Guide to the Classroom Library, Lucy Calkins and the Teachers College Reading and Writing Project, Heinemann, ©2002 Teachers College, Columbia University; http://www.heinemann.com/fieldguides

The True Story of the Three Little Pigs

Jon Scieszka

Book Summary

This is the story of the three little pigs-told from the point of view of the big bad wolf! He claims to have been framed. The wolf explains that he was just making a birthday cake for his granny one day. He needed to borrow a cup of sugar from his neighbor, a pig. When he got to the house and sneezed, the house fell in and the pig apparently died. Not to waste a meal, the wolf ate him. The same thing happened at the next house made of sticks. When the wolf asked at the brick house, the pig made some very rude comments about the wolf's granny and that's what got him all worked up, and that's when the police arrived. That's all. No Big Bad Wolf here-just an innocent wolf framed!

Basic Book Information

This picture book has the bold, modern and funny illustrations of Lane Smith. They also have a complexity that reflects the complexity of the story.

Noteworthy Features

For this book to be fully appreciated, it is absolutely imperative that the reader knows the folk tale *Three Little Pigs* inside and out. Readers should know how the tale is usually told, even down to the repeated phrases that are usually invoked, like "Not by the hairs on my chinny-chin-chin." Without this knowledge of the traditional tale, this story loses its great fun and even its point.

The story of *The Three Little Pigs* by Paul Galdone offers the traditional tale with no frills and no deviations from the expected. Of course, it is better if children have heard more than one version of the story with similar details, over the course of years, but this version of the story can fill in the background for those who haven't had that opportunity.

Teaching Ideas

This story is a good introduction to the concept of point of view. It is easy for readers to realize this is the same story they have heard, but from a different perspective. This experience can provide a model to follow, allowing them to do the same with another story, or a piece of their own writing. The ability to step back and assume another point of view pushes writers' and readers' thinking and deepens their comprehension.

Some readers spend time arguing about whether or not the wolf is lying

Illustrator
Lane Smith

Publisher
Puffin, 1996

ISBN
0140544518

TC Level
7

A Field Guide to the Classroom Library, Lucy Calkins and the Teachers College Reading and Writing Project, Heinemann, ©2002 Teachers College, Columbia University; http://www.heinemann.com/fieldguides

about his version of the story. Can he be trusted? Is he just trying to look good? These are important issues in literature to discuss-if a character is portraying himself accurately or if he is trying to cast himself in a particular light. A great step in comprehending, interpreting, and critiquing literature is realizing that the truth may be different from what is presented to the reader.

This introduction into understanding point of view can lead to an understanding of critique. If children understand different fiction stories have different possible points of view, it is easier for them to imagine that different true stories also can have different points of view depending on the information the teller has, or wishes to get across. Of course, other materials would be necessary to illustrate this for children, for example, different newspaper reports on the same event.

Readers tend to love knowing and finding the inside jokes in this story. Groups of students can point out to each other the funny parts. Kids may also delight in playing with their own thinking-like they too would be seen as big and bad if cheeseburgers were considered cute and fuzzy. As well, the wolf talks in a cool, hip way that kids usually think is funny coming from a mean, old storybook character.

Book Connections

Jon Scieszka has written other twists on folk tales. He has one about the Frog Prince-*The Frog Prince Continued*, and one called *The Stinky Cheese Man and Other Fairly Stupid Stories*, both of which challenge readers to think about old stories from new angles. *The Book that Jack Wrote* goes even further and has readers think about the page layout, typefaces, and fonts the stories are written in! His stories make readers aware of the construction of the stories in a way that is unusual for children's literature.

Genre
Fairy and Folk Tale; Picture Book

Teaching Uses
Independent Reading; Interpretation; Critique

The Very Hungry Caterpillar

Eric Carle

Book Summary

This book portrays the metamorphosis of a caterpillar into a colorful butterfly. The caterpillar starts out as an egg, transforms into a "very hungry caterpillar" and then becomes a beautiful full-grown butterfly. Over the course of the week, the caterpillar eats through many foods: apples, pears, plums, strawberries, and oranges. On the sixth day, he is still hungry and eats an array of junk food and ends up with a terrible stomachache. On the seventh day, after only eating through one leaf, he makes the final transformation into a gorgeous butterfly.

Basic Book Information

This picture book includes 13 die-cut pages. The number of sentences on a page as well as the length of the sentences varies throughout the book. There are many short, repetitive, simple sentences (e.g., "But he was still hungry, on _____, he ate through _____.") But there are also lengthier and more complex sentences and groups of sentences on a page (e.g., "He built a small house, called a cocoon, around himself. He stayed inside for weeks. Then he nibbled a hole in the cocoon, pushed his way out.").

Noteworthy Features

The pages are beautifully illustrated in Carle's trademark collage style. Often the illustrations are dramatically spread across two pages, with text written on only one side. On other pages, the text is set alongside a single page illustration. On many pages, the illustrations are marked with a hole in the middle. This suggests to the reader, none too subtly, that the hungry caterpillar has been nibbling the illustrations, enhancing their understanding of the concept.

Eric Carle successfully takes the sophisticated topic of metamorphosis and simplifies it for the young reader. He begins the book by presenting the image of the egg lying on the leaf at night, and then moves into the daylight. After the first few pages, the text shifts into a repetitive pattern: "On Monday he ate through one apple, but he was still hungry." Each succeeding page is highly predictable. Many young children are cognizant of the days of the week and are able to accumulate the food that is being eaten each day by both the visual representation as well as the expectation of what will follow. On the sixth page, the pattern begins to break down. Many children find some tricky words on this page, since the pictorial representations are more abstract and not as familiar. The book is so engaging that young readers are usually able to comprehend the text even though there are some specific words that might be tricky.

A Field Guide to the Classroom Library, Lucy Calkins and the Teachers College Reading and Writing Project, Heinemann, ©2002 Teachers College, Columbia University; http://www.heinemann.com/fieldguides

Teaching Ideas

This book is an excellent one to include in an author study on Eric Carle. It is similar to Carle's other books about insects-*The Very Busy Spider* and *The Very Quiet Cricket*. After reading many of his books, children will notice that a number of them are about insects, and that though they appear to be nonfiction, they all contain exaggerated truths. Children will notice the repetitive patterns in many of his books and will want to join in on the refrains (e.g., "But he was still hungry.").

Eric Carle books also provide attainable writing models for children. In their own writing, children will want to try out some of Carle's literary techniques such as combing nonfiction and fiction, using repetition and strong, repetitive patterns, and using the paper creatively.

Eric Carle's books lend themselves to partner reading. Often when children are reading this book in a partnership, sitting close together with one book between the two of them, they make a deliberate decision on how to read the repetitive parts. Partners may decide to each read a different page, and then in unison read, "But he was still hungry." Another partnership might decide to each read the entire repetitive part before switching back and forth.

This book might lead to an inquiry study of change. This investigation might last over a period of several weeks, with one part of the study focusing on the process of change from a caterpillar into a butterfly. If the discussion of change involved the eating habits of the caterpillar this might develop into a conversation about whether or not the foods listed in the book were typical foods for a caterpillar. The concept of "exaggeration" might be discussed. This could also lead to a reading center on books about metamorphosis, where children might ponder this question as they look across books, coming to their own conclusions about truth or poetic license.

Book Connections

Other Carle texts include *The Very Busy Spider, The Very Quiet Cricket*, and *The Grouchy Ladybug*.

Genre

Picture Book; Emergent Literacy Book

Teaching Uses

Author Study; Read Aloud; Independent Reading; Partnerships; Interpretation; Teaching Writing

A Field Guide to the Classroom Library, Lucy Calkins and the Teachers College Reading and Writing Project, Heinemann, ©2002 Teachers College, Columbia University; http://www.heinemann.com/fieldguides

The Well-Fed Bear

Tui Simpson

Book Summary

This book begins and almost ends with the words "I am a well-fed bear." In between, there is the repeating sentence, "I had . . ." with various foods filling in the blank. At the very end of the book, the bear reveals he is a bear on a boy's t-shirt, and the boy has been spilling food on him all day-hence his claim that he is a well-fed bear.

Basic Book Information

The book has 8 pages, with one sentence consistently located at the top of each page. Most of it is held together with the repeating pattern, but there is a twist at the end.

Noteworthy Features

The pictures do not help the reader know which food the bear is saying he had to eat. On one page there is a green glob that is supposed to be ice cream, on another there is yellow goo that could be honey, egg, or a variety of foods, but it turns out to be custard. The same is true of the rest of the foods pictured.

To add to the difficulty of figuring out the food from the print, the bear is not eating in a typical way. He isn't eating ice cream from a cone or vegetables from a bowl, and the orange juice is raining down on him in droplets instead of coming to him in a glass. This makes it even harder to use the pictures for support. If readers think they have figured out the word, they can only use the picture in a rough way to confirm whether they're right.

This book has features that provide standard support to early readers in many areas of reading, such as one-to-one matching. The fact that most of the pages begin with the familiar word "I" helps anchor readers in the text. One page, however, begins with "Today I. . . ." This can be tricky.

Teaching Ideas

This can be an excellent choice for use in a mini-lesson designed to help children stop and talk between pages. It can also work well in partnerships, as there is much for a young reader to ponder in this little book. As the reader goes along in it, she may well stop to wonder why the bear is eating in such an odd manner-without bowls and glasses. If it is because he is a wild bear, why is he eating such "human" food? And why does he wear a ribbon? When children get to the end of the book and learn the bear is "fed" by food spilled on him, the earlier questions begin to make sense. However, whole new areas of questions then open. How can the bear move around like he

Illustrator
Ian McNee

Publisher
Rigby, Shortland
Publications, 1988

ISBN
0868677647

TC Level
3

does in the pictures if he is a bear on a shirt? How can he eat? The book is an excellent choice to fuel conversations in the midst of reading.

Genre
Picture Book

Teaching Uses
Independent Reading; Partnerships

This Quiet Lady

Charlotte Zolotow

Book Summary

A young girl who is trying to understand the relationship between her life and her mother's life narrates this picture book. In it the little girl looks through photo albums and framed pictures of her mother's life from baby through childhood, schoolgirl through bride. Until the last two-page spread with both mother and daughter where the text reads, "And here is where I begin." The final single page is of the little girl herself as a baby that's labeled simply, "The Beginning."

Basic Book Information

Charlotte Zolotow is the acclaimed author of many beloved children's book such as *My Grandson Lew* and *William's Doll*. This is a beautifully illustrated 19-page picture book. The text, which consists of one complete sentence broken into three to four lines of type, is consistently placed on the left side of a double-page spread. The text is clearly written in a large black font on a white background.

Noteworthy Features

The book is set up like a photo album with the young narrator shown on the left hand side in a smaller illustration of black, white, and gray, studying a full-page color "picture" of her mother in a chronological sequence of life stages on each page to the right. It's as if the reader as well as the narrator, is examining and learning about the mother's life page by page.

Each double-page spread has one single sentence beneath the narrator's picture. Each sentence repeats, "This..." and ends with, "...is my mother." This sentence structure may support some early readers in getting through the words of this book.

Teaching Ideas

This is a good book to read aloud and discuss with children. Children might notice the cycle of life in this story and think about how this cycle of life happens to parents and children. This book might also bring out family stories of their own. Many children will be eager to share the stories they have heard about the members of their own families. They might also want to bring in photographs from home to share with other students.

Students will also enjoy time to revisit this book independently. They might read the pictures and the words. Children might also create stories that go with the picture illustrations on both pages, which are always rich in detail. The repeated sentence structure of, "This . . . is my mother" and picture clues offer support to young readers

Illustrator
Anita Lobel

Publisher
Harper Trophy, 1992

ISBN
0688175279

 A Field Guide to the Classroom Library, Lucy Calkins and the Teachers College Reading and Writing Project, Heinemann, ©2002 Teachers College, Columbia University; http://www.heinemann.com/fieldguides

This book is also appropriate for use as a model in the writing workshop. In a mini-lesson a teacher might say, "Let's notice the kinds of things that Charlotte Zolotow did as a writer so we can try some of those things ourselves." Children will notice for example, the author's use of descriptive language (e.g., "This baby smiling in her bassinet under the crocheted throw is my mother." or "This bride like a white flower is my mother.").

Teachers may also point out the ending that reveals the circular theme of the story, "And here is where I begin." Here we see the narrator with her dolly in her lap holding a picture of her mother holding her, a newborn baby girl. As readers turn the page, they see the baby and read, "The Beginning." Once children notice these things they might want to try some or all of these techniques in their own writing.

This book might be a good starting point for story reflections on children's younger years, possibly to begin a memoir study.

Book Connections

When I Was Five by Arthur Howard and *When I Was Little: A Four-Year-Old's Memoir of Her Youth* by Jamie Lee Curtis are also books where the narrators reflect back on an earlier life through memoir writing.

Genre
Emergent Literacy Book; Picture Book

Teaching Uses
Independent Reading; Critique; Interpretation; Teaching Writing; Read Aloud

A Field Guide to the Classroom Library, Lucy Calkins and the Teachers College Reading and Writing Project, Heinemann, ©2002 Teachers College, Columbia University; http://www.heinemann.com/fieldguides

Thunder Cake

Patricia Polacco

Book Summary

As a thunderstorm approaches and a little girl grows more and more afraid, her grandmother helps her to overcome her fear by helping her make a special "thunder cake" and then showing her the courage it took to do it. A recipe for the cake is included.

Basic Book Information

This big picture book features Polacco's colorful, friendly, detailed illustrations, and has her gently funny, realistic text to match.

Noteworthy Features

The first page and paragraph of *Thunder Cake* is an introduction and explanation of the story's origins from the author. Without textual markers that say "Introduction" or "Recipe" children are offered an introduction, the text of the story itself and then a recipe at the end, all with illustrations.

The vocabulary is not basic (*horizon, stammered, penned*), but even if these words are unfamiliar to the reader, the story is still understandable. The same is true for the dialogue, a sentence like "Gather them eggs careful-like." may throw some children off, but if they are willing to go with it, they will probably soon realize that's how the talking goes in the story. In making the cake, the little girl does many things children may not be familiar with, from churning the butter to gathering eggs from the hens and fetching ingredients from the dry shed. But, once again, the pictures help explain and most readers can understand with little support in these unfamiliar topics.

Teaching Ideas

In the writing workshop, *Thunder Cake* is an excellent example of how to use dialogue and sounds in writing in order to give stories life and flavor. From the ways dialogue is included with text, to the ways the sounds of thunder are woven throughout, this story provides many examples of the author's craft that children can study and even imitate.

The recipe at the story's end may encourage readers to include his or her parents in the reading process by asking for help in cooking the thunder cake, or in comparing the recipe with the recipes for sweets from home. Parents and child could read the book together.

There are many opportunities for discussion with this read aloud. The Russian American grandmother, Babushka, and her appearance and way of speaking will add to the air of acceptance and appreciation of ethnic difference in any classroom, whether or not her ethnicity is brought up or

Illustrator
Patricia Polacco

Publisher
PaperStar, 1997

ISBN
0698115813

TC Level
4

remains in the background of the story. Often children relate to the little girl in the story easily, and they are eager to discuss fears of their own with each other. The teacher's challenge is then to help the readers see the ways this child overcame her fear and how that could help them overcome their fear as well.

Teachers may want to do some interpretation work with this read aloud story. In discussion, there's a good chance children will decide the story's message is one of being able to be brave when someone shows you how, and of having trust in one another.

Book Connections

Patricia Polacco is also the author of *Uncle Vova's Tree* and *Rechenka's Eggs,* as well as a number of other titles.

Genre
Picture Book

Teaching Uses
Read Aloud; Character Study; Interpretation

A Field Guide to the Classroom Library, Lucy Calkins and the Teachers College Reading and Writing Project, Heinemann, ©2002 Teachers College, Columbia University; http://www.heinemann.com/fieldguides

Titch

Pat Hutchins

Book Summary

Titch is little. He has a sister Mary, who is big, and a brother Peter, who is bigger. Compared to his siblings, everything Titch has is small-until Titch gets a tiny seed. When he plants his seed with Mary's pot and Peter's spade, the seed grows bigger, and bigger, and bigger.

Basic Book Information

Pat Hutchins is a British author of a number of well-known books including *Rosie's Walk* and *Good-Night Owl*. *Titch* is part of a series of books about the same character: *You'll Soon Grow Into Them Titch* and *Tidy Titch*.

Noteworthy Features

It's worthwhile for teachers to understand that a book such as this is written with hopes that a reader will soon "get" how the whole book goes, so the reader already knows that poor Titch will have the smallest item even before it happens.

Teaching Ideas

A teacher may choose to provide an introduction to this book for a particular reader, knowing that by doing so, he might then go on to read other *Titch* books with more independence. One way of introducing this text is by engaging the child in a conversation about what it's like to have a big brother and sister who always seem to have the bigger and better stuff.

A child who is reading books at this level may not need to point to the words anymore; if that is the case, a finger can get in the way, becoming more of a hindrance than help. "Just keep your finger close and bring it out if you get to a hard part," the teacher can say. The hard parts in this book might include the expression, "flew high above" on pages 8 and 9, and, "wooden whistle" on page 15. The word *spade* may also be an unknown word, and if a teacher is close by he or she may want to tell the child that this is a special kind of shovel.

While conferring, teachers might help readers practice putting together all they've learned about the process of using information in the text-searching, checking, and using phonological information-on the run, while reading. For example, on page 2, a student might read, "His sister Mary went a bit bigger," the teacher might prompt the child by saying, "You said 'went a bit bigger,' does that make sense?" Again on the last page, if the child read, "And Titch had the nails," the teacher might prompt the child to check again by saying "You said . . . I'm glad that you made sense, but does that look right?" Alternately, the teacher could simply ask the child to

Series
Titch

Illustrator
Pat Hutchins

Publisher
Macmillan Publishing, 1971

ISBN
0689716885

TC Level
4

reread, "There was something wrong on this line. See if you can find what was wrong." The teacher could also watch the child's word-solving strategies. For example it'll be interesting to see what the child does with compound words such as *pinwheel* and *flowerpot*. If the students are having difficulty with the word *hand*, attention can be focused on parts of it that look like familiar words, like *and*.

Book Connections

Titch is part of a series written by Pat Hutchins. Other books include *You'll Soon Grow Into Them Titch* and *Tidy Titch*. Other books in the library at about the same level include *George Shrinks!* by William Joyce.

Genre
Picture Book; Emergent Literacy Book

Teaching Uses
Read Aloud; Independent Reading; Small Group Strategy Instruction

Tulip Sees America
Cynthia Rylant

Book Summary

Tulip Sees America tells the story of a young man's journey across the United States. The young man has not yet explored outside of Ohio. When is he grown up, he gets a car, packs his belongings, takes his dog, Tulip, and drives west to make a home for himself in Oregon. The story begins by explaining how the young man's mother and father enjoyed being home in Ohio. The young man knows he is different from them and wants to explore the country. The story describes the scenery throughout Iowa, Nebraska, Wyoming, Colorado, Nevada, and Oregon. The story ends, "And this is where we stayed." with the young man painting a portrait of Tulip in Oregon by the ocean on the beach.

Basic Book Information

Cynthia Rylant has written more than sixty books for children. She has been honored with the Newbery Medal and the Boston Globe-Horn Award. Other picture books she has written include *Appalachia*, *When the Relatives Came*, *All I See*, and *Bookshop Dog*. Some of the chapter books she has written are *Missing May*, *A Fine White Dust*, and *The Islander*. Cynthia Rylant drove with her son and two dogs from Ohio to make a home in Oregon. This was the first time they had ever seen the places they drove through and their wonderful trip was inspiration for the book. Cynthia Rylant lives in a green cottage in Oregon with her son and many pets.

Lisa Desimini is known for her innovative style. She has created artwork for seventeen books and many book jackets. For this book, Desimini created layered oil paintings and scanned them in a computer where they were completed. Her last book for The Blue Sky Press, Arnold Adoff's *Love Letters*, received great reviews in School Library Journal and Booklist. Lisa Desimini lives in New York City.

This picture book is thirty pages. Each place visited is described over four pages. The story is told in the first person narrative from the young man's point of view. The illustrations are brightly colored and truly bring meaning to the text with great attention to detail.

Noteworthy Features

This book provides students with a beautiful example of one person's experience and how it inspired her to write, using descriptive language, and based on her observations. The curved print of the sentences on some of the pages creates movement. The multicolored print is shown in the bright illustrations. This book celebrates the uniqueness of each state visited with

Illustrator
Lisa Desimini

Publisher
The Blue Sky Press, 1998

ISBN
0590847449

TC Level
5

detailed descriptions of the particular differences. For example, "There is no ocean like Oregon's." displays that each coastline is special. It also shares the brave and courageous journey of a young man leaving home and taking in his surroundings. Cynthia Rylant lives with and loves her many pets. Pets are characters in many of her books. Cynthia Rylant dedicates the book to Leia and Martha Jane "for being such good dogs on our trip."

Teaching Ideas

The book provides many opportunities for reader response and can be used as a touchstone text. The book starts out with a young man about to embark on a journey. In comparison to his parents who are "homebodies" he says, "But when I grew up, I knew I was different. I wanted to see America." Students can talk about what they know about the character and how they know it based on his actions, feelings, words, and thoughts. The students can begin to predict by asking questions before, during, and after based on the title, author, illustrator, blurb, and reviews. What does he do? What does he see?

This book provides an excellent example of setting. It is also a great example of the genre of memoir and a linear story. Throughout the book, the young man describes what he sees. The descriptions are not told in complete sentences in some of the scenes. Students can discuss why a writer may use poetic language, a significant word, or list of words that can stand alone (for example, "The farms in Iowa. They are pictures: white houses. Red roofs."). A teacher can explain how a writer can use punctuation to make it easier for a reader to understand these lists.

This is a great mentor text to use when writing personal narrative. The story describes the young man's journey in sequential order. It could be used to show how a story is written in order with a connecting theme. Repetition is used in a simple and purposeful way. Students could use the style and structure of the writing in their own writing to connect the text to a central theme and for emphasis.

This book would serve as a good example for students struggling with endless stories and stories with heaps of extraneous details. *Tulip Sees America* has a definite time frame, and a simple way of showing movement through time-the passage from one state to another. There is a short amount of very specific information about each part of the author's journey. The text is balanced.

Book Connections

In *All I See* by Cynthia Rylant a boy is inspired by an artist's observations of his surroundings. In *When the Relatives Came* by Cynthia Rylant, the people travel by car to visit family. In *The Islander* by Cynthia Rylant, the ocean is an integral and significant piece of the story.

Genre
Picture Book

A Field Guide to the Classroom Library, Lucy Calkins and the Teachers College Reading and Writing Project, Heinemann, ©2002 Teachers College, Columbia University; http://www.heinemann.com/fieldguides

Teaching Uses
Author Study; Character Study; Teaching Writing; Language Conventions

A Field Guide to the Classroom Library, Lucy Calkins and the Teachers College Reading and Writing Project, Heinemann, ©2002 Teachers
College, Columbia University; http://www.heinemann.com/fieldguides

Vegetables, Vegetables!

Fay Robinson

Series
Rookie Read-About
Science

Publisher
Children's Press, 1994

ISBN
0516460307

TC Level
5

Book Summary

Vegetables, Vegetables! introduces readers to basic concepts about vegetables. It begins with several examples of vegetables in their different forms: as a leaf (like lettuce), a seed (like peas), a bulb (like onions), a root (like radishes), and as a flower (like broccoli). Vegetables with seeds are defined as fruits. There is a short section about how and where vegetables are grown in gardens and around the world. Vegetables are shown as part of simple recipes and the book ends with directions on how to make a simple salad.

Basic Book Information

This nonfiction book has 30 pages with the text beginning on page 3. While there is not a lot of text overall and the text is relatively simply written, the vocabulary is quite challenging. Much of the text is made up of words that are not easily decoded. There is a section at the end called "Words You Know" that supports readers by repeating vocabulary from the book with matching photographs, serving as a picture glossary.

Noteworthy Features

The sentence structure and vocabulary may be difficult for early and/or emergent readers. There are easier books in this series that are in the same format and style of this book.

There is a glossary of photos and words, and a detailed index in the back of the book. These can be used as an introduction to some of the features of nonfiction reading.

Teaching Ideas

Teachers may model for children how to use various features of nonfiction text-like an index to find specific information and a glossary to find definitions of unfamiliar words.

Teachers may model for children some strategies for reading nonfiction. Readers of nonfiction often have some decisions to make. Narrative fiction is usually read straight through from beginning to end, but with nonfiction, this is not necessarily so. Readers might check the index or table of contents for a particular kind of information and go straight to it if they need to. Readers can practice reading the text in smaller chunks, rather than from start to finish. Readers can practice generating a list of questions based on the title, skimming of the book, or the small chunk they've read. They can then try reading for the information necessary to answer their specific questions.

Vegetables, Vegetables! can be used in a science reading center on vegetables (or farming, gardening, cooking). As readers become more familiar with the topic, they may want to do some very simple cross-referencing to discover what all books about vegetables have in common, or what this particular book lacks or adds to their study of the topic. Teachers may want to use the picture glossary as a model for texts students might construct as they study a subject.

Book Connections

This book can be used in conjunction with other books from the *Rookie Read-About Science* series as part of a nonfiction study. It can also be used in conjunction with other books about vegetables (farming, planting, etc.) at this level. Other series at this level include *Twig Books* and early readers in the Wright Group.

Genre
Nonfiction; Picture Book

Teaching Uses
Independent Reading; Content Area Study; Reading and Writing Nonfiction

A Field Guide to the Classroom Library, Lucy Calkins and the Teachers College Reading and Writing Project, Heinemann, ©2002 Teachers College, Columbia University; http://www.heinemann.com/fieldguides

What You Know First

Patricia MacLachlan

Book Summary

What You Know First tells the story of a little girl and her family who are preparing to move away from the only home the girl has ever known. The farm she lives on is located on the prairie and holds some of her most cherished memories. The young girl reflects on all of the things she loves about this place and how she will say goodbye to them. The sky, the grass, and her tree, are all a part of her and hard to part with. The little girl wants to find a way to hold on to these things so she can share them with her baby brother when he grows up. She is determined to find a way to take these memories with her.

Basic Book Information

Patricia MacLachlan is the author of many well-loved novels and picture books, including *Sarah, Plain and Tall,* winner of the Newbery Medal; it's sequel, *Skylark,* and *All The Places To Love,* illustrated by Mike Wimmer.

Noteworthy Features

The dark, serious, dramatically cropped engravings on these pages lend the book an adult air, which attracts some children and repels others. The small amount of text per page may, for some children, counterbalance the sophisticated air lent by the illustrations. On the other hand, some children see the format of the copy on the page and think the book is poetry, and therefore (sadly) intimidating to read. In most classrooms, especially at the beginning of the year, this book could use an introduction or a promotion or at least a link to another book (perhaps one of MacLachlan's many others) to get it off the shelves and into children's hands.

What You Know First is really more a meditation than a story. It is the thoughts of a girl-a reader can only tell it is a girl from the pictures, not the text, so conceivably it could be a boy-as she adjusts to the fact that she is moving away from the place she loves.

This book is laden with farm-specific vocabulary and images, so, like any book, readers unfamiliar with the places described will undoubtedly have a harder time picturing it, and possibly understanding it, than other readers. Passages that describe the pipits feeding or the geese sky-talking may give some readers pause.

Some of the more interesting facts about this story are based in its creation. Patricia MacLachlan was born on the prairie, and to this day carries a small bag of prairie dirt with her wherever she goes to remind her of what she knew first. One day, shortly after a move to a new home MacLachlan felt unstable. She was having a hard time adjusting to her new surroundings and missed her old home. She was having trouble writing as

Illustrator
Barry Moser

Publisher
Harper Collins, 1995

ISBN
0064434923

TC Level
8

well. At that very time she was to speak to a fourth grade class at the Jackson Street School and worried about what she would say to them in this state of mind. She wound up discussing heavily the topic of "place and landscape" and showed the students her bag of prairie dirt from where she was born. The children were very involved in the discussion because they could relate. Five were foster children, disconnected from their homes. One boy had recently lost everything he had to a fire in his home. Another told her that he was moving in a few days to a place he'd never been. MacLachlan suggested to these students that maybe she should take her prairie dirt and toss it in her new backyard so that the two places could mix together. The children's reactions to this were so strongly against this idea, fearful that the dirt might blow away. One small girl suggested placing the dirt in a bowl and keeping it on the window so that it would be a constant reminder of "what you knew first." When MacLachlan left the school she went home to write this book.

Teaching Ideas

This book starts right in the middle of her thoughts, with no explanation of the characters, situation or setting. If children are confused by this opening, or by books in general that open this way, it may help them to learn that all readers feel that sense of missing knowledge when a book starts in the middle like that. We can tell children that authors know the reader will be wondering about the details of the situation, and the authors use that to get the reader to read more in order to get their questions answered. In order for the words to make sense as the reader does read more, he or she has to read carefully and hold in mind the questions raised by the text. In this case the questions are probably the following: Who is the "I"? Where is it she won't go? Why?

In this book, some of the reader's questions are answered almost right away. It becomes clear that the place the girl doesn't want to go to is a new house, a new place, a land she's never seen. That quick answer to the reader's early question provides some support for the reader unused to reading with questions. For that reason, this book might make a good transitional read for kids who aren't yet able to read fantasy and other-world-type books that require the reader to hold in mind a lot of unanswered questions.

The book leaves some questions for readers to puzzle over, to discuss in groups or reread and think about. The narrator asks to herself why they must leave at all, and the reader may well try to figure that out from the story. It seems the family must leave for monetary reasons, but students can debate over the possibilities that are hinted at in the book.

Like many of MacLachlan's books, this one has a tone of nostalgia for the "good life," one where people live side by side with natural beauty and in perfect harmony with the land. The tone itself can provide fodder for discussion, especially if the tone in this book is compared to the tone in another book that presents another perspective on farm life-one that shows some of the hardships or negative aspects of country living.

This book could appear in a basket with multiple copies. Whether a teacher wishes to introduce Memoir, Poetry or an Author Study of Patricia MacLachlan's literary work, or if a teacher would rather discuss the beautiful language and vivid vocabulary or even the structure of this text, it would make a great mentor text. Not only is it a wonderfully structured book, but it can even be used to ease the anxiety of that new child that appears at each of our classroom doorways in the late winter or early spring. Surely a child such as this could immediately feel comforted after reading the first page ("I won't go, I'll say, To a new house, To a new place, To a land I've never seen").

This book also provides an outstanding opportunity for introducing the concept of studying artifacts in Memoir. The young girl will "take a twig of the cottonwood tree...take a little bag of prairie dirt." One can almost picture the girl sitting with these artifacts later in life and all of her original memories come flooding to her mind:

> Or maybe
> I'll live in a tree.
> The tall cottonwood that was small when Papa was small,
> But grew faster than he did.
> Now it has branches
> And crooks where I can sit
> To look over the rooftop,
> Over the windmill
> Over the prairie...

Book Connections

Patricia MacLachlan is the author of many well-loved novels and picture books, including *Sarah, Plain and Tall,* winner of the Newbery Medal; it's sequel, *Skylark,* and *All The Places To Love,* illustrated by Mike Wimmer.

Genre
Picture Book

Teaching Uses
Read Aloud; Independent Reading; Critique; Teaching Writing; Partnerships

Who Lays Eggs?

Sally Kneidel

Series
Twig Book

Illustrator
Paul Kratter

Publisher
Wright Group

ISBN
0322001706

TC Level
3

Book Summary

Who Lays Eggs? is an emergent level nonfiction book about six egg-laying animals and one mammal. The book illustrates where the animals live and very simply, how they have babies. For example: "The clam lives on the sandy sea floor. She lays her tiny eggs in the sea."

Basic Book Information

This is a Wright Group *Twig* Book. This nonfiction book has 123 words over 16 pages. There is an average of eight words on each page.

Noteworthy Features

The text follows a set pattern until the last two pages where there is a slight variation in the pattern. The placement of text is consistent throughout, with each page having one sentence at the top or the bottom of the page. The title page asks the question, "Who Lays Eggs?" which is the only question in the book.

The book is beautifully illustrated and the illustrations support the text. Teachers will want to notice that some of the illustrations are not quite clear enough for the reader to match the pictures to the text. For example, on one page the text reads, "She lays her stringy eggs in a puddle." and the illustration shows eggs that are round. Or, "She lays her big, white *eggs* in a large nest." and the illustration shows one, rather small, egg. Even though there is a pattern throughout, this book may be a challenge to emergent readers, due to some difficult animal names (e.g., brook trout) and some descriptive language that may be unfamiliar (e.g., "She lays her soft eggs in a gravel nest." "The eagle carries sticks to the fir tree."). The relatively simple, repetitive text supports early reading behaviors such as one-to-one correspondence, directionality, "getting your mouth ready" to say a word, and using familiar sight words to anchor oneself to the text.

Teaching Ideas

In an introduction, a teacher might say, "The title of this book asks a question about which animals lay eggs to have their babies. You can read to find out some answers to that question. Some of the answers may surprise you!" In conferring with readers, teachers may want to talk about what seems to be a mismatch between pictures and words on some pages.

This book may be used as part of a collection of books for a class studying animals and their babies, egg-laying animals, or mammals. The book can be a useful resource for supporting children in drawing conclusions and can generate some lively discussion. For example, is there anything the same about all animals who lay eggs? How are they the same/different from animals that have live babies? Were you surprised by some of the animals that lay eggs? Where can we learn more about these animals?

In writing workshop, children can use the book as a model for writing their own pattern books about nonfiction topics. They can also try using a question mark at the end of their sentences, or using a question as a title to springboard a written piece.

Book Connections

This book is part of the *Twig Books* series published by the Wright Group. Many of the books at the "orange" emergent level are very similar and can be used in conjunction with this book. Similar books can also be found in Level 2 books of the *Hello Reader! Science* series.

Genre
Picture Book; Nonfiction

Teaching Uses
Teaching Writing; Independent Reading; Content Area Study; Reading and Writing Nonfiction

Who Took the Farmer's Hat?

Joan L. Nodset

Book Summary

The book begins, "The farmer had a hat, an old brown hat. Oh, how he liked that old brown hat!/ But the wind took it, and away it went./ The farmer ran fast, but the wind went faster./ So the farmer had to look for it./" This becomes a cumulative tale about the hat which has been taken away by the wind. The farmer asks all the animals if they have seen his hat. "Squirrel, did you see my old brown hat?" the farmer asks, and then later he addresses the question to mouse, fly, goat, and some of the other animals. They all respond, "No." In reality, they have seen it, but the squirrel thinks it is a bird with wings and the mouse thinks it is a mouse hole. Fly thinks it is a hill, goat thinks it is a flowerpot, and duck thinks it is a boat. Finally the farmer finds his hat being used as a bird's nest. Unwilling to disturb the egg in the nest, he goes to the store and buys a new hat.

Basic Book Information

Just as the farmer must pursue his blowing hat through a whole sequence of places before he finds it, so, too, the reader is pulled on and on through lots of long sentences, across sections of the text that are neatly patterned and sections that break the pattern. Some sentences extend across two pages and this spurs children to take in longer chunks of text at a time. Children also need to link the pages together into a coherent story. It helps to have a pattern set within the chronological narrative.

Noteworthy Features

At first glance, some readers expect the book to be in rhyming couplets and the fact that it doesn't rhyme can be discouraging.

Teaching Ideas

When reading this book, children will need to take in the illustrations as well as the text. As in so many books for early readers, the illustrations contain a great deal of information. Without the picture, a reader won't understand that when Mouse says no, he hasn't seen the hat, he *has* in fact seen it and just mistook it for a mousehole. Doing so requires the reader to consider both sources of information and infer what has actually happened.

The teacher can help students practice the process of using information in the text-searching, checking, and using phonological information-on the run, while reading. For example, if the student reads, "I ran to it, but any it went," the teacher might prompt the child to monitor and search by saying, "You said 'any it went.' Does that make sense? Let's check." Again, if the child reads, "the farmer said," rather than, "the farmer saw," the teacher

Illustrator
Fritz Siebel

Publisher
Scholastic, 1963

ISBN
0064431746

TC Level
5

A Field Guide to the Classroom Library, Lucy Calkins and the Teachers College Reading and Writing Project, Heinemann, ©2002 Teachers College, Columbia University; http://www.heinemann.com/fieldguides

might prompt the child to search and check by saying "You said . . . I'm glad that you made sense, but does that look right?" The teacher can then support the child in replacing the word *said* with *saw* and then rereading. Depending on the reader, the teacher might instead prompt the child by saying, "There was something wrong on that line. See if you can find what was wrong."

The text contains compound words including *mousehole* and *flowerpot*. Both of these words can be constructed with magnetic letters and the children can be asked to separate the two words *mouse* and *hole*, *flower* and *pot*. Teachers may encourage students to generate other compound words they know and extend such a study into a whole class inquiry.

If the students are having difficulty with the word *round*, attention can be focused on a word they know like *out*. Construct the word *out* and *round* with magnetic letters and show how they can use a word they know to get to a word that they do not know. Generate other words using the *ou* chunk. Show the children the word *mouse* with the *ou* chunk.

Genre
Picture Book

Teaching Uses
Independent Reading

A Field Guide to the Classroom Library, Lucy Calkins and the Teachers College Reading and Writing Project, Heinemann, ©2002 Teachers College, Columbia University; http://www.heinemann.com/fieldguides

Work

Ann Morris

Book Summary

In this book, people of all ages and from all over the world are working. The jobs range from weaving baskets, to flying airplanes, to selling fruit in a market. Many unusual workplaces, tools, and jobs are presented.

Basic Book Information

Despite the large, well-spaced text font, the use of high frequency words, and the minimal text overall, this book is quite challenging. There are ellipses, sentences that stretch over two to three pages, and some vocabulary that is not easily decoded or gleaned from the context.

Noteworthy Features

Each photograph supports the print in some way, usually in direct correspondence with some part of the text. But the photographs are rich with additional information that isn't directly referred to in the print.

There is an index at the back of the book that describes the type of work, the country, and nationality of the people. The index is written in language that is more complex and the font is quite small. Early readers may need help with this section of the book.

Teaching Ideas

Work can be used as part of an author study of Ann Morris-particularly those that include photographs from around the world. Many of her books have a similar format, with photographs from around the world. Readers will find lots to compare and contrast in all the Ann Morris books.

Work is also available as a Big Book and so may be used in several different ways by teachers with small groups or the whole class, to support early reading behaviors. This book lends itself to word work because there are a lot of high frequency words, as well as some words that are unfamiliar and will be challenging for the early reader. Teachers may use this book to support lessons on one-to-one matching, "getting your mouth ready" for an upcoming word, predicting or figuring out text from looking at the picture, asking oneself, "What would make sense here?"

This book may be used as part of a nonfiction genre study. Teachers may model for the children how we sometimes read nonfiction differently than fiction. Readers can practice reading smaller chunks, perhaps looking for particular information, rather than straight through from start to finish as they would with a story. Teachers may model for children the many opportunities for, and the importance of, frequent and interesting discussions that nonfiction text presents to the reader. While reading to a

Illustrator
Ken Heyman

Publisher
Lothrop, Lee & Shepard
Books, 1998

ISBN
0688148662

TC Level
6; 7; 8

A Field Guide to the Classroom Library, Lucy Calkins and the Teachers College Reading and Writing Project, Heinemann, ©2002 Teachers College, Columbia University; http://www.heinemann.com/fieldguides

group or the class, the teacher can make occasional stops at relevant sections and encourage the children to "say something" to someone about the text read.

Work may be used to support other areas of the curriculum, particularly social studies. Many teachers in early grades do whole class studies of work and workers and/or the similarities and differences among cultures around the world. The subject of traditional dress, tools for work, how work is related to the environment, and work-roles in the family are often included in such studies. This book can serve as a rich and valuable source of information about any of these topics. Each page is loaded with relevant topics for whole class discussions, critical thinking, hypothesizing and drawing conclusions, and simply learning new information. Teachers may show readers how to use this book as a reference for their studies. Teachers may ask readers questions that help them read the book, thinking critically about people, their work, play, and customs. Teachers may lead readers to discover that jobs are determined by the needs of the community, the roles of family members, and the resources in the environment.

Book Connections

There are several other books written by Ann Morris that follow a format similar to *Work*. *Hats* and *Bread, Bread, Bread* are two of them. There are also many other books at this level about work, workers, family, and community roles.

Genre
Picture Book; Nonfiction

Teaching Uses
Content Area Study; Author Study; Partnerships

You'll Soon Grow Into Them, Titch

Pat Hutchins

Book Summary

When Titch outgrows his clothes, his big brother Pete and his big sister Mary give him their hand-me-downs. They always say, "You'll soon grow into them." Mother tells Dad to take Titch shopping and buy him some brand new clothes. At the end of the story, Titch decides to give his hand-me-downs to his new baby brother.

Basic Book Information

This book has 191 words written over twenty-six pages. Sentence structure and phrasing are consistent with early reading patterns and will help beginning readers make meaning.

Full-page color illustrations are on each page. Text is placed consistently on the top. The illustrations provide high to moderate support. This book uses many high frequency words.

Noteworthy Features

Pat Hutchins, the well-known British author of many wonderful children's books, wrote this text and others about Titch.

The cover picture of *You'll Soon Grow Into Them, Titch* is exactly like the picture on the first book, *Titch*, with Titch still wearing a blue tunic-top and brown/red trousers. But this Titch looks much older, with a thinner face and baggy clothes. Titch's siblings, Peter and Mary are each older too, and a cat has joined their family. If a reader looks at the cover and notices that Titch is older now, this observation will lead directly into the first page of the book where Titch can't fit into his trousers anymore.

Throughout this story we see the passage of time illustrated by such things as a bird building a nest and then having babies, and flowers just starting to come up and then blooming.

Teaching Ideas

Children who are able to read *You'll Soon Grow Into Them, Titch* and other similarly challenging books will find that though many of these books continue to have a pattern, the patterns are more complex. This was true, for example, of *Titch* or *Cookie's Week*, which are both structured like lists of repeating episodes. This book has a similar structure. Titch can't fit into his clothes and his bigger siblings give him theirs, which are always too large. Titch instead goes shopping. But soon his newborn baby brother arrives home. Titch does to the baby brother what others had done to him. He gives his old clothes to the baby, saying, "He'll grow into them soon." Students may be able to predict the outcome of the story, by paying close attention to

Series
Titch

Illustrator
Pat Hutchins

Publisher
William Morrow, 1983

ISBN
0688115071

TC Level
5

this pattern. Students may want to read with a partner, sharing and revising predictions about how the story will turn out.

A child who rereads this book may spot various things in the story that change, marking the passage of time. The bulbs grow into plants. The mother knits clothes that the baby soon wears. The bird builds a nest and then has babies. Mary and Pete also grow-into and out of *their* clothes just like everyone else. Teachers may want to encourage other readers to look for evidence of change and the passage of time in their own books, using this text as a model in a mini-lesson. Students may also make text-to-self connections about how they experience similar changes in growth and share similar feelings about hand-me-downs and older siblings in general. Partners or Group may also want to discuss these changes.

While conferring, a teacher will want to monitor reading comprehension. One way to do so is to assess any substitutions the child makes while reading, considering which cueing systems he seems to be using effectively and which he might make better use of. If the student reads, ". . . that Titch *shout* have some new clothes" the teacher might prompt the child to monitor and search by saying, "You said ' *shout* have some new clothes.' The beginning chunk matches, but does that word make sense there?" Again, on the last page, if the child reads, "And Titch *had* the nails," rather than "And Titch *held* the nails," the teacher might prompt the child to search and check by saying, "You said. . . . That makes sense, but does it look right?" Once attention is drawn to the substitution, the child could probably correct the word *had* to *held*. Alternatively, the teacher might also choose to simply prompt the child to find and correct the error by saying, "There was something wrong on that line. See if you can find what was wrong."

Some children discuss issues of fairness raised in the text. Why doesn't Titch have new clothes all for himself? Why might this be?

Book Connections

You'll Soon Grow Into Them, Titch is part of a series written by Pat Hutchins. Other books include *Titch* and *Tidy Titch*.

Genre
Picture Book

Teaching Uses
Independent Reading; Partnerships; Critique

Young Cam Jansen and the Ice Skate Mystery

David A. Adler

Book Summary

As in the other Young Cam Jansen books, chapter one explains how Jennifer Jansen earns her nickname, Cam, because of her good memory. Other characters are introduced, and there is a test where Cam proves her memory prowess. Cam goes ice skating with her friend Eric and his father. Eric wants to be responsible, and asks to hold the key to the locker. After skating for a while, Eric thinks he's lost the key. Cam uses her amazing memory to figure out the location of the lost key. In chapter five, Cam reveals how the key ended up in her pocket.

Basic Book Information

Young Cam Jansen books have a medium size print with comfortable spacing between the lines and the words. The illustrations lend support to the text and include important details. The reader can see what is happening, notice important clues, and gain insight into the thinking going on in Cam's head. The story is composed of simple sentences, most of which end at the end of the line.

Noteworthy Features

There is one major plot for readers to follow - finding the key. Of all the Young Cams, which are somewhat easier than the books in the regular Cam Jansen series, this is the easiest to follow and could make a good place for a reader new to the series to start. The characters are straightforward and include Cam, Eric and his father. The chapter titles are supportive and aid the reader in predicting what will happen (e.g., "Let's Skate" and "Crash"). Readers will need to pay attention to both text and pictures to get the full story. The vocabulary is mostly familiar with an occasional exception (e.g., *lockers* may be unfamiliar to some readers).

Teaching Ideas

A teacher may want to preview the story for an individual or a group of readers in a way that gets them started doing what mystery readers mainly do, which is to act as if they, too, are the crime solvers looking for clues. Conferences with the teacher or book talks between partners might focus on what was learned about how we read mysteries. We'll want them to notice important features, including the fact that readers tend to learn at the very beginning such important elements as the identity of the crime-solver,

Series
Young Cam Jansen books

Illustrator
Susanna Natti

Publisher
Puffin (Easy to Read), 1998

ISBN
0141300124

TC Level
6

A Field Guide to the Classroom Library, Lucy Calkins and the Teachers College Reading and Writing Project, Heinemann, ©2002 Teachers College, Columbia University; http://www.heinemann.com/fieldguides

whether he or she has a sidekick, and what the mystery will be. In coaching young readers to notice such characteristic features of a particular kind of text - in this case a mystery - we set them up to approach their next experience with that kind of text in a more informed way - with a sense of, "I have some ideas about how mysteries go..." We can also help them realize in a general way that proficient readers are always making subtle adjustments in their approach, depending on the type of text as well as their purpose as a reader. If the whole class is studying the genre of mystery, the share at the end of independent reading time provides a good opportunity to collect ideas and observations from across the class and to discuss strategies that helped them read more effectively.

The *Young Cam Jansen* books are great for retelling work because there is similar sequencing in all of them. Typically, objects are mysteriously lost and Cam finds them. Many chapter books at this level are episodic, with each chapter almost a story unto itself - this one is not. It therefore provides some additional challenges, which are likely to require some teaching and discussion. In a conference, teachers can coach partners to stop to retell and talk about one chapter before beginning another, and to talk about how one chapter connects to the previous chapter. Teachers can use the experiences of those reading the Young Cams as material for planning mini-lessons that anticipate upcoming needs of other readers in the class as they, too, transition out of episodic chapter books and into those structured in this cumulative way.

When students are reading independently, they can put Post-its on clues they accumulate along the way. Post-Its can be marked with a "C" for clue, and the reader can jot these clues in his/her reading notebook. After a few chapters, the reader can reread the clues and try to solve the mystery.

In writing workshop, a teacher might have a mini-lesson on the layout of these chapter books. As an introduction to this mini-lesson, a teacher might say, "Yesterday we talked a little about revising our pieces. I noticed some of you were unsure of how to do this, so I thought we'd look at how this author plans the layout of his pieces. Looking more closely at the chapters in his books, I noticed that each chapter is about a specific moment or event in the story. That makes me think that when the author planned out his book, he thought about the story in parts or chunks, and what parts seemed to go together. One way I can imagine he might have done this would have been to read through the draft of his piece and circle all the parts that talk only about one chunk of the story - like getting to the party. We're going to try that today. Please read through your writing draft and circle the parts that seem to go together. If you have different sections use different colors to circle the sections that go together."

Book Connections

Young Cam Jansen and the Ice Skate Mystery is similar to *Amanda Pig*, written byJean Van Leeuwen. Another *Young Cam Jansen* book included in this library is *Young Cam Jansen and the Dinosaur Game*. Good books to read before this are the *Nate the Great* series written by Marjorie Weinman Sharmat. The *Young Cam Jansen* books provide a great transition to the regular *Cam Jansen* series, as well as to the *Marvin Redpost* books written by Louis Sachar.

Genre
Short Chapter Book; Mystery

Teaching Uses
Independent Reading; Small Group Strategy Instruction; Teaching Writing

A Field Guide to the Classroom Library, Lucy Calkins and the Teachers College Reading and Writing Project, Heinemann, ©2002 Teachers College, Columbia University; http://www.heinemann.com/fieldguides

Index

HOW TO USE THIS BOOK

The National Reading Panel defines reading as "a complex system of deriving meaning from print." Even when students read the exact same text, few of them understand it in exactly the same way, or use the exact same strategies to build their understanding, or struggle with it for the exact same reasons. Learning to read involves a number of essential, predictable steps, but the art of teaching reading lies in matching instruction to the unique strengths and needs of each child in a class. Just as there is no one way all readers read, there is no one way all readers learn about reading.

Fortified with the knowledge these write-ups provide, teachers will feel better prepared to make the most of the powerful teaching potential the classroom libraries hold. Though the write-ups highlight many key elements of the books they describe, they don't attempt to cover every turn of phrase that might captivate a student's imagination, or every word that might be a challenge. Instead, they're designed to provide insight into just some of the instructional possibilities each book presents. Teachers are encouraged to adapt the ideas in the Noteworthy Features or Teaching Ideas sections of the write-ups to meet the particular tastes, tendencies and needs of individual students.

The write-ups in this guide aim to help teachers work with the rich range of books provided through the Mayor's Classroom Library Initiative. The write-ups can also serve as templates for teachers to take notes on books that are not described in this publication. After all, many classrooms have developed libraries apart from this project, and students who bring books from home do not come to school with their own write-ups. As a result, teachers must often discover what *they* find noteworthy about a text, and design instruction accordingly. As they read through these write-ups, teachers might notice the kinds of features the write-ups point out. What are some ways illustrations can help or confuse students? What elements come into play when analyzing a book's sentence structures? How might our teaching change when a book is being read aloud to students rather than when students are reading it to themselves?

Making the Guide Your Own
Teachers are encouraged to fill this guide with notes, Post-Its and highlighter markings. Space is provided along the outer margins of the write-ups so that teachers can add their own ideas and observations. Colleagues who have the same books in their classroom libraries might create new write-ups and share them.

Familiarity with Children's Literature
Students often rely on teachers to help them find books that match their tastes and reading levels. Though it's important to develop familiarity with the overall body of children's literature, teachers don't need to read every page their students do in order to know kids books well. For example, teachers can learn the essential elements of a Cam Jansen mystery novel – major characters, plot formula, writing style – by reading and skimming just a few books in the series. Once they know the series in general, teachers can confidently help students determine whether any given Cam Jansen book makes a fitting choice for independent reading, or offer meaningful support during one-on-one instructional meetings with a child reading a Cam Jansen book. Eventually, teachers will want to read as many of their new books as possible, but in the meantime, they should feel comfortable putting out books for students that they themselves have not yet had a chance to read.

Recommendations for Future Learning
This guide synthesizes important points from a number of professional resources, but educators are encouraged to study reading instruction and classroom libraries in much more depth. Teachers may also wish to ask questions of knowledgeable colleagues and select books and articles to read and discuss with their peers in schoolwide study groups.

THE STRUCTURE OF THE CLASSROOM LIBRARIES

Read-Aloud

In each core library, a number of chapter and picture books are suggested for reading aloud to students.   Teachers may wish to plan when and how they might introduce these books to the class over the course of the school year and consider the potential of each for sparking good book talk. Rereading these books will make them quite familiar to students, and many will be able to read them independently later in the year. These read-alouds can eventually make their way into a basket of independent reading titles labeled "Favorite Books."

Read-Aloud: Emergent Literacy

In the A and B libraries, a number of texts have been identified as emergent literacy titles. There are four copies of each of these books, which should be set aside until teachers introduce them, one at a time, to emergent readers. After children have heard these books read aloud at least four times, they can take begin to flip through them and discuss them with partners, engaging in important reading behaviors that mimic those of the teacher, with teachers coaching alongside thoughtfully.

Author Study

Each library has enrichment modules that include multiple copies of several books by the same authors. The purpose of author studies is to help students practice the important skill of noticing the content and style of particular authors. Author studies also support children's ability to talk across books, comparing and contrasting key features from one to another. Younger students can discuss characteristics of authors' books before they can actually decode the print on their own. Therefore, with Classroom Libraries A and B, teachers may read aloud the books designated for author studies. Teachers will want to think about when in the course of the year it makes sense for them to engage in an author study (e.g., at the start of the year as a way to build classroom community, later in the year when children have more practice noticing subtleties in text). To increase the total number of author studies each class can engage in throughout the year, grade-level colleagues may plan to share and trade the books from different modules or libraries.

Shared Reading: Big Book

In order to support shared reading, in which children both hear and see a text, a few oversized "Big Books" have been included, along with accompanying smaller editions. Big books enable a group of students to follow and read along in a single text with their teachers. Teachers will want to think about each book's teaching opportunities and how each book aligns with the strengths, needs and interests of their group of children. After teachers have modeled a strategy with a big book, but before children leave the meeting area to read independently, children may try out the demonstrated strategy with a partner using the accompanying set of little books.

Shared Reading/Poetry and Songs

Each core library has one or more collections of poetry. In libraries A and B, there is a particular emphasis on poetry and song because they play a powerful role in developing phonemic awareness. While the language play of poetry and song furthers their intellectual development, gathering together as a group to recite poems and sing songs furthers the social and emotional development of young children. Poetry can be presented as a read-aloud, made available for independent reading, copied onto chart paper for shared reading, serve as a model for students' own writing, or even spark a word study exploration.

Leveled Texts for Independent and Partner Reading

At least one third of each classroom library collection is composed of leveled texts, both fiction and nonfiction, for independent and partner reading. ECLAS results can help with decisions about which of these texts to put out as the year begins.

Book Clubs

In order to allow students to read the same texts and discuss them in book groups, enrichment modules D3, D5, E3 and E5 contain four or five additional copies of books offered in the core libraries. These extra books enable small groups of students to work together as they read and talk about the same texts.

Nonfiction

Much of what we read in daily life is nonfiction, and the informational texts in the classroom libraries expose children to this important genre. In addition to the nonfiction in the core libraries, modules include small clusters of books on related topics in science and social studies (e.g., insects, the human body, New York). Teachers may want to lay these clusters alongside their yearlong curriculum plan and think about when the best time to introduce them might be. These nonfiction texts can spark interest in a reading, science or social studies center, or as part of an inquiry-based study.

Books in a Particular Genre

In addition to nonfiction texts, other books are labeled by their genre, such as memoir, how-to and list books. When sorted in this way, these books can support a study of a particular genre and serve as models for children of the kind of writing teachers want them to do. While the *Primary Literacy Standards* call for children to read and write in many of these genres, the books do not have to be sorted only by genre. Depending on the teacher's purpose, they can also be sorted by topic, author or style, and can even be sorted different ways at different times of the year to support the reading, science or social studies curriculum.

Alphabet, Number and Concept Books

These books reinforce alphabetic and numerical concepts for young children. Teachers will no doubt want to put at least some of these out as the year begins, given the important role they play in the daily life of the kindergarten and first grade classroom and curriculum. They might become part of an "ABC" or "Counting Book" reading center.

Models for the Writing Workshop

Books with this label are particularly noteworthy for their authors' craft, style and technique. Especially during a read-aloud, these rich texts can provoke discussion not just about what the books say, but how. Once children are familiar with the stories, they can begin to study them with the attentive eyes of writers.

SOME THINGS TO CONSIDER AS YOU SET UP YOUR LIBRARY

As teachers organize the books they have received as part of the Mayor's Classroom Library Initiative, they will want to think about systems and routines that will foster independence and allow children to select books freely and efficiently by themselves. Below are some suggestions:

Sorting and Organizing Books and Book Storage Systems

- Knowing how to pick a book to match their interests and independent reading level is an important skill that encourages students to read on their own. Students cannot practice this skill unless they flip through books themselves. Rather than keeping them tightly packed on a bookshelf where only the spines are visible, it makes sense to gather clusters of books and store them in accessible, labeled baskets with their front covers in easy view. This will help children when they're looking for books to read and save time when they return them.

- Up to one third of the titles in each of the Mayor's Classroom Libraries are intended for independent and partner reading. Teachers may choose to group some or all of these books according to their reading levels, keeping in mind that only about a third of a classroom library should be leveled. These books have already been leveled with a Teachers College Reading and Writing Project group number (TC Group). A chart that aligns these levels with other leveling systems (e.g., Fountas and Pinnell) can be found after this section. In most cases, levels for these titles are listed in this book. Lists for all libraries can be found on the World Wide Web (www.nycenet.edu/dis/11062001/index.html).

- The range of text levels available in each library should reflect a class's current ECLAS results and independent reading levels. Referring to their class roster of results in the reading strand of ECLAS, teachers should think about the range of text levels represented in the collection. As some ECLAS levels cross a range of text difficulty, it is important for teachers to check back in a child's ECLAS folder so they know exactly which book a child read to master a particular level. Of course, teachers will want to confer with children as they read independently in order to confirm that a book is a good match for a child. The class should have access to baskets of independent reading books at a range of levels that go a bit beyond what the most skillful readers can handle in order to allow for growth.

- Teachers need not put out all of their leveled texts for independent reading in the beginning of the year. Instead, they may wish to reserve a few titles on each level in order to add to and refresh the collection throughout the year. In a kindergarten class, leveled texts would probably be introduced late in the fall, as appropriate, with emergent literacy activities occurring in the first half of the year. For further information about managing a leveled library, please see "The Relationship Between the ECLAS Assessment and Leveled Libraries" on page 149 of the 1999 *ECLAS Instructional Guide.*)

- Teachers may decide to label their leveled books with colored dot stickers and/or by writing the corresponding TC Group or the Fountas and Pinnell Guided Reading level discretely inside the front cover. (A colored-coded dot system is most effective if it's consistent across the school.) Teachers should take care not to let the reading levels become too important to the children. Students should not feel pressure to rush from one level to the next, nor should they compete with one another to read harder books. They should, however, know which colored dot or basket contains a 'just right' book for them, what makes it a good fit and why. The purpose of sorting independent reading books is to give children extra support in choosing 'just right' books, and to help them develop their own sense of what makes a book a good fit.

- Other books may be grouped in the library by topic (e.g., "construction," "our neighborhoods," "spiders"), by genre (e.g., list books, how-to texts, memoir, nonfiction, poetry) or by author. Rather than put them all out at once, teachers may want to hold onto some of these books for points in the year when a particular topic or genre is addressed in the reading, writing, science or social studies curriculum. It always adds to the excitement of beginning a study when new books appear to support it.

Managing Systems and Routines

- Teachers have a number of ways of managing children's independent reading books in the primary grades. Some teachers provide cardboard magazine holders for children to store their independent reading books, and others use sturdy, gallon-size plastic bags with zipper locks. Whatever method teachers choose, they should make sure each child's book container is clearly marked with his or her name.

- In order to cut down on transition time and maintain a productive reading workshop, teachers should plan and set up a routine in which on one day each week children spend time choosing a few books for their independent book boxes. Many teachers find that it works well to begin or end the week in this way, because these days tend to feel like natural times in which to start or complete work with a particular batch of books. Management is also easier if children don't trade in their books on other days. Teachers may want to add books to their boxes in between these "book choice" or "shopping" days, but children should not add to their own boxes without teachers' knowledge. A routine like this also helps teachers monitor children's reading. By looking through their individual book boxes when children are not in the room, teachers can get a quick picture of what students are reading. When teachers notice what seem like inappropriate matches – too many books that are either too easy or too hard – they can make a note to themselves to discuss choosing 'just right' books with individual students who may need more help in this area.

- Teachers should try to create a print-rich environment that allows lots of room for children's work and charts that reflect their thinking. Over the course of the year, teachers can use chart paper to keep records of children's thoughts and ideas, books the class has read together, books the class plans to read together, skills or strategies that have been modeled or that children have discovered, and goals the class is trying to achieve. Artifacts from these lessons continue to teach long after the lessons end. When these charts are displayed around the room, children and teachers can refer back to them as useful reminders or to see how much they have grown. Working with children, teachers can create and display a chart of tips for choosing 'just right' books, a class chart of ideas about what make someone a good reader, word walls of frequently used words, records of word-sort activities, a menu of ways to respond to literature, and anything else that documents the learning in the classroom.

Getting Started

- Teachers should take some time to get to know the books themselves and the characteristics of each level. Knowing the supports and challenges that a book provides the reader (e.g., size and placement of the text, picture support, vocabulary, background knowledge expected) can help teaching become more purposeful and focused.

- Once reading workshop has been launched, children should be encouraged to keep books for a few days, rather than working with different books every day. This will give them a chance to get to know well a few books at a time, and to free them up to practice the strategies they are learning in reading workshop with these familiar texts.

- Students who are reading chapter books will likely take several days to complete them. In grades two and three, teachers may want students to keep a reading log in which they record the title and author of the books they are reading. Later in the year, as part of a unit of study on stamina, teachers might also ask that grade two and three children track the number of pages they read daily.

A GUIDE TO BOOK LEVELS

Please note that these levels are approximate and should be used only as a guide.

Grade (Approx.)	ECLAS Text Level	TC Group	Fountas & Pinnell	Reading Recovery	Sunshine Wright Group	Pm Rigby	Foundations
K-1	2 Ms. Popple's Pets	1	A	1	A	Pink	A
K-1	2 I Paint	1	B	2	B	Pink/Red	B
1	3 Things I Like to Do	2	C	3-4	C	Red	C/D
1	3 My Shadow	2	D	5-6	D	Yellow	D/E/F
1		3	E	7-8	E	Yellow	F/G/H
1	4 Baby Bear's Present	4	F	9-10	F	Blue	I/J
1		4	G	11-12	G	Blue/Green	
1		5	H	13-14	H	Green	2
1-2	4 Nowhere and Nothing	5	I	15-16	I	Orange	3
2	5 Lost!	6	J	17-18	J	Turquoise	4/5
2	5 The Wild Woods	7	K	19-20	2	Purple	
2	6 Weekend with Wendell	8	L	21-22	3		
2	6 The Dandelion Seed	8	M	23-24	4		
2		9	N		5		
3		9	O		6		
3		10	P		7		
3		10	Q		8		
4		11	R		9		
4					10		

Created by Lyn Reggett, Staff Developer, Community School District 2. The New York City Primary Literacy Standards set the following benchmarks for the end of the school year: Kindergarten – Level B, Grade 1 – Level I, Grade 2 – Level L, Grade 3 – Level O. These are Fountas & Pinnell levels.